BLACKSTONE'S GUIDE TO
The Corporate Manslaughter a
Homicide Act 2007

BLACKSTONE'S GUIDE TO

The Corporate Manslaughter and Corporate Homicide Act 2007

Richard Matthews

OXFORD
UNIVERSITY PRESS

OXFORD
UNIVERSITY PRESS

Great Clarendon Street, Oxford OX2 6DP

Oxford University Press is a department of the University of Oxford.
It furthers the University's objective of excellence in research, scholarship,
and education by publishing worldwide in

Oxford New York

Auckland Cape Town Dar es Salaam Hong Kong Karachi
Kuala Lumpur Madrid Melbourne Mexico City Nairobi
New Delhi Shanghai Taipei Toronto

With offices in

Argentina Austria Brazil Chile Czech Republic France Greece
Guatemala Hungary Italy Japan Poland Portugal Singapore
South Korea Switzerland Thailand Turkey Ukraine Vietnam

Oxford is a registered trade mark of Oxford University Press
in the UK and in certain other countries

Published in the United States
by Oxford University Press Inc., New York

© Richard Matthews 2008

The moral rights of the author have been asserted
Database right Oxford University Press (maker)

Crown copyright material is reproduced under Class Licence
Number C01P0000148 with the permission of OPSI
and the Queen's Printer for Scotland

First published 2008

All rights reserved. No part of this publication may be reproduced,
stored in a retrieval system, or transmitted, in any form or by any means,
without the prior permission in writing of Oxford University Press,
or as expressly permitted by law, or under terms agreed with the appropriate
reprographics rights organization. Enquiries concerning reproduction
outside the scope of the above should be sent to the Rights Department,
Oxford University Press, at the address above

You must not circulate this book in any other binding or cover
and you must impose the same condition on any acquirer

British Library Cataloguing in Publication Data

Data available

Library of Congress Cataloging-in-publication Data

Data available

Typeset by Cepha Imaging Private Ltd., Bangalore, India
Printed in Great Britain
on acid-free paper by
Ashford Colour Press Limited, Gosport, Hampshire

ISBN 978-0-19-920321-5

1 3 5 7 9 10 8 6 4 2

Contents—Summary

TABLE OF CASES	xi
TABLE OF SECONDARY LEGISLATION	xvii
TABLE OF STATUTES	xix

1. INTRODUCTION: THE ACT, ITS HISTORY, AND THE COMMON LAW	1
2. THE OFFENCE AND THE ORGANIZATIONS SUBJECT TO THE ACT	13
3. THE RELEVANT DUTY OF CARE I: A QUESTION OF LAW FOUNDED UPON THE COMMON LAW OF NEGLIGENCE	31
4. THE RELEVANT DUTY OF CARE II: THE MEANING AND CATEGORIES OF RELEVANT DUTY OF CARE	43
5. THE RELEVANT DUTY OF CARE III: THE EXEMPTIONS IN SECTIONS 3–7	69
6. COMMITTING THE OFFENCE: CAUSATION AND BREACH OF DUTY	89
7. SENTENCE AND ORDERS UPON CONVICTION	119
8. INVESTIGATION AND REPRESENTATION	131

APPENDIX 1. CORPORATE MANSLAUGHTER AND CORPORATE HOMICIDE ACT 2007	137
APPENDIX 2. A GUIDE TO THE CORPORATE MANSLAUGHTER AND CORPORATE HOMICIDE ACT 2007	155
INDEX	171

Contents—Detailed

TABLE OF CASES	xi
TABLE OF SECONDARY LEGISLATION	xvii
TABLE OF STATUTES	xix

1. INTRODUCTION: THE ACT, ITS HISTORY, AND THE COMMON LAW

A. The Corporate Manslaughter and Corporate Homicide Act 2007	1.01
B. The Common Law	1.04
C. Common Law Gross Negligence Manslaughter	1.16
1. Recent authorities	1.19
2. The position of the statutory offence versus the common law offence	1.30
D. The Need for Reform	1.32
E. History of the Act	1.38

2. THE OFFENCE AND THE ORGANIZATIONS SUBJECT TO THE ACT

A. Overview	2.01
B. The Offence:	2.05
1. Definition and elements	2.06
2. Territorial extent	2.09
3. Institution of proceedings	2.12
4. Individual and secondary liability	2.13
5. Convictions under the Act and under health and safety legislation	2.21
6. Commencement and orders	2.26
7. Procedural provisions and consequential amendments	2.33
C. Element 1: By an Organization Subject to the Act	2.47
1. Corporations	2.50
2. Government bodies and the Crown	2.54
3. Police forces	2.66
4. A partnership, trade union, or employer's association that is an employer	2.72
5. Power to extend section 1 to other organizations: s 21	2.82
D. Element 2: The Organization Owed a Relevant Duty of Care to the Deceased	2.83
E. Element 3: The Way in which the Organization's Activities are Managed or Organized: Causation and Breach	2.89

3. THE RELEVANT DUTY OF CARE I: A QUESTION OF LAW FOUNDED UPON THE COMMON LAW OF NEGLIGENCE

A. Overview — 3.01

B. Relevant Duty of Care: a Judicial Determination of Law and Fact — 3.06
  1. Individual gross negligence manslaughter — 3.06
  2. The Corporate Manslaughter and Corporate Homicide Act, s 2(5) — 3.10
  3. The procedure for determining the existence of a 'relevant duty of care' — 3.20
  4. Directing the jury — 3.30

C. The Existence of a Duty of Care in Negligence — 3.33
  1. Development of the common law — 3.33
  2. *Caparo Industries plc v Dickman* [1990] 1 All ER 568 — 3.38
  3. The meaning of the *Caparo* factors — 3.46
  4. Omissions — 3.54

4. THE RELEVANT DUTY OF CARE II: THE MEANING AND CATEGORIES OF RELEVANT DUTY OF CARE

A. Overview — 4.01

B. Meaning of 'Relevant Duty of Care' — 4.04
  1. Superseding statutory duties: s 2(4) — 4.10
  2. Common law limitations disregarded: s 2(6) — 4.14

C. Work, The Duty Owed to Employees and Other Workers: s 2(1)(a) — 4.20
  1. The employer's duty of care to employees — 4.22
  2. Who is an employee? — 4.30
  3. Non-employee workers — 4.42
  4. Distinguishing vicarious liability — 4.43
  5. Statutory health and safety duties — 4.44
  6. *Volenti non fit injuria* — 4.47

D. The Duty as an Occupier of Premises: s 2(1)(b) — 4.49
  1. The nature of the duty under the Occupiers' Liability Act 1957: the common duty of care — 4.57
  2. The Occupiers' Liability Act 1984 — 4.62

E. Duties Owed 'In Connection with' Various Activities: s 2(1)(c) — 4.66
  1. The supply by the organization of goods or services — 4.67
  2. The carrying on by the organization of any construction or maintenance operations — 4.75
  3. The carrying on by the organization of any other activity on a commercial basis — 4.92
  4. The use or keeping by the organization of any plant, vehicle, or other thing — 4.97

F. The 'Custody' Duty of Care: s 2(1)(d) — 4.99
  1. Potential commencement — 4.100
  2. The relevant duty — 4.103
  3. The nature of the common law duty — 4.111

5. THE RELEVANT DUTY OF CARE III: THE EXEMPTIONS IN SECTIONS 3–7

A. Overview	5.01
B. Public Policy Decisions, Exclusively Public Functions, and Statutory Inspections	5.07
1. Public authorities	5.08
2. Public policy: s 3(1)	5.09
3. Exclusively public functions: s 3(2)	5.12
4. Public policy and public functions: relevant common law principles	5.20
5. Summary of the effect of ss 3(1) and 3(2)	5.35
6. Statutory inspections: s 3(3)	5.37
C. Military Activities	5.41
1. The armed forces	5.41
2. Exemption for military 'operations': ss 4(1) and 4(2)	5.42
3. Exemption for special forces: ss 12(3) and 12(4)	5.48
D. Policing and Law Enforcement	5.49
1. Police forces	5.49
2. Exemption for policing 'operations': ss 5(1) and 5(2)	5.50
3. The exemption for all other policing and law enforcement activity: s 5(3)	5.60
E. Emergencies	5.65
1. The exemption created by s 6	5.65
2. The definition of 'emergency circumstances'	5.67
3. The effect of the exemption in s 6	5.73
4. The common law duty of care and emergency response	5.78
5. Rescue at sea: ss 6(5) and 6(6)	5.82
F. Child Protection and Probation Functions	5.84
1. Child protection: ss 7(1) and 7(2)	5.84
2. Probation functions: s 7(3)	5.86
3. The effect of s 7	5.87

6. COMMITTING THE OFFENCE: CAUSATION AND BREACH OF DUTY

A. Overview	6.01
B. Management Failure, Breach, and Senior Management	6.07
C. The Way in which the Organization's Activities are Managed or Organized Caused the Death: s 1(1)(a)	6.10
1. 'The way its activities are managed or organised'	6.12
2. Causation	6.21
3. Causation and 'management failure': summary of position and principles	6.41
D. 'The Way in which its Activities are Managed or Organised' Amounted to a Gross Breach of that Relevant Duty of Care: s 1(1)(b)	6.46
1. The definition of gross breach	6.47

E. Gross Breach: the Jury Factors in s 8	6.59
1. Health and safety legislation: s 8(2)	6.64
2. Health and safety duties and offences	6.78
3. Specific factors which the jury may take into account: s 8(3)	6.105
F. The Senior Management Requirement	6.117
1. The criticism of the 'senior management' requirement	6.121
2. The Government's view of the 'senior management' requirement	6.124
3. The test for 'senior management'	6.128
4. A substantial element of the breach	6.148
5. Summary: the meaning of the 'senior management' requirement	6.157

7. SENTENCE AND ORDERS UPON CONVICTION

A. Overview	7.01
B. Sentence by way of Fine	7.03
1. The Sentencing Advisory Panel consultation paper	7.06
2. Sentence in health and safety cases	7.18
3. Sentencing public bodies and the 'public element'	7.29
4. The means of the organization and relevant financial information	7.33
C. Remedial Orders and Publicity Orders	7.44
1. Remedial orders	7.45
2. Publicity orders	7.53

8. INVESTIGATION AND REPRESENTATION

A. Overview	8.01
B. The Investigation of Corporate Manslaughter	8.05
1. The Home Office regulatory impact assessment	8.07
2. The Work-Related Death Protocol	8.14
3. Coroners Act 1988 s 16 and adjourned inquests	8.22
4. Police powers and corporate manslaughter	8.24
C. Representation	8.32

APPENDIX 1. Corporate Manslaughter and Corporate Homicide Act 2007	137
APPENDIX 2. A Guide to the Corporate Manslaughter and Corporate Homicide Act 2007	155
INDEX	171

Table of Cases

References are to paragraph and Appendix numbers

Alcock v Chief Constable of South Yorkshire Police [1992] 1 AC 310;
 [1991] 4 All ER 907. . . . . 3.43, 5.63
Alexandrou v Oxford [1993] 4 All ER 328. . . . . 3.52, 5.63
AMF International v Magnet Bowling Ltd and another [1968] 1 WLR 1028 . . . . 4.53
Ancell v McDermott [1993] 4 All ER 355 . . . . 5.63
Andrews v DPP [1937] AC 576 (HL) 1.18
Andrews v Hopkinson [1957] 1 QB 229 . . . . 4.71
Anns v Merton London Borough Council [1978] AC 728. . . . . 3.35, 3.37, 4.82
Ashdown v Samuel Williams & Sons Ltd [1957] 1 QB 409. . . . . 4.26
Attorney-General's Reference (No 1 of 1995) [1996] 2 Cr App R 320. . . . . 1.12, 6.150
Attorney-General's Reference (No 2 of 1999) [2000] 2 Cr App R 207. . . . . 1.11, 2.17

Baker v James Bros & Sons Ltd [1921] 2 KB 674. . . . . 4.47
Barrett v Enfield LBC [1999] 3 All ER 193; [2001] 2 AC 550. . . . . 5.31, 5.32
Bernard v Dudley Metropolitan Borough Council and Dudley Magistrates Court
 [2003] EWHC 147 (Admin) 3.28
Birmingham and Gloucester Railway Co. (1842) 3 QB 223. . . . . 1.04
Bolam v Friern Barnet Hospital [1957] 1 WLR 582. . . . . 6.54
Bolton Engineering v TJ Graham & Sons [1957] 1 QB 159 . . . . 1.07
Brook Street Bureau (UK) Ltd v Dacas [2004] EWCA Civ 217;
 [2004] ICR 1437, CA 4.40
Brooks v Metropolitan Police Commissioner & others [2005] 2 All ER 489 (HL). 5.63
Bunker v Charles Brand & Sons Ltd [1969] 2 QB 480 . . . . 4.55

Cable & Wireless plc v Muscat [2006] EWCA Civ 220 . . . . 4.40
Caparo Industries plc v Dickman [1990] 1 All ER 568 . . . . 1.28, 3.03, 3.06, 3.07,
 3.38–3.45, 3.50
Capital and Counties plc v Hampshire CC [1997] 2 All ER 865;
 [1997] QB 1004 . . . . 3.52, 5.79
Carmichael v National Power plc [1999] ICR 1226. . . . . 4.35
Carty v London Borough of Croydon [2005] EWCA Civ 266; [2005]
 2 All ER 517 . . . . 5.33, 5.88
C Evans & Sons Ltd v Spritebrand Ltd [1985] BCLC 105. . . . . 2.15
Costello v Chief Constable of Northumbria Police [1999] 1 All ER 550 (CA). 5.57
Curran v Northern Ireland Co-ownership Housing Association Ltd [1987]
 2 All ER 13 . . . . 3.37

Donoghue v Stevenson [1932] AC 562 . . . . 3.33, 3.55, 4.71
Dorset Yacht Co. Ltd v Home Office *see* Home Office v Dorset Yacht Co. Ltd
Dutton v Bognor Regis UDC [1972] 1 QB 373 . . . . 4.82

Ellis v Home Office [1953] 2 QB 135 .... 3.54
Environmental Agency (formerly National Rivers Authority) v Empress Cars
 (Abertillery) Ltd [1999] 2 AC 22; [1998] 1 All ER 481 .... 6.26, 6.28, 6.30,
 6.31, 6.34, 6.35, 6.36, 6.44, 6.45

Ferguson v Welsh [1987] 1 WLR 1553 .... 4.53
Franks v Reuters Ltd [2003] EWCA Civ 417; [2003] ICR 1166, CA 4.40
Friskies Petcare UK Ltd [2002] 2 Cr App R (S) 401........................... 3.28

Garrard v A E Southey & Co. and Standard Telephones and Cables Ltd
 [1952] 2 QB 4.40
General Cleaning Contractors Ltd v Christmas [1953] AC 180 .... 4.27, 4.29
Gorringe v Calderdale Metropolitan Borough Council [2004]
 UKHL 15; [2004] 1 WLR 1057 .... 4.91, 5.25, 5.28, 5.29, 5.31
Grant v Australian Knitting Mills Ltd [1936] AC 85 .... 4.71
Great North of England Railway Co. (1846) 9 QB 315 .... 1.04

Harris v Birkenhead Corporation [1975] 1 WLR 379 .... 4.52
Haseldine v C A Daw & Son Ltd [1941] 2 KB 343 .... 4.71
Hazell v British Transport Commission [1958] 1 WLR 169...................... 6.53
Herschtal v Stewart & Arden Ltd [1940] 1 KB 155 .... 4.71
Hewlett Packard v O'Murphy [2002] IRLR 4 (EAT).............................. 4.40
Heyes v Pilkington Glass Ltd [1998] PIQR 103................................ 4.29
Hill v Chief Constable of West Yorkshire [1989] 1 AC 53 .... 5.63
Hobbs (Farms) Ltd v Baxenden Chemical Co. Ltd [1992]
 1 Lloyd's Rep 54.. 4.71
Home Office v Dorset Yacht Co. Ltd [1970] 2 All ER 294;
 [1970] AC 1004.. 3.35, 3.41, 5.34
Huckerby v Elliot [1970] 1 ALL ER 189 (DC) 1.13, 6.150
Hudson v Ridge Manufacturing Co. Ltd [1957] 2 QB 348 .... 4.28
Hughes v National Union of Mineworkers [1991] 4 All ER 278 .... 5.56

Interlink Express Parcels Ltd v Night Trunkers Ltd [2001] IRLR 224 (CA) 4.38

Jones v Minton Construction Ltd (1973) 15 KIR 309........................... 4.42

Kealey v Heard [1983] 1 WLR 573 .... 4.46
Kennedy No 2 [2005] 2 Cr App R 23 .... 6.35
Kent v Griffiths [2000] 2 All ER 474.. 5.81
Kirkham v Chief Constable of the Greater Manchester Police [1990]
 2 QB 283... 4.114
Kubach v Hollands [1937] 3 All ER 907 .... 4.71

Lambeth London Borough Council v Grewal (1986) 82 Cr App Rep 301;
 [1986] Crim LR 260 .... 6.132
Lane v Shire Roofing Co. [1995] IRLR 493.................................... 4.39
Latimer v AEC Ltd [1953] AC 643 .... 4.26
Lee Ting Sang v Chung Chi-Keung [1990] 2 AC 374 .... 4.34

Table of Cases

Lennard's Carrying Co. Ltd v Asiatic Petroleum Co. Ltd [1915] AC 705............... 1.07
Lowery v Walker [1911] AC 10 .... 4.57

McDermid v Nash Dredging and Reclamation Co. Ltd [1987] AC 906;
   [1987] 2 All ER 878 (HL) 4.29
Makepeace v Evans Brothers (Reading) (a firm) [2001] ICR 241 .... 4.46
Marc Rich & Co., AG & others v Bishop Rock Marine Co. Ltd & others;
   The Nicholas H [1995] 3 All ER 307; [1996] AC 211..................... 3.41, 5.40
Matthews v Ministry of Defence [2003] UKHL 4; [2003] 2 WLR 435 .... 5.47
Meridian Global Funds Management v Securities Commission [1995]
   2 AC 500.. 1.05, 1.06
Misra and Srivastava (CA) [2004] EWCA Crim 2375 .... 1.20
Montgomery v Johnson Underwood Ltd [2001] EWCA Civ 318;
   [2001] IRLR 269... 4.40
Morris v Breaveglen [1997] EWCA Civ 1662 .... 4.42
Motorola Ltd v Davidson [2001] IRLR 4 (EAT) 4.40
Muirhead v Industrial Tank Specialities Ltd [1985] 3 All ER 705................... 3.49
Mulcahy v Ministry of Defence [1996] QB 732.............................. 3.52, 5.47
Mullaney v Chief Constable of West Midlands Police [2001]
   EWCA Civ 700 .... 5.57, 5.59
Murphy v Brentwood DC [1990] 2 All ER 908; [1991] 1 AC 398 .... 3.50, 4.82, 4.85

Nelhams v Sandells Maintenance Ltd and Gillespie (UK) Ltd [1996]
   PIQR P 52, CA 4.42
Nettleship v Weston [1971] 2 QB 691.. 4.18

OLL Ltd v Secretary of State for Transport [1997] 3 All ER 897 .... 5.80
Orange v Chief Constable of West Yorkshire Police [2002]
   EWCA Civ 611; [2002] QB 347.. 4.118

P & O European Ferries (Dover) Ltd (1991) 93 Cr App R 72
   (Central Criminal Court)... 1.04
Paris v Stepney Borough Council [1951] AC 367................................. 4.25
Peabody Donation Fund v Sir Lindsay Parkinson & Co. Ltd [1984]
   3 All ER 529 .... 3.36
Performing Right Society Ltd v Ciryl Theatrical Syndicate Ltd [1924]
   1 KB 1.. 1.13, 6.150
Perrett v Collins [1998] 2 Lloyd's Rep 255................................. 3.43, 5.40
Phelps v Hillingdon London BC [2000] 4 All ER 504; [2001]
   2 AC 619... 5.31, 5.33
Priestley v Fowler (1837) 3 M & WI 4.24

R (on the application of Amin) v Secretary of State for the
   Home Department (HL) [2003] UKHL 51; [2003] 4 All ER 1264.............. 4.113
R v Adomako (1994) 99 Cr App R 362; [1995]
   1 AC 171... 1.16, 1.17, 1.18, 1.20, 6.52
R v Associated Octel Ltd [1996] 4 All ER 846 (HL) 1.10

Table of Cases

R v Balfour Beatty Rail Infrastructure Services Ltd [2006]
  EWCA Crim 1586 .... 7.19, 7.20, 7.24–7.27
R v Bateman (1925) 19 Cr App R 8 (CCA) 1.18
R v Beedie [1997] 2 Cr App R 167 .... 2.24
R v Board of Trustees of Science Museum [1993] 3 All ER 853 (CA) 6.78, 6.86
R v Brintons Ltd (CA 22 June 1999) 7.43
R v British Steel plc [1995] 1 WLR 1356; [1995] IRLR 310 .... 1.08, 6.89
R v Cato [1976] 62 Cr App R 41 .... 6.27
R v Colthrop Board Mills Ltd [2002] EWCA Crim 520; [2002]
  2 Cr App R (S) 359 .... 7.19
R v Curley (1909) 2 Cr App R 96 .... 6.27
R v Dant (1865) L & C 567 .... 6.40
R v Egan (1992) 95 Cr App R 278 .... 6.143
R v Great Western Trains Company Ltd (unreported)
  Central Criminal Court, 30 June 1999 .... 1.13, 6.150
R v Howe & Sons (Engineers) Ltd [1999] 2 Cr App R (S) 37 .... 6.71, 6.73, 7.07,
                                              7.18, 7.19, 7.20, 7.21, 7.31, 7.33, 7.40
R v HTM Ltd [2006] EWCA Crim 1156 .... 6.89, 6.97, 6.98
R v Hutchinson (1864) 9 Cox 555 .... 6.40
R v Jarvis Facilities Ltd [2005] EWCA Crim 1382; [2006] Cr App R (S) 44 ... 7.19, 7.32
R v Jefferson (1994) 99 Cr App R 13 (CA) 2.16
R v Jones (1870) 11 Cox 544 .... 6.40
R v Keltbray Ltd [2000] 1 Cr App R (S) 132 .... 7.43
R v Kew and Jackson (1872) 12 Cox 355 .... 6.40
R v Latif [1996] 2 Cr App R 92 .... 6.33
R v Lloyd (1966) 50 Cr App R 61 .... 6.142, 6.154
R v Milford Haven Port Authority [2000] 2 Cr App R (S) 423 .... 7.18, 7.30, 7.32
R v Misra and Srivastava [2004] EWCA Crim 2375; [2005] 1 Cr App R 21 ..... 6.52
R v Nelson Group Services (Maintenance) Ltd [1999] 1 WLR 1526 (CA) 2.40
R v P and another [2007] All ER (D) 173 (Jul) 1.13, 6.150
R v Railtrack plc and others (unreported) 1 September 2004 .... 3.07
R v Swindall and Osbourne (1846) 2 C & K 230 .... 6.40
R v Transco plc [2006] EWCA Crim 838 .... 7.19, 7.24, 7.28, 7.34, 7.38
R v Wacker [2002] EWCA Crim 1944; [2003] 2 Cr App R 22 .... 1.21, 4.15
R v Warburton-Pitt (1990) 92 Cr App R 136 (CA) 3.28
R v Yaqoob [2005] EWCA Crim 1269; [2005] All ER (D) 109 (Aug) 6.52
Ramsden v Secretary of State for Work and Pensions [2003] EWCA Civ 32 .... 6.135
Ready Mixed Concrete Ltd v Minister of Pension and National Insurance
  [1968] 2 QB 497 .... 4.37
Reeves v Commissioner of Police of the Metropolis [2000] 1 AC 360 .... 4.115
Robertson v Riley [1989] 2 All ER 474 .... 4.52

Saunders v Edwards [1987] 1 WLR 1116 .... 1.24
Singh [1999] Crim LR 582 (CA) 1.26
Smith v Baker [1891] AC 325 .... 4.47
Smith v Eric S Bush (a firm) [1990] 1 AC 831 (HL) 4.42
Smith v Littlewoods Organisation Ltd [1987] 2 AC 241 .... 3.54
Smith v Raker [1891] AC 325 .... 4.27

Table of Cases

South Yorkshire Transport Ltd and another v Monopolies and Mergers
    Commission and another [1993] 1 All ER 289 (HL) 6.138
Spring v Guardian Assurance plc (1994) 3 All ER 129 .... 3.52
Stennett v Hancock [1939] 2 All ER 578 .... 4.71
Stephenson v Delphi Diesel Systems Ltd [2003] ICR 471 .... 4.40
Stovin v Wise (Norfolk CC, third party) [1996] 3 All ER 801;
    [1996] AC 923 .... 1.27, 3.51, 3.54, 4.91, 5.26, 5.27, 5.28, 5.31
Sutherland Shire Council v Heyman (1985) 60 ALR 1 .... 3.40, 3.48
Swain v Buri [1996] PIQR P442 .... 4.63
Swinney v Chief Constable of Northumbria Police [1997] QB 464 .... 5.63

Targett v Torfaen BC [1992] 3 All ER 27 .... 4.82
Tesco Supermarkets Ltd v Nattrass [1972] AC 153 (HL) 1.07

Vacwell Engineering Co. Ltd v BDH Chemicals Ltd [1971] 1 QB 88 .... 4.71
Vellino v Chief Constable of Greater Manchester [2002] 3 All ER 78 .... 4.119

Waters v Commissioner of Police for the Metropolis [2000] 1 WLR 1607 .... 5.58
Watson v British Boxing Board of Control [2001] QB 1134 .... 5.40
Watson v Buckley, Osborne Garrett & Co. Ltd [1940] 1 All ER 174 .... 4.71
Wheat v Lacon & Co. Ltd [1966] 1 QB 335; [1966] AC 552 .... 4.52, 4.53
Wheeler v Copas [1981] 3 All ER 405 .... 4.46
White v St Albans City and District Council, *The Times*, 12 March 1990 .... 4.63
Williams and another v Natural Life Health Foods Ltd [1998]
    2 All ER 577 (HL) 1.13, 2.15, 6.150
Williams and another v Natural Life Health Foods Ltd and another
    [1997] 1 BCLC 131 (CA) 1.13, 2.15, 6.150
Williams v Birmingham Battery and Metal Co. [1899] 2 QB 338 .... 4.47
Willoughby [2005] 1 Cr App R 29 .... 1.27, 1.29, 3.09, 3.19
Wilson v Tyneside Window Cleaning Co. [1958] 2 QB 110 .... 4.26, 4.29
Wilsons and Clyde Coal Co. Ltd v English [1938] AC 57 .... 4.25, 4.29

X and others (minors) v Bedfordshire County Council [1995] 3 All ER 353;
    [1995] 2 AC 633 .... 1.27, 3.52, 5.31, 5.32

Yewens v Noakes (1880) 6 QBD 530 .... 4.39
Yuen Kun Yeu v A-G of Hong Kong [1987] 2 All ER 705 .... 3.37

Table of Secondary Legislation

References are to paragraph and Appendix numbers

Children (Northern Ireland) Order
   1995 (SI 1995/755) (NI 2)
   Pt 5 .... 5.85
   Pt 6 .... 5.85
Construction (Design and
   Management) Regulations 2007
   (SI 2007/320) 4.46, 4.80, 6.68
Control of Asbestos Regulations 2006
   (SI 2006/2739) 6.68
Criminal Procedure Rules 2005
   (SI 2005/384)
   r 4 .... 2.36
   r 4.3 .... 2.36
   r 4.3(1)(b) 2.38
   r 4.4 .... 2.37
   r 4.4(1) 2.38
   r 4.4(2)(b) 2.38
   r 4.7 .... 2.38

Health and Safety at Work
   (Northern Ireland) Order 1978
   (SI 1978/1039) (NI 9) 6.65, 7.49

Industrial Relations (Northern Ireland)
   Order 1992 (SI 1992/807) (NI 5)
   Art 3 .... 2.75
   Art 4 .... 2.76

Lifting Operations and Lifting
   Equipment Regulations 1998
   (SI 1998/2307) 6.68
Management of Health and Safety
   at Work Regulations 1999
   (SI 1999/3242)
   reg 3(1) 6.100
   reg 21 ....6.97, 6.98
Mental Health (Care and
   Treatment) (Scotland)
   Act 2003 (Consequential
   Provisions) Order 2005
   (SI 2005/2078)
   Art 11 .... 4.105
Mental Health (Northern Ireland)
   Order 1986 (SI 1986/585)
   (NI 4) 4.105
   Art 131 .... 4.105

Probation Board (Northern Ireland)
   Order 1982 (SI 1982/713)
   (NI 10)
   Art 4 .... 5.86

Work at Heights Regulations 2005
   (SI 2005/735) 6.68

Table of Statutes

References are to paragraph and Appendix numbers

Administration of Justice
(Miscellaneous Provisions)
Act 1933
   s 2 .... 2.40

Building Act 1984
   s 38 .... 4.81

Carriage by Air Act 1961 .... 4.11, 4.13
   s 4 .... 4.13
Children Act 1989
   Pt 4 .... 5.85
   Pt 5 .... 5.85
Children (Scotland) Act 1995
   Pt 2 .... 5.85
Civil Aviation Act 1982
   s 92 .... 2.09
Consumer Protection Act 1987 .... 4.70
Coroners Act 1988
   s 11(6) 2.46
   s 16 .... 8.22
   s 16(1)(a)(i) 2.46
   s 16(7) 8.23
   s 17(1)(a) 2.46
   s 17(2)(a) 2.46
Corporate Manslaughter and
   Corporate Homicide Act 2007 .... 1.01,
                                    1.37, 1.48, App 1
   s 1 .... 2.01, 2.05, 2.09, 2.26,
                       2.48, 2.65, 2.82, 6.09
   s 1(1) 2.06, 2.07, 2.08,
                   6.07, 6.08, 6.36, 6.43, 6.117
   s 1(1)(a) 2.06, 2.90, 6.01,
                 6.07, 6.11, 6.18, 6.41, 6.46
   s 1(1)(b) 2.06, 2.90, 6.01,
                     6.07, 6.18, 6.46, 6.55
   s 1(2) 2.06, 2.07, 2.08, 2.47
   s 1(2)(a)–(b) 2.06
   s 1(2)(c) 2.06, 5.49
   s 1(2)(d) 2.06, 2.72, 2.73

   s 1(3) 2.06, 2.07, 2.08,
                   2.90, 6.01, 6.08, 6.117,
                   6.137, 6.148, 6.151
   s 1(4) 5.01
   s 1(4)(b) 2.91, 3.31, 6.47, 6.55
   s 1(4)(c) 2.95, 6.02, 6.06, 6.119,
                   6.129, 6.131, 6.144
   s 1(5)(a)–(b) 2.05
   s 1(6) 7.03
   s 2 .... 2.57, 2.58, 2.67, 2.83,
                   2.86, 3.04, 4.01, 4.12,
                   4.55, 5.01, 5.21, 5.41
   s 2(1) 2.84, 2.88, 4.04, 5.01,
                   5.06, 5.14, 5.35, 5.63
   s 2(1)(a) 4.20, 4.80, 5.12, 5.37,
               5.60, 5.65, 5.82, 5.83, 5.84
   s 2(1)(b) 5.12, 5.37, 5.60, 5.65,
                 5.82, 5.83, 5.84, 6.91
   s 2(1)(c) 4.66–4.98
   s 2(1)(c)(i) 4.66, 4.67, 4.80
   s 2(1)(c)(ii) 4.66, 4.75
   s 2(1)(c)(iii) 4.66, 4.80, 4.92
   s 2(1)(c)(iv) 4.66, 4.77, 4.97, 5.38
   s 2(1)(d) 1.48, 2.30, 2.87,
                 4.09, 4.99–4.121, 5.12,
                 5.16, 5.60, 5.84
   s 2(2) 2.84, 2.87, 4.04, 4.105,
                 4.106, 4.107–4.110, 5.02
   s 2(2)(a)–(c) 4.104, 4.105
   s 2(2)(d)–(e) 4.104
   s 2(3) 5.01
   s 2(4) 4.10–13
   s 2(5) 2.85, 3.02, 3.10–3.19,
                 3.20, 5.46
   s 2(6) 3.30, 4.10,
                 4.14–4.19, 4.55, 4.59,
                 4.64, 4.117, 4.121, 6.58
   s 2(6)(a) 4.17
   s 2(6)(b) 4.16, 4.17, 4.48, 4.49–4.56
   s 2(7) 4.51, 4.76, 4.87, 4.105

… Table of Statutes

Corporate Manslaughter and Corporate
 Homicide Act 2007 (*cont.*)
s 3 . . . . 2.57, 2.58, 2.67,
 2.88, 3.42, 3.52, 4.12,
 4.78, 4.91, 4.112, 5.01,
 5.03–5.06, 5.07, 5.21
s 3(1) 5.09–5.11, 5.35–36
s 3(2) 4.112, 5.12–5.19,
 5.35–5.36, 5.38, 5.39,
 5.44, 5.63, 5.87
s 3(3) 4.30, 5.37–5.40
s 3(4) 5.13, 5.37
s 4 . . . . 2.57, 2.58, 2.67, 2.88,
 3.42, 3.52, 4.12, 4.74,
 4.78, 4.112, 5.01, 5.03–5.06,
 5.21, 5.42, 5.43
s 4(1) 5.44
s 4(1)(c) 5.46
s 4(2) 5.42
s 5 . . . . 2.57, 2.58, 2.67, 2.88, 3.42,
 3.52, 4.12, 4.74, 4.78, 4.112,
 5.01, 5.03–5.06, 5.21, 5.50
s 5(1) 5.52, 5.55
s 5(2) 5.51
s 5(3) 5.60, 5.62
s 5(4) 5.61
s 6 . . . . 2.57, 2.58, 2.67, 2.73,
 2.88, 3.42, 3.52, 4.12, 4.74,
 4.78, 4.112, 5.01, 5.03–5.06,
 5.21, 5.65, 5.73
s 6(1) 5.65
s 6(2) 5.65, 5.66
s 6(3) 5.70
s 6(4) 5.71
s 6(5) 5.82
s 6(6) 5.82, 5.83
s 6(7) 5.67
s 6(8) 5.66, 5.69, 5.72, 5.77
s 7 . . . . 2.57, 2.58, 2.67, 2.88, 3.42,
 3.52, 4.12, 4.74, 4.112, 5.01,
 5.03–5.06, 5.21, 5.84, 5.87
s 7(2) 5.85
s 7(3) 5.86
s 8 . . . . 3.30, 4.45, 6.03, 6.59,
 6.60, 6.68, 6.113, 6.152
s 8(1) 6.60
s 8(2) 6.64, 6.66, 6.67, 6.78,
 6.104, 6.105

s 8(2)(a) 6.72
s 8(2)(b) 6.75–6.77
s 8(3) 6.63, 6.105, 6.153
s 8(3)(a) 6.20, 6.152, 6.153
s 8(4) 6.63, 6.77
s 8(5) 6.113
s 9 . . . . 7.45, 7.47
s 9(1) 7.48
s 9(2) 7.49, 7.50
s 9(3) 7.49
s 9(4) 7.51, 7.59
s 9(5) 7.52
s 10 . . . . 7.53
s 10(1) 7.55
s 10(2) 7.57
s 11 . . . . 2.55–2.63, 5.04, 5.21
s 11(1) 2.55
s 11(2) 2.56
s 11(2)(b) 2.53
s 11(3) 2.58, 6.102
s 11(3)(a)(i) 2.57
s 11(3)(b)(i) 2.57
s 11(4) 2.57, 5.21
s 11(5) 2.57
s 12 . . . . 5.04, 5.41
s 12(2) 5.41, 6.102
s 12(3)–(4) 5.48
s 13 . . . . 2.66, 2.67, 5.04, 5.49
s 13(1) 2.66
s 13(1)(a) 2.68
s 13(1)(d) 2.68
s 13(1)(f) 2.68
s 13(2) 2.67
s 13(3) 2.68, 2.69, 6.102
s 13(4) 2.68
s 13(5)–(6) 2.67
s 13(7) 2.69
s 14 . . . . 2.81
s 14(1) 2.79
s 14(2)–(3) 2.80
s 14(4) 2.81
s 15 . . . . 2.30, 2.33, 2.35
s 15(2) 2.34
s 16 . . . . 2.30
s 16(2) 2.59
s 16(3) 2.61
s 16(4) 2.63
s 16(5) 2.62

s 16(6)–(7) 2.63	s 33(6) 2.44
s 17 . . . . 2.12	Criminal Justice Act 1991
s 18 . . . . 2.16	s 80 . . . . 4.105
s 18(1)–(2) 2.13	Criminal Justice Act 2003
s 19(1) 2.21	Pt 10 . . . . 2.45
s 19(2) 2.23, 2.24	s 58 . . . . 3.26
s 19(3) 2.21	s 62 . . . . 2.45
s 20 . . . . 2.05, 2.17, 2.27, 2.28	s 142 . . . . 7.26
	s 162 . . . . 7.35
s 21 . . . . 2.30, 2.48, 2.82	s 164 . . . . 7.38
s 21(3) 2.48	Criminal Justice and Court Services Act 2000
s 22 . . . . 2.64	
s 22(1) 2.30	Pt 1 . . . . 5.86
s 22(2) 2.64	Criminal Justice and Public Order Act 1994
s 22(3) 2.30	
s 23 . . . . 2.30	s 34(1)–(2) 8.31
s 23(1)–(3) 4.109	s 102 . . . . 4.105
s 24 . . . . 4.110	s 118 . . . . 4.105
s 24(1) 2.29	Criminal Procedure and Investigations Act 1996
s 24(2) 2.32	
s 24(3) 2.31	s 29 . . . . 3.27
s 25 . . . . 2.50, 2.51, 2.52, 2.71, 2.75, 2.76, 2.77, 2.86, 4.31, 4.33, 4.50, 5.08, 6.65, 6.81, 7.49	s 35 . . . . 3.27
	Criminal Procedure (Scotland) Act 1995 . . . . 4.105
s 27(1) 2.29	s 200 . . . . 4.105
s 27(2) 2.30, 2.87, 4.09, 4.99, 5.16	Crown Proceedings Act 1947 . . . . 5.21
	Crown Proceedings (Armed Forces) Act 1987 . . . . 5.47
s 27(3) 2.26	
s 27(4) 2.27	
s 27(5) 2.28	Defective Premises Act 1972 . . . . 4.01, 4.51, 4.52
s 28 . . . . 2.09	
s 28(3) 2.09	s 1 . . . . 4.85
s 28(4) 2.10	s 1(1) 4.84
Sch 1 . . . . 2.03, 2.33, 2.49, 2.54, 2.56, 2.57, 2.58, 2.59, 2.64–2.65, 3.42, 5.21, 6.102	s 1(2) 4.86
	s 3(1)–(2) 4.83
	s 4(1) 4.88
	s 4(3) 4.89
Sch 2 . . . . 2.45, 2.46, 8.22	
Guide. . . . . 1.49, 2.11, 6.19, 6.120, 6.127, 6.131, App 2	Employment Rights Act 1996 . . . . 4.41
	s 230 . . . . 4.33
Countryside and Rights of Way Act 2000 . . . . 4.62	
	Fair Trading Act 1973
Crime and Disorder Act 1998 Sch 3	s 64(1)(a) 6.138
para 2(1) 3.24	s 64(3) 6.138
para 2(5) 3.24	Finance Act 1988 Sch 6
Criminal Justice Act 1925	
s 33(3) 2.43	para 1 . . . . 4.95

Table of Statutes

Health and Safety at Work etc.
  Act 1974 . . . . 1.25, 4.44, 6.65,
            6.67, 6.78, 6.81, 6.82, 6.101,
            7.06, 7.13, 7.14, 7.17, 7.49
  s 2 . . . . 1.25, 6.66, 6.68, 6.69,
            6.79, 6.82, 6.85, 6.89, 6.90
  s 2(1) 6.84
  s 3 . . . . 1.10, 1.25, 6.66, 6.68,
            6.69, 6.79, 6.82, 6.85,
            6.89, 6.90, 7.16, 7.25, 7.28
  s 3(1) 1.08, 6.84
  s 3(2) 6.79
  s 4 . . . . 1.25, 6.68, 6.69, 6.80,
            6.82, 6.85, 6.91, 6.92
  s 4(4) 6.92
  s 5 . . . . 1.25, 6.69, 6.82, 6.85
  s 6 . . . . 1.25, 6.69, 6.80,
            6.82, 6.85, 6.93
  s 7 . . . . 6.85
  s 15 . . . . 6.67, 6.94
  s 16 . . . . 6.114
  s 17 . . . . 6.115
  s 20 . . . . 8.26
  s 20(2)(j)–(k) 8.26
  s 21 . . . . 7.46
  s 22 . . . . 7.46
  s 33(1)(a) 6.69, 6.83
  s 33(1)(c) 6.69, 6.95
  s 33(3)(b)(i) 6.69
  s 33(4) 6.69
  s 37 . . . . 2.25
  s 40 . . . . 6.88, 6.104
  s 42 . . . . 7.45
  s 47(1)(a) 6.85
  s 53(1) 4.33, 6.93
Highways Act 1980 . . . . 5.26
Homicide Act 1957
  s 2(1) 6.141
Hovercraft Act 1968 . . . . 2.09
Human Rights Act 1998 . . . . 5.08
  s 6 . . . . 5.08
  s 6(3)(a)–(b) 5.08
  s 6(4) 5.08

Immigration Acts 5.61
Immigration and Asylum Act 1999
  s 147 . . . . 4.105
  s 156 . . . . 4.105

Income and Corporation Taxes
  Act 1988
  s 53 . . . . 4.95
  s 297 . . . . 4.95

Law Reform (Contributory Negligence)
  Act 1945
  s 1(1) 6.38
  s 4 . . . . 6.39
Law Reform (Personal Injuries)
  Act 1948
  s 1 . . . . 4.24
Limited Liability Partnerships
  Act 2000 . . . . 2.51
Limited Partnerships Act 1907 . . . . 2.77
Local Government (Miscellaneous
  Provisions) Act 1982
  Sch 3
    para 4(1) 6.132

Magistrates' Courts Act 1980 . . . . 2.39
  s 46 . . . . 2.39
  Sch 3 . . . . 2.39
    para 1 . . . . 2.40
    para 1(1) 2.40
    para 2 . . . . 2.40
    para 2(a) 2.41
    para 3 . . . . 2.42
    para 3(1)–(2) 2.42
Mental Health Act 1983 . . . . 4.106
  Pt 2 . . . . 4.105
  Pt 3 . . . . 4.105
  s 137 . . . . 4.105
Mental Health (Care and Treatment)
  (Scotland) Act 2003
  s 13 . . . . 4.105
Merchant Shipping Act 1995
  Part 2 . . . . 2.09
  Sch 3
    para 4 . . . . 5.83
  Sch 3A 5.83

Occupiers' Liability Act 1957 . . . . 4.01,
            4.17, 4.51, 4.52,
            4.57, 4.65, 6.91
  s 1(3)(a) 4.54
  s 2 . . . . 4.58
  s 2(3)–(4) 4.60

Table of Statutes

s 2(5) 4.17, 4.59
s 2(6) 4.57
Occupiers' Liability
    Act 1984 . . . . .4.01, 4.51, 4.52,
                              4.62, 4.65, 6.91
s 1(1)(A). 4.62
s 1(3) 4.62
s 1(3)(a)–(b). 4.62, 4.63
s 1(3)(c) 4.62
s 1(4) 4.62
s 1(6) 4.64

Partnership Act 1890 . . . . 2.77
Petroleum Act 1998
    s 10(1) 2.09
Police Act 1996 . . . . 2.66
Police and Criminal Evidence
    Act 1984 . . . . 8.00, 8.03, 8.24
    s 8 . . . . 8.25
    s 24 . . . . 8.28
Police (Northern Ireland) Act 2000
    ss 39–40. . . . . 2.68
    s 42 . . . . 2.68
Police (Scotland) Act 1967. . . . . 2.66

Sale of Goods Act 1979
    s 14 . . . . 4.70
Sale and Supply of Goods
    Act 1994 . . . . 4.70

Serious Organised Crime and
    Police Act 2005
    Pt 2 . . . . 5.61
Social Security (Contributions Benefits)
    Act 1992
    s 72(1)(a)(i) 6.135
Social Work (Scotland) Act 1968
    s 27 . . . . 5.86
Supply of Goods and Services 1982
    s 4 . . . . 4.70

Trade Union and Labour Relations
    (Consolidation) Act 1922
    s 1 . . . . 2.75
    s 122 . . . . 2.76

Unfair Contract Terms Act 1977
    s 1(1)(c) 4.61
    s 1(3) 4.61
    s 2(1) 4.61
    s 6 . . . . 4.70

Water Resources Act 1991
    s 85(1) .6.28, 6.29

International Legislation

European Convention on
    Human Rights
    Art 7 . . . . 1.20

1
INTRODUCTION: THE ACT, ITS HISTORY, AND THE COMMON LAW

A. The Corporate Manslaughter and Corporate Homicide Act 2007	1.01
B. The Common Law	1.04
C. Common Law Gross Negligence Manslaughter	1.16
1. Recent authorities	1.19
2. The position of the statutory offence versus the common law offence	1.30
D. The Need for Reform	1.32
E. History of the Act	1.38

A. THE CORPORATE MANSLAUGHTER AND CORPORATE HOMICIDE ACT 2007

1.01 The Corporate Manslaughter and Corporate Homicide Act 2007 sweeps away the common law offence of manslaughter by gross negligence in its application to organizations which are subject to the Act. Those organizations include corporate bodies but also others, some of which had no potential liability at common law, such as Government departments and Crown bodies, from whom Crown immunity in this respect is removed, and partnerships.

1.02 In respect of these organizations that are subject to the Act, in place of the common law which will still apply to individuals, the offence of corporate manslaughter has been created. The test for liability in the Act is focused on the way that an organizations' activities were managed or organized, which must be the cause of a person's death and found the 'gross' breach of a relevant duty of care owed in negligence. 'Gross' breach is given the meaning of having fallen far below what could have reasonably been expected by the organization in the circumstances.

1.03 Furthermore, the way such activities were managed or organized must have been a substantial element in the breach. As Lord Bassam of Brighton told the House of Lords during the passage of the Bill through Grand Committee, this requirement for the involvement of senior management in the offence is there to limit liability, 'we put the requirement in the Bill that there was a failure at the senior level.

We think that this is important because we believe that without such clarity the offence could lead to risk aversion; we also think that it is right in principle that organisations cannot be guilty of corporate manslaughter without fault at the senior level.'[1]

B. THE COMMON LAW

1.04 If it was ever seriously contended that companies and other corporate bodies were not liable to be prosecuted for criminal offences, the myth has long since been dispelled.[2] However, corporate criminal liability has been plagued by the issue of how and through whom such a body becomes criminally liable.

1.05 Lord Hoffmann, in *Meridian Global Funds Management v Securities Commission* [1995] 2 AC 500, giving the judgment of the Privy Council, described the issue in the following way:

A rule may be stated in language primarily applicable to a natural person and require some act or state of mind on the part of that person 'himself', as opposed to his servants or agents. This is generally true of the rules of the criminal law, which ordinarily impose liability only for the *actus reus* and *mens rea* of the defendant himself. How is such a rule to be applied to a company? One possibility is that the court may come to the conclusion that the rule was not intended to apply to companies at all; for example, a law which created an offence for which the only penalty was community service. Another possibility is that the court might interpret the law as meaning that it could apply to a company only on the basis of its primary rules of attribution, ie if the act giving rise to liability was specifically authorised by a resolution of the board or a unanimous agreement of the shareholders. But there will be many cases in which neither of these solutions is satisfactory; in which the court considers that the law was intended to apply to companies and that, although it excludes ordinary vicarious liability, insistence on the primary rules of attribution would in practice defeat that intention. In such a case, the court must fashion a special rule of attribution for the particular substantive rule. This is always a matter of interpretation: given that it was intended to apply to a company, how was it intended to apply? Whose act (or knowledge, or state of mind) was for this purpose intended to count as the act etc of the company? One finds the answer to this question by applying the usual canons of interpretation, taking into account the language of the rule (if it is a statute) and its content and policy.[3]

---

[1] *Hansard*, HL, Grand Committee, column 134 (11 January 2007).

[2] See, eg, the comprehensive review of the authorities by Turner J, in *P & O European Ferries (Dover) Ltd* (1991) 93 Cr App R 72, 73 (Central Criminal Court), on the liability or otherwise of companies to be prosecuted. In *P & O*, Turner J outlined the incremental development of corporate criminal liability. The historical position was that an indictment could lie against a corporation: *per* Paterson J, in *Birmingham and Gloucester Railway Co.* (1842) 3 QB 223; *per* Denman CJ, in *Great North of England Railway Co.* (1846) 9 QB 315. Exceptions to this general rule were noted, such as that a corporation could not be indicted, *inter alia*, for treason or felony or perjury, or any offence involving personal violence.

[3] [1995] 2 AC 500, at 506C.

B. The Common Law

Lord Hoffman described: 1.06

It is a question of construction in each case as to whether the particular rule requires that the knowledge that an act has been done, or the state of mind in which it was done, should be attributed to the company.[4]

One of the competing theories of attribution was the 'identification' doctrine,[5] which was developed by *Tesco Supermarkets Ltd v Nattrass* in which, at 170E, Lord Reid said: 1.07

A living person has a mind which can have knowledge or intention or be negligent and he has hands to carry out his intentions. A corporation has none of these: it must act through living persons though not always one or the same person. Then the person who acts is not speaking or acting for the company. He is acting as the company and his mind which directs his acts is the mind of the company. There is no question of the company being vicariously liable. He is not acting as a servant, representative, agent or delegate. He is an embodiment of the company or, one could say, he hears and speaks through the persona of the company, within his appropriate sphere, and his mind is the mind of the company. If it is a guilty mind then that guilt is the guilt of the company.

The alternative approach to corporate attribution can be found in *R v British Steel plc* [1995] IRLR 310, a case in which the defendant company was prosecuted for a breach of the duty under the Health and Safety at Work Act 1974, s 3(1), to do all that was reasonably practicable to ensure safety. A worker was killed because of the collapse of a steel platform during a repositioning operation which a competent supervisor would have recognized was inherently dangerous. The defence was that the workmen had disobeyed instructions and, even if the supervisor was at fault, the company at the level of its directing mind had taken all reasonably practicable steps. In the Court of Appeal, Steyn LJ described the issue at 313: 1.08

Counsel for British Steel plc concedes that it is not easy to fit the idea of corporate criminal liability only for acts of the 'directing mind' of the company into the language of s 3(1). We would go further. If it be accepted that Parliament considered it necessary for the protection of public health and safety to impose, subject to the defence of reasonable practicability, absolute criminal ability, it would drive a juggernaut through the legislative scheme if corporate employers could avoid criminal liability where the potentially harmful event is committed by someone who is not the directing mind of the company...that would emasculate the legislation.

In a commentary on this decision in [1995] Criminal Law Review 655 Professor Sir John Smith said in relation to the 'directing mind' argument 1.09

Where a statutory duty to do something is imposed upon a particular person (here an employer) and he does not do it, he commits the actus reus of an offence. It may be that he has failed to fulfil his duty because his employee or agent has failed to carry out his duties properly, but this is not a

---

[4] [1995] 2 AC 500, at 511D.
[5] The origins of which are said to lie in the speech of Viscount Haldane LC in *Lennard's Carrying Co. Ltd v Asiatic Petroleum Co. Ltd* [1915] AC 705 at 713; and the judgment of Denning LJ in *Bolton Engineering v TJ Graham & Sons* [1957] 1 QB 159 at 172.

case for vicarious liability. If the employer is held liable, it is because he personally has failed to do what the law requires him to do and he is personally not vicariously liable. There is no need to find someone—in the case of a company, the brains and not merely the hands—for whose act the person with the duty be held liable. The duty on the company in this case was to ensure, ie to make certain, that persons are not exposed to risk. They did not make it certain. It does not matter how; they were in breach of their statutory duty and, in the absence of any requirement for mens rea, that is the end of the matter.

1.10 This was an approach adopted by Lord Hoffman in *R v Associated Octel Ltd* [1996] 4 All ER 846 [HL] where he described the view that 'attribution', in the context of statutory duties involved finding a person whom the company is responsible or as being:

'based on what seems to me a confusion between two quite different concepts: an employer's vicarious liability for the tortious act of another and a duty imposed upon the employer himself. Vicarious liability depends (with some exceptions) on the nature of the contractual relationship between the employer and the tortfeasor. There is liability if the tortfeasor was acting within the scope of his duties under a contract of employment. Otherwise, generally speaking, the employer is not vicariously liable. But s 3 is not concerned with vicarious liability. It imposes a duty upon the employer himself. That duty is defined by reference to a certain kind of activity, namely, the conduct by the employer of his undertaking. It is indifferent to the nature of the contractual relationships by which the employer chooses to conduct it.'

1.11 The apotheosis of the issue was reached with the Court of Appeal's ruling in *Attorney General's Reference (No 2 of 1999)* [2000] 2 Cr App Rep 207, affirming that of the trial judge Scott-Baker J (as he then was) in the manslaughter prosecution of a train company following the death of seven people in what was known as the Southall rail disaster. There, many of the above passages were considered, before it was definitively decided that unless an identified individual's conduct, as opposed to the aggregated conduct of individuals, characterized as gross criminal negligence, could be attributed to a company, the company was not, liable for common law manslaughter. Civil negligence rules, it was held, were not apt to confer criminal liability on a company, rather, the 'identification' doctrine remained the only basis in common law for corporate liability for gross negligence manslaughter.

1.12 Gross negligence manslaughter at common law involves the gross breach of a duty of care owed to the deceased under the law of negligence. Thus the identification doctrine, in its application to gross negligence manslaughter and corporations, provided that only the gross breach of an individual 'directing mind', and not the aggregated lesser failings of more than one such 'directing mind', could attach to the corporation.[6]

1.13 The further limitation on potential liability this provided was that, at common law, while a corporation would owe primary duties of care in negligence directors and be vicariously liable for breaches of duties of care by its employees, those who manage a company do not owe a duty of care to any third party by reason of holding

---

[6] *Attorney-General's Reference* (No 1 of 1995) [1996] 2 Cr App R 320.

papercavalier

252 Java Street,
Suite 120
Brooklyn, NY 11222
United States

Biscuit Factory
Block J Unit 112A
100 Clements Road
London SE16 4DG
Great Britain

Hello. Here's your receipt:

```
      Sales channel: Amazon.co.uk
          Order no: 204-3499442-6297919
        Order date: October 01, 2018
           Bill to: Hamish Stark
        Deliver to: Hamish Stark
                    15 DA VINCI WALK
                    ROYAL WOOTTON BASSETT Wiltshire SN4 7FG
                    United Kingdom
This package contains: Blackstone&#39;s Guide to the Corporate
                    Manslaughter and Corp...
         Condition: New
             Price: GBP 16.50
          Delivery: GBP 2.80
              VAT: 0
            Total: GBP 19.30
            Paid in full
```

Find the best deals on new and used books online: http://www.part.ly

---

such an office,[7] nor do they owe a duty of care in relation to the company's compliance with laws, certainly not such a duty of care in respect of the company's non-delegable statutory health and safety duties as employer,[8] and will only owe any duty of care as a result of some particular assumption or appointment of responsibility.[9]

1.14 Thus while a company could only be grossly negligent through its directors, nonetheless proving the existence of a duty of care owed by such a director was very difficult.

1.15 For the purposes of establishing liability, the doctrine made it practically impossible to identify, in anything but a very small company, a 'directing mind' who owed and was in breach of a duty of care and thus under whose auspices the company's gross breach was committed. Between 1992 and 2005 some 34 manslaughter prosecutions were launched against corporations, of which six resulted in a conviction. Each of the six was just such a small company that operated and was managed wholly through an identified director.

C. COMMON LAW GROSS NEGLIGENCE MANSLAUGHTER

1.16 The existing common law offence of gross negligence manslaughter, which will continue to apply to individuals, crystallized in the judgement of Lord Mackay in *R v Adomako* [1995] 1 AC 171.

1.17 *Adomako*[10] authoritatively established that the ordinary principles of the law of negligence apply to determine whether a defendant was in breach of a duty of care towards the victim. Where a defendant can be proved to be in breach of a duty of care towards a deceased victim, which was a substantial cause of the death of the victim, then, if having regard to the risk of death involved, the defendant's conduct can be proved to have been 'so bad in all the circumstances as to amount to a criminal act or omission', he will be guilty of manslaughter by gross negligence.

1.18 How 'bad' the conduct is judged to be is ultimately a question for a jury: in *Adomoko*[11] it was held that it is always eminently for a jury to decide whether, having regard to the risk of death involved, the defendant's conduct was so bad in all the circumstances as to amount to a criminal act or omission.[12] Such allegations of manslaughter can, and often are, based upon an alleged omission

---

[7] *Performing Right Society Ltd v Ciryl Theatrical Syndicate Ltd* [1924] 1 KB 1 at 14; *Williams and another v Natural Life Health Foods Ltd and anothet* [1997] 1 BCLC 131 (CA); *Williams and Another v Natural Life Health Foods Ltd* (HL) [1998] 2 All ER 577.
[8] *Huckerby v Elliot* [1970] 1 ALL ER 189, DC; *R v P and another* [2007] All ER (D) 173 (Jul).
[9] *R v Great Western Trains Company Ltd* (unreported) Central Criminal Court, 30 June 1999, per Scott-Baker J; *Williams and Another v Natural Life Health Foods Ltd* (HL) [1998] 2 All ER 577.
[10] [1995] 1 AC 171.
[11] ibid.
[12] Following *R v Bateman* (1925) 19 Cr App R 8 (CCA) and *Andrews v DPP* [1937] AC 576 (HL).

to act in circumstances where a defendant is alleged to have been under a duty to act.

1. Recent authorities

1.19 The uncertainties that remains in common law manslaughter are illustrated by recent authorities which have centred around resolving four key issues:

(a) What are the 'ordinary principles of negligence'?
(b) What is the relevance of any statutory duty owed by a defendant to a duty of care?
(c) What is the relevant test for establishing whether a duty of care exists?
(d) Is the question whether a duty of care exists one of fact or law?

1.20 The Court of Appeal held in *Misra and Srivastava* that the common law offence was sufficiently certain and did not offend Article 7 of the ECHR. As Lord Justice Judge stated, 'The ingredients of the offence have been clearly defined, and the principles decided in the House of Lords in *Adomako*. They involve no uncertainty.'[13] However, the principles decided in *Adomako* were equally imprecise. It was held in *Adomako*[14] that 'the ordinary principles of the law of negligence apply to ascertain whether or not the defendant has been in breach of a duty of care towards the victim who has died.'[15] Yet, apparently some principles are more ordinary than others.

1.21 In *Wacker*[16] the Court of Appeal was concerned with the infamous lorry driver who had been convicted of conspiracy to facilitate the entry in the UK of illegal immigrants and of 58 offences of manslaughter by gross negligence following the horrific discovery of the asphyxiated bodies of 58 illegal immigrants within a container on his trailer at Dover.

1.22 Following the close of the prosecution case at trial, the defence submitted that one of 'the ordinary principles of the law of negligence', known by the Latin maxim of *ex turpi causa non oritur actio*, was that the law of negligence did not recognize the relationship between those involved in a criminal enterprise as giving rise to a duty of care owed by one participant to another.

1.23 The trial judge ruled that that the concept was as much a part of the law of manslaughter as other principles of the law of negligence. However, he found a distinction in the roles and responsibilities of the drivers and the immigrants and ruled that there was a case to answer.

1.24 This approach found no favour with the Court of Appeal who held that *ex turpi causa* was not an ordinary principle of negligence in common law gross negligence

---

[13] [2004] EWCA Crim 2375 at para 64.
[14] *R v Adomako* (1994) 99 Cr App R 362.
[15] P 369 and 187B.
[16] [2003] 1 Cr App R 22.

C. Common Law Gross Negligence Manslaughter

manslaughter; rather, that the civil courts had introduced the concept as a matter of public policy as the courts will not 'promote or countenance a nefarious object or bargain which it is bound to condemn.'[17] Kay LJ went on to state that when Lord Mackay referred to ordinary principles of negligence, 'He was doing no more than holding that in an "ordinary" case of negligence, the question whether there was a duty of care was to be judged by the same legal criteria as governed whether there was a duty of care in the law of negligence.'

1.25 Statutory duties under the Health and Safety at Work etc. Act 1974 (HSWA) impose strict liability save for the qualification of 'reasonable practicability'. HSWA specifically excludes civil liability in respect of breaches of the general duties created in ss 2–6 of the Act. Common law duties of care in negligence require a different and lower standard than that imposed by these statutory duties.

1.26 In *Singh* [1999] Crim LR 582 CA, the appellant was found to have been under a duty to ensure the safety of gas equipment and convicted of gross negligence manslaughter. The appellant submitted to the Court of Appeal that the trial judge had failed to make clear to the jury what the extent of that duty was. Was it the absolute duty required under the statutory health and safety provisions or a common law duty to take reasonable care? The Court accepted the importance of the distinction and the possibility of different verdicts on the same facts dependent on the standard imposed. However, the Court found that the judge's summing up had not been wrong and that there was no risk that the jury had been unclear as to which standard applied, namely reasonable care. What the Court of Appeal failed to address was what relevance, if any, the statutory duties owed by the defendant had on the issues the jury had to determine.

1.27 In negligence, the existence of a statutory duty is not determinative of the existence of a duty of care. Indeed, in a number of cases civil courts have determined that no duty of care arose in such circumstances.[18] A statutory duty does no more than place a potential defendant in a situation of proximity to a potential claimant and may inform the extent of any duty of care found to arise. Unfortunately, the clarity of this position does not sit comfortably with dicta from the Court of Appeal's decision in *Willoughby*[19] which suggested that there may be cases where a duty arises because Parliament has imposed a statutory duty.[20]

1.28 In September 2004, Mr Justice Mackay, dismissing counts of manslaughter against directors of a number of companies in the prosecution that followed the Hatfield train crash, reviewed the conflicting authorities on the issue of how and by whom the existence of a duty of care is determined in individual gross negligence manslaughter. He identified how the offence was founded upon the 'ordinary principles of negligence' and, as such, the question of the existence of a duty care must

---

[17] Bingham *LJ in Saunders v Edwards* [1987] 1 WLR 1116 at 1134.
[18] See, eg, the House of Lords in *Stovin v Wise* [1996] AC 923 and *X and others (minors) v Bedfordshire CC* [1995] 3 All ER 353.
[19] [2005] 1 Cr App R 29.
[20] Para 23.

be resolved in accordance with the tripartite test set out in the leading authority, namely *Caparo Industries plc v Dickman*,[21] which explicitly recognized how the ingredients of this test, 'are not susceptible of any such precise definition as would be necessary to give them utility as practical tests.'[22]

1.29 It was just months later on the 1 December 2004, the host of conflicting authorities in respect of whether the existence of a duty of care in a charge on individual gross negligence manslaughter was a question of law for the judge, a question of fact for the jury or involved both questions of law and fact was reviewed by the Court of Appeal in *Willoughby* [2005] 1 Cr App R 29. The judgment of Rose LJ purported to decide, once and for all, that, 'Whether a duty of care exists is a matter for the jury once the judge has decided that there is evidence capable of establishing a duty.'[23]

2. The position of the statutory offence versus the common law offence

1.30 The Act does achieve a means of either resolving these issues or avoiding them for the offence of corporate manslaughter:

- The judge will decide whether a relevant duty of care was owed by the organization, as a matter of law, and will decide all questions of fact necessary so to do.
- To be a relevant duty of care it must be one owed under the law of negligence that falls within certain defined categories. The operation of various principles, such as *ex turpii causa*, are excluded.
- Health and safety duties owed under statute are relevant where they relate to an organization's breach of the relevant duty of care and are a matter a jury must consider when deciding the issue of gross breach.

1.31 The stark differences that will exist between the statutory offence of corporate manslaughter and the common law gross negligence manslaughter may prove challenging if ever an individual is indicted with the common law offence alongside an organization indicted with the statutory offence.

D. THE NEED FOR REFORM

1.32 The late 1980s and early 1990s saw a series of public disasters where many lives were lost. *The Herald of Free Enterprise* capsized in March 1987 killing 187; this was followed in November of that year with the death of 31 people in the King's Cross Fire. In July 1988 the *Piper Alpha* oil platform disaster claimed the lives of 167; later in that year 35 died as a result of the Clapham rail crash. The following year saw

---

[21] [1990] 1 All ER 568.
[22] [1990] 1 All ER 568 at 574.
[23] [2005] 1 Cr App R 29 at para 24.

D. The Need for Reform

51 people die when the *Marchioness* pleasure boat sank in the Thames. More recently, 49 people were killed as a result of the rail disasters at Southall, near Paddington, Hatfield and Potters Bar.

1.33 Perhaps infamously, none of these disasters was followed by a successful prosecution for gross negligence manslaughter of a company involved in the conduct of the undertaking responsible for the tragedy. Public outrage seemed to grow as what appeared to be companies with inadequate safety systems in place at the fatal times avoided conviction for manslaughter, although in a number of instances very substantial fines were imposed in respect of health and safety offences.

1.34 In each prosecution that was brought, what proved insurmountable was the common law doctrine of identification. This required the prosecution to prove that the act or omission causing the death was the act or omission in breach of a duty of care owed by an individual who was the embodiment of the corporation.

1.35 Government, the unions and practitioners had each observed that the law needed reform. Industry, too, acknowledged that the common law offence provided no certainty in respect of liability.

1.36 In 2006, John Reid, the then Home Secretary, declared that, 'Companies and other organisations must be held property to account for gross corporate negligence that has led to loss of life.'[24] He further defended the need to legislate for a new corporate offence, stating that 'it is not enough for those failings to be punished under health and safety law'.[25]

1.37 However, the Corporate Manslaughter and Corporate Homicide Act 2007 comes with a disclaimer. The reasons why proceedings such as those that followed in the wake of public disasters proved unsuccessful 'are complex'.[26] The implementation of the 2007 Act will 'not mean that each of these cases would now necessarily be successfully prosecuted'.[27] Instead, the new Act is aimed at 'tackling the key difficulties'[28] the old law presented. It remains to be seen whether the next public disaster that involves large scale lose of life will result in a prosecution under the new Act. That the way in which an organization's activities are managed or organized by its senior management must have been a 'substantial element' in any gross breach of a duty of care for liability to arise may mean that a conviction for corporate manslaughter will prove almost as elusive as it did under the common law.

---

[24] *Hansard*, House of Commons, 10 October 2006, col 194.
[25] ibid.
[26] Corporate Manslaughter: The Government's Draft Bill for Reform (Cm 6497), Introduction, at para 10.
[27] ibid.
[28] ibid.

E. HISTORY OF THE ACT

1.38 The real foundations of the Act go back to the 1996 Law Commission report *Legislating the Criminal Code: Involuntary Manslaughter* (Law Com No 237).[29]

1.39 The Commission recommended that for the purposes of a proposed offence of corporate killing, a death should be regarded as having been caused by the conduct of a corporation if it was caused by a failure in the way which the corporation's activities are managed or organized, to ensure the health and safety of persons employed in or affected by those activities;[30] and, that the offence should be committed only where the defendant's conduct in causing death fell far below what could reasonably be expected.[31]

1.40 The Commission took the view that the existing common law reliance upon the existence of a duty of care was problematic:

> ...the terminology of 'negligence' and 'duty of care' is best avoided within the criminal law because of the uncertainty and confusion that surround it.[32]

1.41 Following the 1997 Labour manifesto commitment to reform the law of corporate manslaughter and to remove Crown immunity, the government published its proposals in May 2000.[33] These were largely based upon the 1996 Law Commission's recommendations, however, the proposals set out a number of issues and posed various questions upon which the government thereafter started a protracted period of consultation. These issues surrounded whether and to what extent liability should be extended to organizations beyond corporations and the limiting of Crown immunity.

1.42 It was not until 23 March 2005 that the Home Office published a draft Corporate Manslaughter Bill.[34] The Bill proposed that the offence of corporate manslaughter would be committed by an organization if the way in which its activities were managed or organised by its senior management caused a death and amounted to a gross breach of a duty of care owed in negligence. A list of Government departments and Crown bodies which were to be organizations subject to the Act was included as a proposed schedule 1 to the Act; whether an organization owed a duty of care was proposed to be a matter for the judge to decide.

1.43 Having heard oral and written evidence from a wide panel of witnesses and various interest groups, on 20 December 2005, the Joint Committees of the Home Affairs and Work and Pensions Committees of the House of Commons

---

[29] The report is available at <http://www.lawcom.gov.uk/files/lc237.pdf>.
[30] Recommendation 11(4).
[31] Recommendation 11(2).
[32] *Legislating the Criminal Code: Involuntary Manslaughter* (Law Com No 237, 1996).
[33] Reforming the Law on Involuntary Manslaughter: the Government Proposals (May 2000).
[34] Corporate Manslaughter: The Government's Draft Bill for Reform (Cm 6497).

E. History of the Act

published a three-volume report[35] scrutinizing the government's draft Corporate Manslaughter Bill. The Joint Committees report contained many recommendations and called for a further review by the government. Principally, the Joint Committees recommended:

- the abandonment of 'relevant duty of care' and a return to the Law Commission's proposals;
- a rethink of the 'senior management' requirement;
- the inclusion of secondary individual liability.

1.44 The government published its response to the Joint Committees Report on 8 March 2006[36] and thereafter a draft Bill[37] was introduced to the House of Commons on 20 July 2006. The Government's amended Bill was proposed to extend across all the jurisdictions of the United Kingdom; a relevant duty of care in negligence remained at the heart of the offence, with the categories of potential duty broadened; individual liability under the Act was precluded; and, most importantly, the way that the organization's activities were managed or organized by senior management now had only to be a 'substantial element' in the breach.

1.45 The government set the tone for the progress of the Bill, by stating that it was 'firmly committed to taking the process of reform through to completion'. It indicated that time was of the essence for the new corporate offence: '. . .we will be looking to introduce a bill without delay as soon as parliamentary time allows'.[38]

1.46 The Bill received broad cross-party support and passed through the House of Commons, reaching the House of Lords on 5 December 2006.

1.47 Thereafter, the Bill ultimately spent nearly five months being passed to and fro between the Commons and the Lords as the scope of the final Act was fought upon in a protracted 'ping-pong' stage. The amendments tabled by the Lords included both the semantic and those which would significantly alter the Act's operation. Many significant amendments entered the Act without contention, such as the inclusion of employing partnerships, trade unions and employers' associations to the category of organizations subject to the offence. The sticking point became the Lords insistence of the immediate inclusion in the Act of the duty owed to those persons in custody and the Commons rejection of the same.

1.48 The stand-off lasted throughout the spring of 2007 with neither House making any significant movement over the issue. The Lords dug their heels in and the final

---

[35] First Joint Report from the Home Affairs and Work and Pensions Committees Session 2005–06 (HC-540).
[36] Government Response to the First Joint Report from the Home Affairs and Work and Pensions Committees Session 2005–06. (Cm 6755).
[37] Corporate Manslaughter and Homicide Bill (Bill 220).
[38] Government Response to the First Joint Report from the Home Affairs and Work and Pensions Committees Session 2005–06. (Cm 6755), p 1.

Act that received Royal Assent on 26 July 2007 provided for a duty of care to be owed to those detained in custody. 'Custody' is given a wide enough interpretation to include the Lords' original proposals. However, the provision, which is contained in s 2(1)(d), can only be brought into force by an Order approved by a vote of both Houses of Parliament.

1.49 In October 2007, the Ministry of Justice published *A Guide to the Corporate Manslaughter and Corporate Homicide Act 2007*,[39] being non-statutory guidance. That document promised that the majority of the provisions of the Act would be brought into force on 6 April 2008.

---

[39] See App 2.

2
THE OFFENCE AND THE ORGANIZATIONS SUBJECT TO THE ACT

A. Overview	2.01
B. The Offence:	2.05
1. Definition and elements	2.06
2. Territorial extent	2.09
3. Institution of proceedings	2.12
4. Individual and secondary liability	2.13
5. Convictions under the Act and under health and safety legislation	2.21
6. Commencement and orders	2.26
7. Procedural provisions and consequential amendments	2.33
C. Element 1: By an Organization Subject to the Act	2.47
1. Corporations	2.50
2. Government bodies and the Crown	2.54
3. Police forces	2.66
4. A partnership, trade union, or employer's association that is an employer	2.72
5. Power to extend section 1 to other organizations: s 21	2.82
D. Element 2: The Organization Owed a Relevant Duty of Care to the Deceased	2.83
E. Element 3: The Way in which the Organization's Activities are Managed or Organized: Causation and Breach	2.89

A. OVERVIEW

The offence of corporate manslaughter is created by s 1 of the Corporate Manslaughter and Homicide Act 2007 (CMCHA). The Act abolishes common law liability for gross negligence manslaughter in respect of organizations subject to the Act and precludes individual liability for the new offence. Individuals will continue to be subject to the common law offence of gross negligence manslaughter.

2.02 The offence can be broken into three elements, with the first being the definition of an organization subject to the Act, which is considered in detail in this chapter. The remaining two elements, namely the 'relevant duty of care' and 'causation and breach', are considered in summary in this chapter and in detail in separate subsequent chapters.

2.03 Four types of organization are subject to the Act and thus capable of committing the offence of corporate manslaughter, namely:

- corporations;
- Government departments and bodies listed in Sch 1;
- police forces; and
- partnerships, trade unions and employers' associations that are employers.

2.04 Jurisdiction in respect of an offence of corporate manslaughter arises solely through and in relation to harm resulting in death that occurs within the territory of the United Kingdom. Proceedings for an offence of corporate manslaughter may not be instituted in England and Wales without the consent of the Director of Public Prosecutions.

B. THE OFFENCE

2.05 The Act creates the offence which is to be known in England and Wales and Northern Ireland as 'corporate manslaughter'[1] and in Scotland as 'corporate homicide'.[2] By s 20, the common law offence of manslaughter by gross negligence is abolished in its application to corporations, and in any application it has to other organizations to which s 1 applies.

1. Definition and elements

2.06 The offence is created by ss 1(1)–1(3) of the Act, which provide:

(1) An organisation to which this section applies is guilty of an offence if the way in which its activities are managed or organised—
   (a) causes a person's death, and
   (b) amounts to a gross breach of a relevant duty of care owed by the organisation to the deceased.
(2) The organisations to which this section applies are—
   (a) a corporation;

---

[1] CMCHA, s 1(5)(a).
[2] CMCHA, s 1(5)(b).

B. The Offence

    (b) a department or other body listed in Schedule 1;
    (c) a police force;
    (d) a partnership, or a trade union or employers' association, that is an employer.
(3) An organisation is guilty of an offence under this section only if the way in which its activities are managed or organised by its senior management is a substantial element in the breach referred to in subsection (1).

Thus, the offence created by ss 1(1)–1(3) will be committed: 2.07

1. by an organization subject to the Act, where;
2. the organization owed a relevant duty of care to the deceased; and
3. the way in which its activities are managed or organised:
    i. caused a person's death;
    ii. amounted to a gross breach of that duty of care;
    iii. by its senior management is a substantial element in the breach.

Many of the subsequent provisions of the Act relate to the meaning, interpretation and consideration by a judge and jury of elements of the offence created by ss 1(1)–1(3) (see table 2.1).   2.08

2. Territorial extent

By s 28, the Act extends to England and Wales, Scotland and Northern Ireland. Section 28(3) provides that s 1, the provision creating the offence, applies if the harm resulting in death is sustained in the United Kingdom or—   2.09

(a) within the seaward limits of the territorial sea adjacent to the United Kingdom;
(b) on a ship registered under Part 2 of the Merchant Shipping Act 1995 (c. 21);
(c) on a British-controlled aircraft as defined in section 92 of the Civil Aviation Act 1982 (c. 16);
(d) on a British-controlled hovercraft within the meaning of that section as applied in relation to hovercraft by virtue of provision made under the Hovercraft Act 1968 (c. 59);
(e) in any place to which an Order in Council under section 10(1) of the Petroleum Act 1998 (c. 17) applies (criminal jurisdiction in relation to offshore activities).

Section 28(4) additionally provides that for these purposes, harm sustained on a ship, aircraft or hovercraft includes harm sustained by a person who—   2.10

(a) is then no longer on board the ship, aircraft or hovercraft in consequence of the wrecking of it or of some other mishap affecting it or occurring on it, and
(b) sustains the harm in consequence of that event.

Thus jurisdiction in respect of an offence of corporate manslaughter arises solely through and in relation to harm resulting in death that occurs within the territory of the United Kingdom: neither the location or place of incorporation of the organization nor the place where any management failure or breach of a relevant duty occurs affects jurisdiction concerning an alleged offence. As the *Guide to the Corporate*   2.11

Table 2.1 Elements of the offence and associated provisions

	Element	Section	Provides:	Other Relevant Sections
(1)	'organisation'	s 1(2)	Organizations to which the offence applies: (a) corporation (b) department/body listed in Sch 1 (c) police force (d) partnership, trade union, or employers' association, that is an employer.	s 25, interpretation, provides: • 'corporation' does not include corporation sole but includes any body corporate wherever incorporated; • employee means an individual who works under a contract of employment or apprenticeship (whether express or implied and, if express, whether oral or in writing); • 'police force' has the meaning given by CMCHA, s 13; • 'partnership' means a partnership within Partnership Act 1890, a limited partnership registered under Limited Partnerships Act 1907 or a firm or entity of a similar character formed under the law of a country or territory outside the UK; • 'employers' association' has the meaning given by Trade Union and Labour Relations (Consolidation) Act 1992, s 122 or Industrial Relations (Northern Ireland) Order 1992,[1] Art 4.
(2)	'relevant duty of care'	s 1(4)(a)	Has the meaning given by s 2, read with ss 3–7	• s 2 provides definition, categories of relevant duty and means of determining existence of a duty of care • ss 3–7 provides exemptions based upon public policy, public functions, military activity, police and law enforcement activity, emergencies and child protection
	'causes a person's death'	s 1(1)		
	'gross breach'	s 1(4)(b)	the conduct alleged to amount to a breach of the duty falls far below what can reasonably be expected of the organization in the circumstances	s 8 provides definition, relevant factors which a jury must take into account and identifies some factors which the jury may take into account, when deciding if a breach is gross
(3)	'the way in which its activities are managed or organised'			
	'by its senior management is a substantial element in the breach'	s 1(3)	Guilty of the offence only if the way in which its activities are managed or organized by senior management is a substantial element in the breach	s 1(4)(c) defines 'senior management' to mean those who play significant roles in: (i) the making of decisions about how the whole or a substantial part of its activities are to be managed or organised (ii) the actual managing or organizing of the whole or a substantial part of those activities.

[1] (SI 1992/807 (NI 5))

B. The Offence

Manslaughter and Corporate Homicide Act 2007, which was published by the Ministry of Justice in October 2007, states:

In the majority of cases, the injury causing the death and the death will occur at the same time, in the same location. But death may occur some time after an injury or harm takes place. The courts will still have jurisdiction for the new offence if the death has occurred abroad, provided the relevant harm was sustained in the UK. In the case of fatalities connected with ships, aircraft and hovercraft, the new offence will still apply if the death does not actually occur on board (for example, the victim drowns), provided it relates to an on-board incident.[3]

3. Institution of proceedings

Section 17 of the Act provides that proceedings for an offence of corporate manslaughter may not be instituted in England and Wales without the consent of the Director of Public Prosecutions and may not be instituted in Northern Ireland without the consent of the Director of Public Prosecutions for Northern Ireland.

2.12

4. Individual and secondary liability

Section 18(1) of the Act provides that an individual cannot be guilty of aiding, abetting, counselling or procuring the commission of an offence of corporate manslaughter. In respect of the Scottish offence, s 18(2) similarly provides that an individual cannot be guilty of aiding, abetting, counselling or procuring, or being art and part in, the commission of an offence of corporate homicide.

2.13

Therefore, there can be no secondary liability for directors, managers or officers of an organization for the offence of corporate manslaughter. Such persons will continue to be subject to the common law offence of individual gross negligence manslaughter.

2.14

(a) *Company directors and individual gross negligence manslaughter*
The history of prosecutions against company directors is marked by very few successes, those exclusively being in relation to small companies with a director essentially identifiable as having direct control over the day to day affairs of the company. The difficulty is, and will remain, that the common law of negligence does not impose a duty of care towards third parties upon such individuals by operation of holding the office of director. The position is best illustrated by Hirst LJ in the Court of Appeal[4] in *Williams and another v Natural Life Health Foods Ltd and another* [1997] 1 BCLC 131 (CA), where he conducted a review of the authorities and cited,

2.15

---

[3] *Guide to the Corporate Manslaughter and Corporate Homicide Act 2007* (Ministry of Justice) October 2007, p 17.

[4] Hurst LJ's analysis of the authorities was approved by the House of Lords, where, however, the Court of Appeal's application of the law to the facts was overturned: *Williams and another v Natural Life Health Foods Ltd (HL)* [1998] 2 All ER 577.

in particular, a passage from the judgment of Slade LJ in *C Evans & Sons Ltd v Spritebrand Ltd*:

> The authorities...clearly show that a director of a company is not automatically to be identified with his company for the purpose of the law of tort, however small the company may be and however powerful his control over its affairs. Commercial enterprise and adventure is not to be discouraged by subjecting a director to such onerous potential liabilities. In every case where it is sought to make him liable for his company's torts, it is necessary to examine with care what part he played personally in regard to the act or acts complained of.[5]

(b) *Secondary liability in respect of non-natural persons*

2.16 The terms of s 18 exclude secondary liability in respect of an 'individual' but leave the secondary liability of other non-natural legal persons, such as corporations, untouched. Common law secondary liability has been held to be of general application to all offences, unless expressly or impliedly excluded by statute[6] and thus, arguably, such other legal persons are capable of being guilty of aiding, abetting, counselling or procuring the commission of an offence of corporate manslaughter.

2.17 If this is the position, then in the absence of express statutory provision, such a legal person would be subject to the common law 'identification doctrine' that haunted what will be the abolished common law offence of manslaughter by gross negligence in it application to corporations, whereby only the acts of the directing minds of the legal person could be attributed to it.[7]

2.18 In such circumstances, the legal person, if an organization subject to the Act, would be more likely to attract primary liability for the offence than be demonstrably guilty as an aidor or abettor of another organization's offence: there may well be situations where more than one organization in breach of a relevant duty of care owed to a deceased, which may have amounted to a cause of a death.

2.19 During the Act's passage through the Grand Committee stage in the House of Lords attempts were made to introduce a form of secondary liability for holding or parent companies. The Government, in rejecting the proposed amendment, made clear its view that such organizations were not exempt from the offence, but would attract liability in such circumstances through primary liability. The problem with any other approach was described, on behalf of the Government, by Lord Bassam in the following terms:

> A subsidiary company has its own legal persona, and the directors of such a company must act in the interests of that company. If the actions, or failings, of a subsidiary company cause the death of a person in breach of its duty of care, that company would properly be liable to the new offence... The parent company in a group of companies is a separate legal entity and, as such, is not subject to any legal obligation to prevent those subsidiaries committing any crime. Clearly, there are reputational risks for any parent company if one of its subsidiaries is prosecuted,

---

[5] [1985] BCLC 105 at 110.
[6] *R v Jefferson* 99 Cr App R 13 (CA).
[7] See *Attorney-General's Reference* (No 2 of 1999) [2000] 2 Cr App R 207.

B. The Offence

but that self-interest is quite different from having a direct legal responsibility for the way in which a subsidiary conducts its business.[8]

However, thereafter Lord Bassam continued by suggesting that secondary liability would apply to a holding or parent company:

2.20

> Under the existing criminal law, there are clear principles of secondary liability for holding one person to account for their contributory actions to another person's crime, but such principles do not generally impose a duty to prevent criminality by others. The principles of secondary liability will apply to holding or parent companies in the case of the offence of corporate manslaughter as they apply elsewhere. We are not persuaded that there is a compelling argument for taking a different approach in the Bill.[9]

5. Convictions under the Act and under health and safety legislation

Section 19(1) provides that where in the same proceedings there is a charge of corporate manslaughter or corporate homicide arising out of a particular set of circumstances and a charge against the same defendant of a health and safety offence[10] arising out of some or all of those circumstances the jury may, if the interests of justice so require, be invited to return a verdict on each charge.

2.21

This provision is uncontroversial and does no more than confirm what would be the position in any event: a health and safety offence may be alleged as an alternative, but will not be a mutually exclusive alternative, to corporate manslaughter.

2.22

Section 19(2) provides that an organization that has been convicted of corporate manslaughter or corporate homicide arising out of a particular set of circumstances may, if the interests of justice so require, be charged with a health and safety offence arising out of some or all of those circumstances.

2.23

The principle of 'double jeopardy' as interpreted in *R v Beedie* [1997] 2 Cr App R 167 has placed an effective stop on the institution of successive sets of proceedings against a defendant for a health and safety offence and a manslaughter offence arising out of substantially the same facts. Section 19(2) is addressed to proceedings in respect of a health and safety offence following a conviction for a corporate manslaughter offence, a move that is less likely to be instituted than where a trial has resulted in an acquittal for manslaughter. Furthermore, it does no more than confirm that such proceedings may occur 'if the interests of justice so require'.

2.24

The apparent intention behind and perceived need[11] for this provision is to ensure that a conviction for corporate manslaughter would not preclude the conviction in subsequent proceedings of an individual on a secondary basis, pursuant to the Health and Safety at Work etc. Act 1974 (HSWA), s 37, for having consented, connived or caused through neglect the health and safety offence of a corporation.

2.25

---

[8] *Hansard*, HL (pt 008, Column GC166) (11 January 2007).
[9] ibid.
[10] Meaning an offence under any health and safety legislation: CMCHA, s 19(3).
[11] See Explanatory Notes on Lords Amendments to Bill 70 prepared by the Home Office, para 20.

2. The Offence and the Organizations Subject to the Act

However, it is very doubtful that either proceedings or a conviction in respect of the principal, namely the corporation, is required in order to pursue a secondary party pursuant to HSWA, s 37.[12]

6. Commencement and orders

2.26 The Act provides that the offence created by s 1 does not apply in relation to anything done or omitted before the commencement of that section (s 27(3)).

2.27 The abolition of liability for organizations that are subject to the Act in respect of manslaughter at common law, provided by s 20, 'does not affect any liability, investigation, legal proceeding or penalty for or in respect of such a common law offence committed wholly or partly before the commencement of that section' (s 27(4)).

2.28 The Act defines that an offence is committed wholly or partly before the commencement of s 20, 'if any of the conduct or events alleged to constitute the offence occurred before that commencement' (s 27(5)).

2.29 Section 27(1) provides that the provisions of the Act will come into force with provision made by order by the Secretary of State and s 24(1) provides that a power of the Secretary of State to make an order under the Act is exercisable by statutory instrument.

2.30 Section 27(2) provides that an order bringing into force section 2(1)(d), the 'custody' category of relevant duty of care,[13] is subject to the affirmative resolution procedure. Various other sections create powers of amendment exercisable by the Secretary of State through order subject either to the affirmative resolution procedure (ss 21, 22(1) and 23) or the negative resolution process (ss 15, 16 and 22(3))

2.31 Section 24(3) provides that, 'Where an order under this Act is subject to "affirmative resolution procedure" the order may not be made unless a draft has been laid before, and approved by a resolution of, each House of Parliament.'

2.32 Section 24(2) provides that 'Where an order under this Act is subject to "negative resolution procedure" the statutory instrument containing the order is subject to annulment in pursuance of a resolution of either House of Parliament.'

7. Procedural provisions and consequential amendments

2.33 Section 15 provides that any statutory provision (whenever made) about criminal proceedings applies, (subject to any adaptations or modifications prescribed by an order made by the Secretary of State), in relation to proceedings under the Act against:

(a) a department or other body listed in Sch 1,
(b) a police force,

---

[12] For a consideration of HSWA, s 37 see *Health and Safety Enforcement: Law and Practice* (2nd edn, Oxford University Press, October 2007) paras 5.46–5.76.
[13] See paras 4.99–4.102 and 4.103–4.121 generally.

B. The Offence

(c) a partnership,
(d) a trade union, or
(e) an employers' association that is not a corporation,
    as it applies in relation to proceedings against a corporation.

By s 15(2) the term 'provision about criminal proceedings' includes: 2.34

(a) provision about procedure in or in connection with criminal proceedings;
(b) provision about evidence in such proceedings;
(c) provision about sentencing, or otherwise dealing with, persons convicted of offences;

(a) *Provisions about procedure against corporations*
There are various procedural provisions relating to corporations that, pursuant to 2.35
s 15, will apply to organizations, subject to any order that may be made in this respect by the Secretary of State.

The Criminal Procedure Rules, rule 4, makes provision in respect of the service 2.36 of documents on persons and includes specific provision for service in respect of corporations. The relevant part of rule 4.3, service by handing over a document, provides:

(1) A document may be served on
   (b) a corporation by handing it to a person holding a senior position in that corporation;
   (c) an individual or corporation who is legally represented in the case by handing it to that representative

The relevant part of rule 4.4, which concerns service by leaving or posting a document, provides: 2.37

(1) A document may be served by leaving it at the appropriate address for service under this rule or by sending it to that address by first class post or by the equivalent of first class post
(2) The address for service under this rule on—
   (b) a corporation is its principal office in England and Wales, and if there is no readily identifiable principal office then any place in England and Wales where it carries on its activities or business;
   (c) an individual or corporation who is legally represented in the case is that representative's office

Rule 4.7, makes provision in respect of documents that must be served only by 2.38 handing them over, leaving or posting them, and, specifically in respect of corporations it provides that various documents, but principally summonses, can only be served upon a corporation under rule 4.3(1)(b) or rule 4.4(1) and (2)(b), above.

The procedure on charge of offence against corporation is provided for by 2.39 Magistrates' Courts Act 1980, s 46 which provides that the provisions of Sch 3 to that Act have effect where a corporation is charged with an offence before a magistrates' court. Schedule 3 provides that, subject to the provisions of the schedule, provisions of the Magistrates' Courts Act 1980 relating to the inquiry into, and trial of indictable offences apply to a corporation as they apply to an adult.

2.40 The provisions in the schedule include para 1, which provides:

1(1) A magistrates' court may commit a corporation for trial by an order in writing empowering the prosecutor to prefer a bill of indictment in respect of the offence named in the order.[14]
(2) An order under this paragraph shall not prohibit the inclusion in the bill of indictment of counts that under section 2 of the Administration of Justice (Miscellaneous Provisions) Act 1933 may be included in the bill in substitution for, or in addition to, counts charging the offence named in the order.

2.41 Paragraph 2(a) of the schedule provides that a representative may on behalf of a corporation make before examining justices such representations as could be made by an accused who is not a corporation.

2.42 Paragraph 3 of the schedule provides:

(1) Where a representative appears, any requirement of this Act that anything shall be done in the presence of the accused, or shall be read or said to the accused, shall be construed as a requirement that that thing shall be done in the presence of the representative or read or said to the representative.
(2) Where a representative does not appear, any such requirement, and any requirement that the consent of the accused shall be obtained for summary trial, shall not apply.

2.43 The Criminal Justice Act 1925, s 33(3) provides that on arraignment of a corporation, the corporation may enter in writing by its representative a plea of guilty or not guilty, and if either the corporation does not appear by a representative or fails to enter any plea, 'the court shall order a plea of not guilty to be entered, and the trial shall proceed as though the corporation had duly entered a plea of not guilty.'

2.44 Section 33(6) provides that the expression 'representative' in relation to a corporation means a person appointed by the corporation to represent it for these purposes before the court. Furthermore, the subsection provides:

A representative for the purposes of this section need not be appointed under the seal of the corporation and a statement in writing purporting to be signed by a managing director of the corporation, or by any person (by whatever name called) having, or being one of the persons having, the management of the affairs of the corporation, to the effect that the person named in the statement has been appointed as the representative of the corporation for the purposes of this section shall be admissible without further proof as prima facie evidence that that person has been so appointed.

(b) *Minor and consequential amendments*

2.45 Schedule 2 to the Act provides that the offence of corporate manslaughter is a qualifying offence in respect of Criminal Justice Act, s 62 (prosecution right of appeal in

---

[14] In *R v Nelson Group Services (Maintenance) Ltd* [1999] 1 WLR 1526, CA it was held that the signature by committing magistrates of a certificate in the form appropriate for the committal for trial of an individual is sufficient compliance with paragraph 1(1).

respect of evidentiary rulings)[15] and Pt 10 (Cases that may be retried following acquittal).

2.46 Schedule 2 further amends the Coroners Act 1988 ss 11(6), 16(1)(a)(i), 17(1)(a) and 17(2)(a), to incorporate corporate manslaughter onto the same footing as manslaughter in respect of inquests: principally, the effect is that an inquest will be adjourned pending the conclusion of proceedings for corporate manslaughter.

C. ELEMENT 1: BY AN ORGANIZATION SUBJECT TO THE ACT

2.47 Section 1(2), as enacted, defines four types of organization which are subject to the provisions of the Act and thus can commit the offence of corporate manslaughter.

2.48 Section 21, creates a power, exercisable by the Secretary of State, to amend s 1 so as to extend the categories of organization to which the section, and thus the offence, applies. The power is exercisable through an order that is subject to the affirmative resolution process.[16]

2.49 The four types of organization subject to the Act are:

a) corporation,
b) a department or other body listed in Sch 1,
c) a police force,
d) a partnership, or trade union, or employers' association, that is an employer.

1. Corporations

2.50 The interpretation section of the Act, s 25, provides that corporation does not include a corporation sole but includes any body corporate wherever incorporated.

2.51 In respect of United Kingdom corporations this includes limited liability companies, public limited companies, limited liability partnerships (formed under the Limited Liability Partnerships Act 2000) and companies limited by guarantee. The latter being common vehicles through which charities operate. The definition of corporation extends to bodies, such as local authorities, incorporated by statute or Royal Charter but s 25 expressly excludes a corporation sole, being a vehicle used to create an office that is held successively by different individuals. Many such offices are religious but a number of such corporations sole have been recently created by statute in respect of the office of chief constable of various police forces and the commissioner of various public bodies.

2.52 Importantly, s 25 defines a corporation to include a body corporate 'wherever incorporated' and thus such a foreign incorporated company who activities cause harm resulting in death sustained in the United Kingdom will be subject to the offence.

---

[15] At date of publication, not in force.
[16] CMCHA s 21(3).

2.53 Corporations that are agents or servants of the Crown are not immune from prosecution under the Act by reason of the operation of any Crown immunity.[17]

2. Government bodies and the Crown

2.54 Schedule 1, as enacted, sets out 48 organizations being Government departments or Crown bodies that are deemed to be organizations subject to the Act. These range from all the various Departments of Government, including the Attorney-General's Office, Home Office and Ministry of Defence, to such bodies as the National Audit Office and Office for National Statistics.

(a) *Crown immunity and the application of the Act to Crown bodies: s 11*

2.55 Section 11 deals explicitly with Crown immunity and provides for the application of the Act to Crown bodies. Section 11(1) provides that, 'An organisation that is a servant or agent of the Crown is not immune from prosecution under this Act for that reason.'

2.56 Section 11(2) provides that for the purposes of this Act both a department or other body listed in Sch 1 and a 'corporation that is a servant or agent of the Crown' is to be treated as owing whatever duties of care it would owe if it were a corporation that was not a servant or agent of the Crown'.

2.57 Section 11(4) provides that for the purposes of ss 2 to 7, the relevant duty of care, anything done purportedly by a department or other body listed in Sch 1, although in law by the Crown or by the holder of a particular office, is to be treated as done by the department or other body itself.[18]

2.58 Of the potential categories of relevant duty of care under the Act,[19] those arising from the relationship of employer to employees and workers[20] and those arising from the occupation of premises[21] are likely to be the most pertinent to the activities of such Government departments and Crown bodies listed in Sch 1. In this regard s 11(3) provides that for the purposes of s 2, and the relevant duty of care:

(a) a person who is—
  (i) employed by or under the Crown for the purposes of a department or other body listed in Schedule 1, or

---

[17] CMCHA, s 11(2)(b) and paras 2.55–2.56.
[18] Section 11(5) provides that ss 11(3)(a)(i), 11(3)(b)(i) and 11(4) apply in relation to a Northern Ireland department as they apply in relation to a department or other body listed in Sch 1.
[19] See paras 4.01–4.19 for the relevant duty of care and paras 5.01–5.88 for the limitations created by ss 3–7 many of which are directly pertinent to the activities of Crown bodies.
[20] See paras 4.20–4.48 for the duty of care as employer.
[21] See paras 4.49–4.65 for the duty of care as occupier of premises.

C. Element 1: By an Organization Subject to the Act

    (ii) employed by a person whose staff constitute a body listed in that Schedule, is to be treated as employed by that department or body;
(b) any premises occupied for the purposes of—
    (i) a department or other body listed in Schedule 1, or
    (ii) a person whose staff constitute a body listed in that Schedule, are to be treated as occupied by that department or body.

(b) *Transfer of functions*

2.59 Section 16 makes detailed provision in relation to the transfer of functions and the change of identity of a 'relevant public organisation', being a department or body listed in Sch 1; a corporation that is a servant or agent of the Crown; or a police force.[22]

2.60 The section applies where

(a) a person's death has occurred, or is alleged to have occurred, in connection with the carrying out of functions by a relevant public organisation, and
(b) subsequently there is a transfer of those functions, with the result that they are still carried out but no longer by that organisation.

2.61 Section 16(3) provides that any proceedings instituted against a relevant public organization after the transfer for an offence under the Act in respect of the person's death are to be instituted against the relevant public organization, if any, by which the functions are currently carried out or, if no such organization currently carries out the functions, then the relevant public organization by which the functions were last carried out.

2.62 Section 16(5) provides that where such a transfer occurs while proceedings for an offence of corporate manslaughter are in progress against a relevant public organization, the proceedings are to be continued against the relevant public organization, if any, by which the functions are carried out as a result of the transfer; or, where as a result of the transfer no such organization carries out the functions, the same organization as before.

2.63 Sections 16(4) and 16(6) provide for orders to be made by the Secretary of State in relation to a particular transfer of functions, to provide that the proceedings may be instituted, or (if they have already been instituted) may be continued, against the organization that no longer carries out the function, or such other relevant public organization as may be specified in the order.[23]

(c) *Amendment of Schedule 1*

2.64 Section 22 provides a detailed procedure relating to the powers for the Secretary of State to amend Sch 1. Section 22(2) provides that a statutory instrument containing such an order is subject to the affirmative resolution procedure,[24] unless the only

---

[22] CMCHA, s16 (2).
[23] Such orders are subject to the negative resolution procedure: CMCHA, s 16(7).
[24] See para 2.31.

2. The Offence and the Organizations Subject to the Act

amendments to Sch 1 fall within the terms of subsection (3), when in such case the instrument is subject to the negative resolution procedure.[25]

2.65 An amendment falls within the terms of subsection (3) if:

(a) it is consequential on a department or other body listed in Sch 1 changing its name,
(b) in the case of an amendment adding a department or other body to Sch 1, it is consequential on the transfer to the department or other body of functions all of which were previously exercisable by one or more organisations to which s 1 applies, or
(c) in the case of an amendment removing a department or other body from Schedule 1, it is consequential on—
　(i) the abolition of the department or other body, or
　(ii) the transfer of all the functions of the department or other body to one or more organisations to which s 1 applies.

3. Police forces

2.66 Section 13 Act makes specific provision for the application of the Act to police forces and s 13(1) defines 'police force' to mean:

(a) a police force within the meaning of—
　(i) the Police Act 1996 (c.16), or
　(ii) the Police (Scotland) Act 1967 (c. 77);
(b) the Police Service of Northern Ireland;
(c) the Police Service of Northern Ireland Reserve;
(d) the British Transport Police Force;
(e) the Civil Nuclear Constabulary;
(f) the Ministry of Defence Police.

2.67 Section 13 provides that for the purposes of the Act a police force is to be treated as owing whatever duties of care it would owe if it were a body corporate;[26] any premises occupied for the purposes of a police force are to be treated as occupied by that force;[27] and, for the purposes of ss 2–7 (the relevant duty of care) anything that would be regarded as done by a police force if the force were a body corporate is to be so regarded.[28]

2.68 Furthermore, s 13(3) provides that:

- a member[29] of a police force is to be treated as employed by that force;
- a special constable appointed for a police area in England and Wales is to be treated as employed by the police force maintained by the police authority for that area;

---

[25] See paras 2.32.
[26] CMCHA, s 13(2).
[27] CMCHA, s 13(5).
[28] CMCHA, s 13(6).
[29] In the case of Scottish police forces, a reference to a member of a force is to be treated as a reference to a constable of that force: s 13(4).

C. Element 1: By an Organization Subject to the Act

- a special constable appointed for a police force mentioned in s 13(1)(d) or (f) is to be treated as employed by that force;
- a police cadet undergoing training with a view to becoming a member of a police force mentioned in s 13(1)(a) or (d) is to be treated as employed by that force;
- a police trainee or a police cadet appointed under, respectively, Police (Northern Ireland) Act 2000, ss 39 or 42, is to be treated as employed by the Police Service of Northern Ireland;
- a police reserve trainee appointed under Police (Northern Ireland) Act 2000, s 40 is to be treated as employed by the Police Service of Northern Ireland Reserve;
- a member of a police force seconded to the Serious Organised Crime Agency or the National Policing Improvement Agency to serve as a member of its staff is to be treated as employed by that Agency.

Section 13(7) provides that where, by virtue of s 13(3), a person is treated by the Act as employed by a police force, and by virtue of any other statutory provision he is, or is treated as, employed by another organization, then 'the person is to be treated for those purposes as employed by both the force and the other organisation'. 2.69

This rather inelegantly drafted subsection contemplates 'dual simultaneous employers', a notion that has germinated in a series of Court of Appeal decisions concerned with 'agency' workers, who, under employment protection legislation appeared to be employed by no one.[30] In the context of the Act, it is difficult to envisage how such simultaneous employment could sensibly be construed: it would involve the judge making a finding as to the extent of the duties of care owed by each employer, presumably based upon the extent of control of the employees, premises or activity that founds the duty of care under consideration. Another difficulty is posed by the phrase in the subsection, 'for those purposes': which purposes? The Act, the 'other statutory provision' or both? 2.70

Having excluded a corporation sole from the ambit of the Act,[31] presumably this section is intended to make the police force the employer under the Act and apply all statutory responsibilities that are cast upon the office of the chief constable or commissioner of the police force, which is often a corporation sole and deemed by such statutory provision to be the employer. 2.71

4. A partnership, trade union, or employer's association that is an employer

Three types of organization were added to the Act by s 1(2)(d) as a result of amendments by the House of Lords following the third reading of the Act in the House of Commons, namely, 'a partnership, or trade union or employers' association, that is an employer'. 2.72

---

[30] See para 4.42.
[31] CMCHA, see s 25 and see para 2.51.

2. The Offence and the Organizations Subject to the Act

2.73 A number of other organizations, such as the emergency services, are subject to express limitation on the activities that can give rise to a relevant duty of care other than one owed as employer to employees and workers or as occupier of premises.[32] The three types of organization added by s 1(2)(d) are limited to those that are an employer;[33] however, where such an organization is an employer, its potential liability arises in respect of all relevant duties of care, not solely those arising as employer.

2.74 Of the three organizations, most, if not all trade unions and employers' association are likely to be employers and therefore subject to the Act but in respect of partnerships this is not the case, with the distinction between employing partnerships and non-employing partnerships appearing to be both arbitrary and capable of exploitation.

2.75 Trade Union is defined by s 25 as having the meaning given by Trade Union and Labour Relations (Consolidation) Act 1922, s 1 or Industrial Relations (Northern Ireland) Order 1992 (SI 1992/807 (NI5)), Art 3.

2.76 Employers' association, pursuant to s 25, has the meaning given by the Trade Union and Labour Relations (Consolidation) Act 1992, s 122 or Industrial Relations (Northern Ireland) Order 1992 (SI 1992/807 (NI 5)), Art 4.

(a) *Specific provisions related to partnerships*

2.77 Section 25 defines partnership to mean:

(a) a partnership within the Partnership Act 1890 (c. 39), or
(b) a limited partnership registered under the Limited Partnerships Act 1907 (c. 24), or a firm or entity of a similar character formed under the law of a country or territory outside the United Kingdom.

2.78 Much of the debate in the House of Lords concerning the need to include partnerships within the terms of the Act was focused upon concern that otherwise many organizations with multi-million pound turnovers would escape potential liability: in reality, most if not all of these concerns are Limited Liability Partnerships which fall within the Act as corporations.

2.79 Section 14(1) provides that for the purposes of the Act a partnership is to be treated as owing whatever duties of care it would owe if it were a body corporate.

2.80 Section 14(2) provides that proceedings for an offence under the Act alleged to have been committed by a partnership are to be brought in the name of the partnership (and not in that of any of its members) and s 14(3) provides that a fine imposed on a partnership upon conviction of an offence under the Act is to be paid out of the funds of the partnership. A partnership is not a legal person at common law and proceedings in respect of health and safety offences can only be brought against individual partners or all of them.

---

[32] CMCHA, s 6 and paras 5.42–5.88.
[33] See paras 4.30–4.45 for a consideration of employer and employment.

D. Element 2: The Organization Owed a Relevant Duty of Care to the Deceased

Section 14(4) provides that the terms of s 14 do not apply to a partnership that is a legal person under the law by which it is governed.   2.81

5. Power to extend section 1 to other organizations: s 21

Section 21 provides that the Secretary of State may by order amend section 1 so as to extend the categories of organization to which that section applies and that such an order may make any amendment to this Act that is incidental or supplemental to, or consequential on, such an amendment. An order under this section is subject to affirmative resolution procedure.   2.82

D. ELEMENT 2: THE ORGANIZATION OWED A RELEVANT DUTY OF CARE TO THE DECEASED

Section 2 defines 'relevant duty of care', provides categories of relevant duty of care and sets out the means by which the existence of a relevant duty of care is to be determined.   2.83

Section 2(1) provides that, A 'relevant duty of care', in relation to an organization, means any of the following duties owed by it under the law of negligence—   2.84

(a) a duty owed to its employees or to other persons working for the organisation or performing services for it;
(b) a duty owed as occupier of premises;
(c) a duty owed in connection with—
 (i) the supply by the organisation of goods or services (whether for consideration or not),
 (ii) the carrying on by the organisation of any construction or maintenance operations,
 (iii) the carrying on by the organisation of any other activity on a commercial basis, or
 (iv) the use or keeping by the organisation of any plant, vehicle or other thing;
(d) a duty owed to a person who, by reason of being a person within subsection (2), is someone for whose safety the organisation is responsible.

By s 2(5) the existence of a relevant duty of care is a matter of law for the judge. The determination of this issue and the application of the law of negligence are considered at paras 3.01–3.56.   2.85

The categories of relevant duty of care are defined in subsections of s 2 and by operation of the interpretation section, s 25 (see table 2.1). The meaning and categories of relevant duty of care are considered at paras 4.01–4.121.   2.86

Section 2(1)(d), the 'custody' category of relevant duty of care, which is defined in s 2(2), can only be brought into force by an order of the Secretary of State that is subject to the affirmative resolution process.[34]   2.87

The relevant duty of care defined by s 2(1) is subject to exclusions set out in ss 3 to 7. These exclusions related to public policy and public functions (s 3); military activities (s 4); policing and law enforcement (s 5); emergencies (s 6); and,   2.88

---

[34] CMCHA, s 27(2).

child protection and probation functions (s 7). These provisions are considered in detail at paras 5.01–5.88.

E. ELEMENT 3: THE WAY IN WHICH THE ORGANIZATION'S ACTIVITIES ARE MANAGED OR ORGANIZED: CAUSATION AND BREACH

2.89 The third element of the offence is concerned with causation and breach, it is composed of requirements drawn from various different subsections and is considered in detail in paragraphs 6.01–6.157.

2.90 An organization subject to the Act (element one) that owed the deceased a relevant duty of care (element two) will be guilty of the offence if the third element is proved, namely:

3. i) the way in which its activities are managed or organised caused a person's death (s 1(a));
   ii) the way in which its activities are managed or organised amounted to a gross breach of that relevant duty of care (s 1(b)); and:
   iii) the way in which its activities are managed or organised by its senior management is a substantial element in the breach (s 1(3)).

2.91 A breach of a duty of care by an organization is a 'gross' breach where the conduct alleged to amount to a breach of that duty falls far below what can reasonably be expected of the organization in the circumstances (s 1 (4)(b)).

2.92 Section 8 provides factors that the jury must take account when assessing 'gross' breach, factors that they may take into account and how the jury may have regard to any other matters they consider relevant.

2.93 A factor the jury must consider is whether the evidence shows that the organization failed to comply with any health and safety legislation that relates to the alleged breach of relevant duty of care, and if so, how serious that failure was and how much of a risk of death it posed.

2.94 A jury may consider the extent to which the evidence shows that there were 'attitudes, policies, systems or accepted practices within the organization' that were likely to have encouraged or produced tolerance of any such failure to comply with any health and safety legislation. The jury may also have regard to any health and safety guidance that relates to the alleged breach.

2.95 The 'senior management' requirement, whereby an organization is only guilty of an offence if the way its activities are managed or organized by its senior management is a substantial element in the gross breach, rests upon a definition of 'senior management' in s 1(4)(c). Section 1(4)(c) defines 'senior management' to mean those who play significant roles in:

i) the making of decisions about how the whole or a substantial part of its activities are to be managed or organized
ii) the actual managing or organizing of the whole or a substantial part of those activities.

3

THE RELEVANT DUTY OF CARE I: A QUESTION OF LAW FOUNDED UPON THE COMMON LAW OF NEGLIGENCE

A. Overview	3.01
B. Relevant Duty of Care: a Judicial Determination of Law and Fact	3.06
1. Individual gross negligence manslaughter	3.06
2. The Corporate Manslaughter and Corporate Homicide Act, s 2(5)	3.10
3. The procedure for determining the existence of a 'relevant duty of care'	3.20
4. Directing the jury	3.30
C. The Existence of a Duty of Care in Negligence	3.33
1. Development of the common law	3.33
2. *Caparo Industries plc v Dickman* [1990] 1 All ER 568	3.38
3. The meaning of the *Caparo* factors	3.46
4. Omissions	3.54

A. OVERVIEW

The new offence is intended to apply only in circumstances where an organization owed a duty of care to a deceased victim under the law of negligence at common law.   3.01

The vexed issue of by whom and how the existence of a duty of care is decided in gross negligence manslaughter has resulted in a series of conflicting Court of Appeal judgments, which have approached the issue rather in the manner of dressing the Emperor in his new clothes. These authorities will continue to apply to the common law offence of individual gross negligence manslaughter. In respect of the corporate offence, a striking feature of the Act found in s 2(5), provides that the existence of a duty of care in a particular case is a matter of law for the judge to decide and that, 'the judge must make any findings of fact necessary to decide that question.'   3.02

3.03 The determination of the existence of a relevant duty of care by the judge will require recourse to the principles and precedents from the decided cases that constitute the law of negligence. The current position of the common law rests upon the three stage test set out by Lord Bridge in *Caparo Industries plc v Dickman* [1990] 1 All ER 568 which involves forseeability of damage, a relationship of 'proximity' and a situation considered by the court for it to be fair, just and reasonable to found the existence of a duty of care. The elements of this test are no more than convenient labels for describing how a court assesses the facts of any case in order to reach a decision as to the existence of a legal relationship known as 'a duty of care'.

3.04 Section 2 of the Corporate Manslaughter and Corporate Homicide Act 2007 (CMCHA) is concerned with defining what is a 'relevant duty of care' owed in negligence, of which a gross breach may result in the commission of an offence. The relevant duty of care for the offence is limited to one arising out of certain specific functions performed by the organization. These meaning of 'relevant duty of care' and the ambit of these categories is considered at paras 4.01–4.120.

3.05 The Act provides a series of exclusions relating to the ambit of relevant duties of care owed by public authorities, in emergency situations and by Crown bodies. These and the liability of such organizations generally are considered in paras 5.01–5.88.

B. RELEVANT DUTY OF CARE: A JUDICIAL DETERMINATION OF LAW AND FACT

1. Individual gross negligence manslaughter

3.06 In September 2004, Mr Justice Mackay, dismissing counts of manslaughter against directors of a number of companies in the prosecution that followed the Hatfield train crash, reviewed the conflicting authorities on the issue of how and by whom the existence of a duty of care is determined in individual gross negligence manslaughter. He identified how the offence was founded upon the 'ordinary principles of negligence' and, as such, the question of the existence of a duty care must be resolved in accordance with the tripartite test set out in the leading authority, namely *Caparo Industries plc v Dickman*,[1] which explicitly recognized how the ingredients of this test, 'are not susceptible of any such precise definition as would be necessary to give them utility as practical tests.'[2]

3.07 Mr Justice Mackay commented how he, 'found great difficulty in seeing how a jury could be helped to find its way through the tripartite *Caparo* test and in particular how the direction should be framed, if the exercise is as that case tells us an incremental one building on established examples of other duty situations.'[3]

---

[1] [1990] 1 All ER 568.
[2] [1990] 1 All ER 568 at 574.
[3] Mackay J, *R v Railtrack plc & others* (unreported) 1 September 2004, transcript p 19.

B. Relevant Duty of Care: a Judicial Determination of Law and Fact

As a result, the prosecution in that case submitted that the question of the existence of a duty of care was a matter of law which he should resolve and thereafter direct the jury upon.

However, just months later on 1 December 2004, the host of conflicting authorities in respect of whether the existence of a duty of care in a charge on individual gross negligence manslaughter was a question of law for the judge, a question of fact for the jury or involved both questions of law and fact was reviewed by the Court of Appeal in *Willoughby* [2005] 1 Cr App R 29. The judgment of Rose LJ purported to decide, once and for all, that, 'Whether a duty of care exists is a matter for the jury once the judge has decided that there is evidence capable of establishing a duty.'[4]

2. The Corporate Manslaughter and Corporate Homicide Act, s 2(5)

The Act, in respect of corporate manslaughter, provides in s 2(5) that:

For the purposes of this Act, whether a particular organization owes a duty of care to a particular individual is a question of law. The judge must make any findings of fact necessary to decide that question.

Thus the Act sweeps away the fiction that this is a simple question of fact that a jury can determine through application of directions of law. In its place, the Act provides no more than a bare statement of principle and details no mechanism or procedure to be adopted for this novel course.

Following the publication of the draft Bill[5] in 2005, a joint committee of the Home Affairs and Work and Pensions Committees scrutinized the Bill, hearing evidence from various parties before publishing a report.[6] Lord Justice Judge, the President of the Queen's Bench Division, gave evidence to the committee and was asked about the confusion a jury may feel when faced with the term 'duty of care'.

He responded:

If you open up the standard textbook on the duty of care in the law of negligence in the civil world, it is not quite as big as that, but it is a very large amount of literature. The issue has gone to the House of Lords for decision very many times in the past ten years. I was very troubled about the possible consequences. However, if you make this a question of law for the judge, depending on whatever facts he has to find... I do not think it presents a problem. I think in truth it identifies that there is a duty that you are concerned with neglect. It has that strength, provided it is for the judge to decide whether it is a duty situation.[7]

Lord Justice Judge apparently recognized how both the determination of the facts and the appropriate legal conclusion may be far from straightforward.

---

[4] [2005] 1 Cr App R 29 at para 24.
[5] Draft Corporate Manslaughter Bill (Cm 6497).
[6] First Joint Report from the Home Affairs and Work and Pensions Committees Session 2005–06 (HC540).
[7] First Joint Report from the Home Affairs and Work and Pensions Committees Session 2005–06. Minutes of Evidence–Vol III (HC 540-III) Q 507.

3.15 The Explanatory Notes[8] to the Act describe how this provision, 'reflects the heavily legal nature of the tests relating to the existence of a duty of care in the law of negligence. Because the judge will be deciding whether the circumstances of the case give rise to a duty of care, he will need to make certain determinations of fact that are usually for the jury.'

3.16 The Notes continue by expressing what may be more of a hope than an expectation:

> The questions of fact that the judge will need to consider will generally be uncontroversial and in any event will only be decided by the judge for the purposes of the duty of care question.[9]

3.17 There appears to be an inconsistency between assurances from the Home Office that the duty of care test represents a settled standard that organizations well understand and the Government's justification for the adoption of this novel approach of having the judge decide the very existence of such a duty of care: that justification being that the issues are too complex for a jury and have been the subject of numerous appellate decisions.

3.18 The intention of the section could not be clearer: the judge alone will determine whether a duty of care existed; he will do so as a matter of law, having made whatever determinations of facts are necessary; he will direct the jury, as a matter of law, on the existence of a duty of care.

3.19 Where, as is envisaged, directors of organizations or other individuals are charged with individual gross negligence manslaughter upon the same indictment as an organization, he may then find difficulty in directing the jury, in accordance with the judgement in *R v Willoughby*,[10] that the existence of a duty of care in respect of such individuals is matter for them.

3. The procedure for determining the existence of a 'relevant duty of care'

3.20 The bare words of s 2(5) providing that whether a particular organization owes a duty of care to a particular individual is a question of law and how the judge must make any findings of fact necessary to decide that question are not supplemented by provisions on the procedure to be adopted. The corporate offence under the Act is unique in including an element of the offence to be determined by a judge who will then direct the jury of its existence, as a matter of law.

3.21 In the face of the Act's silence, it must be that the prosecution bear the burden of proving the existence of a duty of care and that, in making findings of fact, the judge will have to be satisfied to the criminal standard, that is, so that he is sure.

3.22 The same witnesses of fact and exhibits relevant to the issue of the gross breach of any duty of care are likely to be those which the judge will have to take account of

---

[8] Corporate Manslaughter and Corporate Homicide Bill [HL 19], Explanatory Notes para 24.
[9] ibid.
[10] [2005] 1 Cr App R 29 and see para 1.29.

B. Relevant Duty of Care: a Judicial Determination of Law and Fact

in making any findings of facts necessary to conclude that a defendant owed any particular relevant duty of care. When should he make such a determination?

When the Bill passed through the Committee stage of the House of Commons, the Government stated how it was satisfied that no special procedure for determining the issue was required:

3.23

> Criminal proceedings will often involve questions that need to be decided by the judge as a matter of law and this matter will fall to be decided in the same way. It is worth remembering that in the majority of cases whether or not a duty existed would be a straightforward matter — for example, when the person killed was an employee or a train passenger. In cases of uncertainty a defendant can apply before the case reaches the court for it to be dismissed on the grounds that there is no case to answer. If it is not dealt with then, it can be raised as a preliminary point at the start of the proceedings in the way that points of law generally can be raised for the judge to consider. In the vast majority of cases, it should be straightforward.[11]

There being nothing usual about a judge determining the existence of an element of a criminal offence, it is difficult to see how the 'usual' procedure can be adopted. Firstly, it must be open to a defendant organization to apply to have dismissed, pursuant to Crime and Disorder Act 1998, Sch 3, para 2(1), the charge of corporate manslaughter on the basis that 'the evidence against the applicant would not be sufficient for him to be properly convicted', specifically that the prosecution's case on the papers does not disclose sufficient evidence capable of satisfying the judge to the requisite standard of the existence of a relevant duty of care owed by the organization. The Crime and Disorder Act 1998, Sch 3, para 2(5) provides that, 'oral evidence may be given on such an application only with the leave of the judge or by his order; and the judge shall give leave or make an order only if it appears to him, having regard to any matters stated in the application for leave, that the interests of justice require him to do so.' Thus the judge could hear witness evidence called by either or both parties. At such a stage what would the appropriate test be? Presumably the judge would only look for sufficient evidence capable of establishing a duty of care and would make no final positive determination of the existence of a duty of care.

3.24

Equally, during trial, following the close of the prosecution case, it could be submitted by a defendant that the prosecution case had failed to establish sufficient evidence capable of satisfying the judge of the existence of a relevant duty of care. A defendant organization may thereafter call evidence in its defence relevant to the issues of forseeability of risk and proximity of relationship and thus relevant to both the existence and nature of a duty of care and whether there had been a gross breach of the same. In this way, it could only be at the close of all the evidence that the judge could finally determine whether he was satisfied to the requisite standard of the existence of a duty of care.

3.25

---

[11] Corporate Manslaughter and Corporate Homicide Bill in Standing Committee B, 4th sitting, 24 October 2006, Col. 105, Mr Gerry Sutcliffe MP (Parliamentary Under-Secretary of State for the Home Department).

3.26 A ruling that no such relevant duty of care either was capable of being established or that no such relevant duty of care had been established would be a terminating ruling and subject to the provisions of Criminal Justice Act 2003, s 58 concerning prosecution appeals of such matters.

3.27 Pursuant to Criminal Procedure and Investigations Act 1996, s 29 (as amended), a judge may order a preparatory hearing before the jury are sworn, and at such a hearing can determine any question of law. Thus, a pre-trial hearing could be held to determine the issue of existence of a duty of care: presumably, both parties would be afforded the opportunity to call evidence, cross-examine witnesses and make submissions. At the conclusion, the judge would make a ruling, based on the evidence heard, as to whether he was satisfied as to the existence of a relevant duty of care. Such rulings would be capable of potential appeal, by either party, prior to trial pursuant to Criminal Procedure and Investigations Act 2003, s 35.

3.28 Both the Court of Appeal and Divisional Court have stressed the importance of proper particularization in cases where criminal allegations involve allegations of breach of duty/negligence.[12]

3.29 If the existence of a duty of care is a question of law for the judge, then the determination of this question will involve identifying the nature of any duty of care found to exist. There may be different duties of care capable of being found to exist or, more strictly, a duty of care founded on alternative or multiple bases and of a wider or narrower extent. It appears that the prosecution will have to particularize the nature of any duty of care alleged to have existed, whether in the indictment or in a separate document.

4. Directing the jury

3.30 Pursuant to s 2(6) the existence of a relevant duty of care is matter of law to be decided by the judge, who must decide all facts necessary to make that determination; whether the way an organization's activities are managed or organized amount to a 'gross' breach of the relevant duty of care is a matter for the jury, who must apply various factors set out in s 8.[13] Thus it appears that following the close of all the evidence, in summing up to the jury, the judge will direct the jury as to the existence of the relevant duty of care owed by the organization. This will involve identifying what the relevant duty of care was and may involve identifying to what it extended.

3.31 Section 1(4)(b) provides that, 'a breach of a duty of care by an organization is a "gross" breach if the conduct alleged to amount to a breach of that duty falls far

---

[12] See the judgment in *Bernard v Dudley Metropolitan Borough Council and Dudley Magistrates Court* [2003] EWHC 147 Admin (considering the Court of Appeal decision in *Friskies Petcare Uk Ltd* [2002] 2 Cr App R (S) 401) and the case of *R v Warburton-Pitt* 92 Cr App R 136, CA.

[13] See paras 6.59–6.116.

below what can reasonably be expected of the organization in the circumstances'. This test would appear to involve the determination of two questions by the jury:

- What was reasonably expected of the organization in the circumstances?; and
- Did the conduct of the organization, the way in which its activities were managed or organized, fall far below that standard?

3.32 Directing the jury upon and defining the existence of a relevant duty of care, may necessarily involve the trial judge directing the jury as to the answer, at least in part, to the first question.

C. THE EXISTENCE OF A DUTY OF CARE IN NEGLIGENCE

1. Development of the common law

3.33 Before 1932 there was no general duty of care in negligence. In *Donoghue v Stevenson* [1932] AC 562 a bare majority of the House of Lords opined that the manufacturer of ginger beer could be liable in negligence for injury to a consumer of the product as a result of its defective condition, namely the alleged remains of a snail in the bottle, the consumption of which caused the plaintiff's illness. Thus, it was held, the negligent manufacturer of a defective article owed a duty of care to a person with whom he was not in a contractual relationship. In the course of his speech Lord Atkin formulated a general principle apparently encompassing all the circumstances in which the courts had previously held that there could be liability for negligence:

The rule that you are to love your neighbour becomes in law, you must not injure your neighbour; and the lawyer's question, Who is my neighbour? receives a restricted reply. You must take reasonable care to avoid acts or omissions which you can reasonably foresee would be likely to injure your neighbour. Who, then, in law is my neighbour? The answer seems to be-persons who are so closely and directly affected by my act that I ought reasonably to have them in contemplation as being so affected when I am directing my mind to the acts or omissions which are called in question.[14]

3.34 However, it has never been the position that the infliction of foreseeable damage in all circumstances is actionable in negligence: the finding of a duty of care involves the determination of whether such foreseeable damage is actionable.

3.35 In *Home Office v Dorset Yacht Co. Ltd* [1970] AC 1004, the law had developed to the point where Lord Reid was able to state that Lord Atkin's dictum applied in all circumstances unless there was some justification or valid explanation for its exclusion.[15] This was confirmed by the House of Lords in *Anns v Merton London Borough Council* [1978] AC 728 where Lord Wilberforce opined:

in order to establish that a duty of care arises in a particular situation, it is not necessary to bring the facts of that situation within those of previous situations in which a duty of care has been held

---

[14] [1932] AC 562, at p 580.
[15] [1970] AC 1004, at p 1027.

to exist. Rather the question has to be approached in two stages. First one has to ask whether, as between the alleged wrongdoer and the person who has suffered damage there is a sufficient relationship of proximity or neighbourhood such that, in the reasonable contemplation of the former, carelessness on his part may be likely to cause damage to the latter-in which case a prima facie duty of care arises. Secondly, if the first question is answered affirmatively, it is necessary to consider whether there are any considerations which ought to negative, or to reduce or limit the scope of the duty or the class of person to whom it is owed or the damages to which a breach of it may give rise.[16]

3.36 However, in *Peabody Donation Fund v Sir Lindsay Parkinson & Co. Ltd* [1984] 3 All ER 529, Lord Keith in the House of Lords warned against the danger of treating these statements as definitive: 'A relationship of proximity in Lord Atkin's sense must exist before any duty of care can arise, but the scope of the duty must depend on all the circumstances of the case', and 'in determining whether or not a duty of care of particular scope was incumbent on a defendant it is material to take into consideration whether it is just and reasonable that it should be so...'[17]

3.37 In *Curran v Northern Ireland Co-ownership Housing Association Ltd* [1987] J 2 All ER 13, 17 Lord Bridge described *Anns v Merton London Borough Council*[18] as the 'high-water mark' of a trend of cases that had elevated Lord Atkin's neighbour principle, 'into one of general application from which a duty of care may always be derived unless there are clear countervailing considerations to exclude it'. This was followed in *Yuen Kun Yeu v A-G of Hong Kong* [1987] 2 All ER 705, where Lord Keith in a Privy Council judgment stated: 'Their Lordships venture to think that the two-stage test formulated by Lord Wilberforce for determining the existence of a duty of care in negligence has been elevated to a degree of importance greater than it merits, and greater perhaps than its author intended.'[19]

2. *Caparo Industries plc v Dickman* [1990] 1 All ER 568

3.38 The accepted starting-point for determining the existence of a duty of care in negligence is now generally considered to be the three-fold approach formulated by Lord Bridge in *Caparo Industries plc v Dickman* [1990] 1 All ER 568 in which he summarized the effect of this series of previous decisions of the House of Lords, Court of Appeal and Privy Council in relation to the duty of care as follows:

...in addition to the forseeability of damage, necessary ingredients in any situation giving rise to a duty of care are that there should exist between the party owing the duty and the party to whom it is owed a relationship characterised by the law as one of 'proximity' or 'neighbourhood' and that the situation should be one in which the court considers it fair, just and reasonable that the law should impose a duty of a given scope upon the one party for the benefit of the other.[20]

---

[16] [1978] AC 728 at p 751–752.
[17] [1984] 3 All ER 529 at p 534.
[18] [1978] AC 728.
[19] *Yuen Kun Yeu v A-G of Hong Kong* [1987] 2 All ER 705, at p 710.
[20] [1990] 1 All ER 568 at 574.

C. The Existence of a Duty of Care in Negligence

However, Lord Bridge acknowledged that these ingredients were insufficiently precise to be used as practical tests, and were 'little more than convenient labels to attach to the features of specific situations which, on a detailed examination of all the circumstances, the law recognizes pragmatically as giving rise to a duty of care of a given scope.' 3.39

Lord Bridge approved the opinion of Brennan J. in the High Court of Australia in *Sutherland Shire Council v Heyman*[21] that the law should develop novel categories of negligence incrementally and by analogy with established categories. 3.40

In *Marc Rich & Co. AG & others v Bishop Rock Marine Co. Ltd & others; the Nicholas H* [1995] 3 All ER 307, Lord Steyn confirmed that the *Caparo* factors apply whatever the nature of the harm sustained: 'Since the decision in *Dorset Yacht Co. Ltd v Home Office* [1970] AC 1004 it has been settled law that the elements of forseeability and proximity as well as considerations of fairness, justice and reasonableness are relevant to all cases whatever the nature of the harm sustained by the plaintiff.'[22] 3.41

Whilst it appears that all three *Caparo* factors are relevant to the determination of the existence of a duty of care, arguably the third can only affect the determination in a novel situation, where no such duty of care is well established in previous case law. The offence created by the Act, through its definition of what is a 'relevant duty of care' appears intended to encompass situations in which duties of care in negligence exist arising from settled and established relationships and situations. Thus it is likely that this factor will be potentially most relevant in relation to alleged offences under the Act committed by public authorities or the Crown bodies listed in Sch 1, in respect of which ss 3–7 apply to limit and exclude various activities and circumstances from founding a relevant duty of care under the Act.[23] 3.42

In any event, in a number of negligence authorities where the nature of the harm sustained is direct physical damage, it has been suggested that the third *Caparo* factor plays no part.[24] 3.43

The position is best summarized by Lord Roskill in *Caparo Industries plc v Dickman* [1990] 1 All ER 568, where he commented how: 3.44

It has now to be accepted that there is no simple formula or touchstone to which recourse can be had in order to provide in every case a ready answer to the questions whether, given certain facts, the law will or will not impose liability for negligence or, in cases where such liability can be shown to exist, determine the extent of that liability. Phrases such as 'forseeability', 'proximity', 'neighbourhood', 'just and reasonable', 'fairness', 'voluntary acceptance of risk' or 'voluntary assumption of responsibility' will be found used from time to time in the different cases. But. . .such phrases are not precise definitions. At best they are but labels or phrases descriptive of the very different factual situations which can exist in particular cases and which must be carefully examined in each

---

[21] (1985) 60 ALR 1 at 43–44.
[22] [1995] 3 All ER 307 at 326.
[23] See paras 5.01–5.88.
[24] *Alcock v Chief Constable of South Yorkshire Police* [1992] 1 AC 310 at p 396; *Perrett v Collins* [1998] 2 Lloyd's Rep 255.

case before it can be pragmatically determined whether a duty of care exists and, if so, what is the scope and extent of that duty.[25]

3.45 The Act, by providing that the existence of a duty of care is a matter of law to be decided by the judge who must make necessary findings of fact, has at least recognized that the determination of the issue requires careful examination in each case before it can be 'pragmatically determined'.

3. The meaning of the *Caparo* factors

(a) *Forseeability of harm*

3.46 The concept of reasonable forseeability relates to reasonable foresight of the harm, of the kind which in fact occurred, that might result to a class of persons that includes the victim. It focuses on the knowledge that someone in the defendant's position would be expected to possess. This requires the court to consider what a reasonable person in the defendant's position should have foreseen. Whether the defendant did foresee the risk is not relevant in establishing whether there was a duty of care. The test is objective but takes account of the characteristics of the defendant in determining what is foreseeable.

3.47 It is not the precise manner of an accident that should be forseeable, rather that the type of harm could be occasioned, that is physical harm in respect of a 'relevant duty of care' under the Act, that must be forseeable. In respect of an offence under the Act, the risk of death is, pursuant to s 8, relevant not to whether a duty of care existed but only in the context of an organization's failure to comply with any health and safety legislation and whether such a breach of duty is a gross one.

(b) *Proximity*

3.48 Proximity focuses on the relationship between the victim and the defendant. Mr Justice Deane, in the Australian case of *Sutherland Shire Council v Heyman*, described the proximity requirement as involving:

> The notion of nearness or closeness and embraces physical proximity (in the sense of space and time) between the person or property of the plaintiff and the person or property of the defendant, circumstantial proximity such as an overriding relationship of employer and employee or of a professional man and his client and what may (perhaps loosely) be referred to as causal proximity in the sense of the closeness or directness of the causal connection or relationship between the particular act or course of conduct and the loss or injury sustained. It may reflect an assumption by one party of a responsibility to take care to avoid or prevent injury, loss or damage to the person or property of another or reliance by one party upon such care being taken by the other in circumstances where the other party knew or ought to have known of that reliance.[26]

---

[25] [1990] 1 All ER 568 pp 581–582.
[26] (1985) 60 ALR 1 at pp 55–60.

C. The Existence of a Duty of Care in Negligence

Thus the concepts of forseeability and proximity overlap: the more an injury to a particular victim is forseeable, the more likely such a victim will be deemed to be sufficiently proximate. Physical proximity may be relevant but it is not an essential requirement: the manufacturer is probably many miles from the consumer but there is a relationship of proximity if the product causes injury. In *Muirhead v Industrial Tank Specialities Ltd* [1985] 3 All ER 70S Goff LJ said that proximity is used as a convenient label to describe a relationship between the parties by virtue of which the defendant can reasonably foresee that his act or omission is liable to cause damage to the claimant of the relevant type. 3.49

In *Caparo Industries plc v Dickman* [1990] 1 All ER 568, 599 Lord Oliver commented that proximity 'is an expression used not necessarily as indicating literally "closeness" in a physical or metaphorical sense but merely…a convenient label to describe circumstances from which the law will attribute a duty of care' and in *Murphy v Brentwood District Council* [1990] 2 All ER 908, at 935 he further commented how proximity is an expression which 'persistently defies definition'. 3.50

Thus proximity may consist of various forms of closeness: physical, temporal circumstantial or causative. There are established categories of proximity, such as an employer to his employees in respect of their health and safety and a manufacturer of defective goods to the ultimate consumer, for instance. Where physical harm is caused to a person, proximity will almost inevitably arise although this is not necessarily so in the case of an omission.[27] 3.51

(c) *Whether it is just and reasonable to impose a duty of care*
The 'fair, just and reasonable' criterion appears potentially determinative only where a Court is concerned with novel circumstances.[28] This factor encompasses public policy as well as considerations of fairness, reasonableness and justice. It has played a prominent part in consideration of the existence of a duty of care in various cases on the part of the emergency services,[29] social services in relation to child protection[30] and in relation to the activities of soldiers during a battle.[31] These situations and activities are the subject of ss 3–7, which provide limitations and exclusions in relation to the foundation of relevant duties of care under the Act.[32] 3.52

In other cases, considerations under this head have included: whether imposing a duty would result in a flood of claims, placing too heavy a burden on a particular class of defendant and/or insurance companies and whether imposing a duty might lead defendants to give up a socially-beneficial activity altogether or to take unnecessary and costly safety precautions. 3.53

---

[27] *Stovin v Wise (Norfolk CC, a third party)* [1996] AC 923.
[28] *Spring v Guardian Assurance plc* (1994) 3 All ER 129, see Lord Keith pp 133–142.
[29] *Alexandrou v Oxford* [1993] 4 All ER 328 (police); *Capital and Counties plc v Hampshire CC* [1997] QB 1004 (fire service).
[30] *X and others (minors) v Bedfordshire County Council* [1995] 3 All ER 353, 2 AC 633.
[31] *Mulcahy v MoD* [1996] QB 732.
[32] See paras 5.01–5.88.

4. Omissions

3.54 According to Lord Goff in *Smith v Littlewoods Organisation Ltd*, 'the common law does not impose liability for what are called pure omissions'.[33] Thus there is no general duty of care in negligence to prevent harm occurring to another. In a number of specific situations affirmative duties in negligence do arise. A number of these are 'relevant duties of care' under the Act, such as the duties of employers in relation to the health and safety of their employees while at work and the duties of occupiers to ensure that their property is safe for lawful visitors. Other relationships with the potential to give rise to affirmative duties include those where there is a special relationship between the victim and the defendant, such as with organizations with a responsibility for the care of others.[34] In each case the scope of the potential duty imposed on the responsible person can be twofold: to see to the safety of the other person in the relationship and to see that the other does not cause harm to third parties.

3.55 The distinction between acting and failing to act or between *misfeasance* and *nonfeasance* is said to be fundamental but, in practice it can prove difficult to discern. Thus, in *Donoghue v Stevenson*[35] was it the manufacturer's positive act of supplying a dangerous product or his failure (omission) to properly check the contents of the bottle which caused the plaintiff's illness? However, it is in situations in which the damage is brought about through the actions either of a third party or of the victim himself and where the defendant could have acted to avert the harm but failed to do so, that this issue can arise in an acute form.

---

[33] [1987] 2 AC 241, 171; see also the judgment of Lord Hoffmann in *Stovin v Wise* [1996] AC 923.
[34] See, by way of example, *Ellis v Home Office* [1953] 2 QB 135.
[35] [1932] AC 562.

4

THE RELEVANT DUTY OF CARE II: THE MEANING AND CATEGORIES OF RELEVANT DUTY OF CARE

A. Overview	4.01
B. Meaning of 'Relevant Duty of Care'	4.04
1. Superseding statutory duties: s 2(4)	4.10
2. Common law limitations disregarded: s 2(6)	4.14
C. Work, The Duty Owed to Employees and Other Workers: s 2(1)(a)	4.20
1. The employer's duty of care to employees	4.22
2. Who is an employee?	4.30
3. Non-employee workers	4.42
4. Distinguishing vicarious liability	4.43
5. Statutory health and safety duties	4.44
6. *Volenti non fit injuria*	4.47
D. The Duty as an Occupier of Premises: s 2(1)(b)	4.49
1. The nature of the duty under the Occupiers' Liability Act 1957: the common duty of care	4.57
2. The Occupiers' Liability Act 1984	4.62
E. Duties Owed 'In Connection with' Various Activities: s 2(1)(c)	4.66
1. The supply by the organization of goods or services	4.67
2. The carrying on by the organization of any construction or maintenance operations	4.75
3. The carrying on by the organization of any other activity on a commercial basis	4.92
4. The use or keeping by the organization of any plant, vehicle, or other thing	4.97
F. The 'Custody' Duty of Care: s 2(1)(d)	4.99
1. Potential commencement	4.100
2. The relevant duty	4.103
3. The nature of the common law duty	4.111

A. OVERVIEW

4.01 Section 2 of the Corporate Manslaughter and Corporate Homicide Act 2007 (CMCHA) is concerned with defining the 'relevant duty of care' owed in negligence, of which a gross breach may result in the commission of an offence. The section specifically provides that the Occupiers' Liability Acts 1957 and 1984 and the Defective Premises Act 1972 are included within the ambit of the law of negligence.

4.02 The relevant duty of care for the offence is limited to one arising out of certain specific functions performed by the organization: it will arise only where an organization owed a common law duty of care as an employer; as an occupier of land; as a result of the supply of goods or services; in connection with carrying out of construction or maintenance work; by its keeping or use of plant, vehicles, or any other thing or when carrying out other activities on a commercial basis.

4.03 A further category was added to the Act at the insistence of the House of Lords, namely a duty owed to a person in detention for whose safety the organization is responsible. This provision, in s 1(d), can only be brought into force following an order of the Secretary of State contained in a statutory instrument that must be affirmed by a vote in both Houses of Parliament.

B. MEANING OF 'RELEVANT DUTY OF CARE'

4.04 For the purposes of an offence under the Act, s 2(1) provides that:

A 'relevant duty of care', in relation to an organization, means any of the following duties owed by it under the law of negligence—

a) a duty owed to its employees or to other persons working for the organisation or performing services for it;
b) a duty owed as occupier of premises;
c) a duty owed in connection with—
   i) the supply by the organisation of goods or services (whether for consideration or not),
   ii) the carrying on by the organisation of any construction or maintenance operations,
   iii) the carrying on by the organisation of any other activity on a commercial basis, or
   iv) the use or keeping by the organisation of any plant, vehicle or other thing.
d) a duty owed to a person who, by reason of being a person within s 2(2) (detention/custody), is someone for whose safety the organisation is responsible.

4.05 Thus the subsection creates five broad activity based categories from which a relevant duty of care may arise, namely, employing or controlling workers; occupying premises; the supply of goods or services; any other commercial activity; and the detention of a person in custody.

4.06 During debates in Grand Committee of the House of Lords, the Government claimed, 'The principle that lies behind providing a list of categories is to provide a

B. Meaning of 'Relevant Duty of Care'

more readily accessible offence, the application of which can be resolved in many circumstances without detailed resort to the law of negligence.'[1]

The categories themselves do little to advance this aim, rather investigators and the courts will have to identify the existence of a relevant duty of care and then ensure it fits into one of the categories. Often an activity may be capable of fitting two or more of the categories; some of the categories include concepts that have proved troublesome in the law of negligence. In reality, these categories have more to do with the aim of limiting the scope of the offence in its application to public bodies than providing 'a more readily accessible offence.' 4.07

As the Explanatory Notes[2] state: 4.08

Many functions that are peculiarly an aspect of government are not covered by the offence because they will not fall within any of the categories of duty of care in this clause. In particular, the offence will not extend to circumstances where public bodies perform activities for the benefit of the community at large but without supplying services to particular individuals.

The duty of care added by s 2(1)(d), namely that owed to a person detained or in custody ('the custody duty') is an exception to this but found its way into the Act following a long and hard fought campaign in the House of Lords. It can only be brought into force by an order of the Secretary of State through a statutory instrument approved by a vote of both Houses of Parliament.[3] 4.09

1. Superseding statutory duties: s 2(4)

Section 2(4) of the Act provides that a reference to a relevant duty of care owed under the law of negligence, 'includes a reference to a duty that would be owed under the law of negligence but for any statutory provision[4] under which liability is imposed in place of liability under that law.' 4.10

The Explanatory Notes[5] identify the purpose of this subsection as to extend the potential relevant duty of care to one owed where, 'liability in the law of negligence has been superseded by statutory provision imposing strict liability', such as, the Notes suggest, that of carriers under the Carriage by Air Act 1961. 4.11

This provision is not intended to open up 'relevant duty of care' to the host of statutory duties the breach of which provide a basis for civil liability to an injured party, indeed, much of the drafting of ss 2 to 7 is designed to avoid just that eventuality. The test under s 2(4) of the Act for such a statutory duty to fulfil in order to be potentially a relevant duty of care must be whether liability under the statutory provision, 'is imposed in place of liability' under the law of negligence. 4.12

---

[1] *Hansard*, HL Grand Committee, Column 182, Lord Bassam of Brighton (15 January 2007).
[2] Corporate Manslaughter and Corporate Homicide Bill [HL 19], Explanatory Notes para 23.
[3] CMCHA, s 27(2).
[4] s 2(6) provides that 'statutory provision' means provision contained in, or in an instrument made under, any Act, any Act of the Scottish Parliament or any Northern Ireland legislation.
[5] Corporate Manslaughter and Corporate Homicide Bill [HL 19], Explanatory Notes para 21.

4.13 Thus the Carriage by Air Act 1961, s 4 limits the civil liability of air carriers to that provided under the Carriage by Air Act 1961, which amounts 'to the aggregate liability of the carrier in all proceedings which may be brought against him under the law of any part of the United Kingdom, together with any proceedings brought against him outside the United Kingdom.'[6]

2. Common law limitations disregarded: s 2(6)

4.14 Section 2(6) provides, that for the purposes of the Act, there is to be disregarded:

(a) any rule of the common law that has the effect of preventing a duty of care from being owed by one person to another by reason of the fact that they are jointly engaged in unlawful conduct;

(b) any such rule that has the effect of preventing a duty of care from being owed to a person by reason of his acceptance of a risk of harm.

(a) *Ex turpi causa*

4.15 It is a principle, known by the Latin maxim of *ex turpi causa non oritur actio*, that the law of negligence does not recognize the relationship between those involved in a criminal enterprise as giving rise to a duty of care owed by one participant to another. The Court of Appeal, in *R v Wacker*,[7] held that the civil law had introduced this concept as a matter of public policy as the courts will not, 'promote or countenance a nefarious object or bargain which it is bound to condemn', but that it was clear that the criminal law adopted a different approach and in relation to individual gross negligence manslaughter the principle had no application. The Act provides that this is the position in respect of the corporate manslaughter offence.

(b) *Volenti non fit injuria*

4.16 The doctrine of voluntary assumption of risk, *volenti non fit injuria*, prevented an injured party claiming damages in negligence in respect of injury arising from a risk which he had agreed or chosen to accept. Section 2(6)(b) provides that, for the purposes of the Act, 'any such rule' is to be disregarded.

4.17 The words 'any such' in s 2(6)(b) appear to refer to s 2(6)(a) and specifically, 'any rule of the common law'. The Occupiers' Liability Act 1957 provides a statutory definition of the duty of care owed to visitors by an occupier. The Occupiers' Liability Act 1957, s 2(5) provides that this duty, 'does not impose on an occupier any obligation to a visitor in respect of risks willingly accepted as his by the visitor

---

[6] Carriage by Air Act 1961, s 4.
[7] *R v Wacker* [2003] 2 Cr App R 22.

C. Work, the Duty Owed to Employees and Other Workers: s 2(1)(a)

(the question whether a risk was so accepted to be decided on the same principles as in other cases in which one person owes a duty of care to another)'. This statutory limitation appears to have escaped the provisions of s 2(6) of the Corporate Manslaughter and Corporate Homicide Act 2007.

4.18 The common law rule of voluntary assumption of risk is in any event of very narrow application. It once played a central part in employee injury cases but in respect of all torts, as Lord Denning described in *Nettleship v Weston*,[8] 'it has been severely limited'.[9] Lord Denning explained:

> Knowledge of the risk of injury is not enough. Nor is a willingness to take the risk of injury. Nothing will suffice short of an agreement to waive any claim for negligence. The plaintiff must agree, expressly or impliedly, to waive any claim for any injury that may befall him due to the lack of reasonable care by the defendant.[10]

4.19 Bearing in mind quite how limited the common law rule is, it is not immediately apparent why those who drafted the Act felt it necessary to include a provision requiring a judge to disregard this rule when considering whether an organization owed a duty of care to such a person. Whilst s 2(6) states that the rule should be 'disregarded', this is only in respect of its, 'effect of preventing a duty of care from being owed to a person': there is nothing that prevents a jury considering such a factor when considering whether there has been a gross breach of the duty by the organization.

C. WORK, THE DUTY OWED TO EMPLOYEES AND OTHER WORKERS: s 2(1)(a)

4.20 This first, 'employer', category of relevant duty of care is likely to be one of the most frequent bases for the foundation of an offence under the Act. In 2005/06 there were 212 fatal injuries to workers in the United Kingdom, 59 of which were to construction workers and 45 of which were to those working in manufacturing industry.[11] With many of these fatalities, a 'management failure' on the part of an organization has been at least an arguable cause.

4.21 The Explanatory Notes describe how this category, 'will include an employer's duty to provide a safe system of work for its employees. An organization may also owe duties of care to those whose work it is able to control or direct, even though they are not formally employed by it. This might include contractors or volunteers. The new offence does not impose new duties of care where these are not currently owed.'[12]

---

[8] [1971] 2 QB 691.
[9] [1971] 2 QB 691 at 701.
[10] [1971] 2 QB 691 at 701.
[11] Source HSE statistics for fatal injuries reported in 2005/06.
[12] Corporate Manslaughter and Corporate Homicide Bill [HL 19], Explanatory Notes para 22.

1. The employer's duty of care to employees

4.22 In law, an organization as an employer, will owe different duties and be potentially liable for breaches on the following bases:

- Primary liability for breach of a personal, non-delegable, duty of care.
- Vicariously liable for torts committed by employees in the course of employment.
- Liability for breach of a statutory duty.

4.23 It is the first of these that is the relevant duty of care under the Act. An organization may also owe a relevant duty of care arising from work to those workers who are not strictly employees and to those who provide services to it.

4.24 For many years the doctrine of 'common employment' precluded a worker's action against his employer for harm inflicted by fellow employees. This doctrine, which stemmed from the decision in *Priestley v Fowler* (1837) 3 M & WI and held sway until it was finally abolished by the Law Reform (Personal Injuries) Act 1948, s 1, was based on a judicial fiction that an employee impliedly agreed to accept the risks incidental to his employment, including the risk of negligence by other employees. As a result, the concept of an employer's personal, non-delegable duty of care for the safety of his workers developed.

4.25 The employer's duty is considered to include a duty to provide and maintain a safe place of work and equipment; to provide competent employees; and to establish and enforce a safe system of work. This is a personal, non-delegable duty of care. The primary duty arises by virtue of the employment relationship and exists, 'whether or not the employer takes any share in the conduct of the operations'.[13] Thus he can delegate the performance of the duty to others, whether employees or independent contractors, but not responsibility for its negligent performance. This is the case even where a statute requires him to delegate the task to a suitably qualified person.[14] The duty is owed to each individual employee and must take account of his circumstances.[15]

4.26 An employer must take such steps as are reasonable to see that work premises are safe[16] and this duty can extend to the means of access.[17] The employer is also under a duty with respect to the premises of a third party even though he has no control over the premises, but obviously the steps required to discharge such a duty of reasonable care will vary with the circumstances.[18]

4.27 An employer has a 'duty of taking reasonable care to provide proper plant, appliances and equipment, and to maintain them in a proper condition'.[19] The duty

---

[13] Lord Wright in *Wilsons and Clyde Coal Co. Ltd v English* [1938] AC 57 at 84.
[14] *Wilsons and Clyde Coal Co. Ltd v English* [1938] AC 57.
[15] *Paris v Stepney Borough Council* [1951] AC 367.
[16] *Latimer v AEC Ltd* [1953] AC 643.
[17] *Ashdown v Samuel Williams & Sons Ltd* [1957] 1 QB 409, at 430 CA.
[18] *Wilson v Tyneside Window Cleaning Co.* [1958] 2 QB 110, 124 per Parker LJ.
[19] *Smith v Baker* [1891] AC 325, 362 per Lord Herschell.

C. Work, the Duty Owed to Employees and Other Workers: s 2(1)(a)

obviously extends to the provision of safety appliances, and to maintaining such equipment in a proper state of repair. An employer owes a duty to take reasonable care to provide employees with proper instruction in the use of equipment.[20]

The employer must take reasonable care to select competent employees and this is a continuing duty which can require the dismissal of incompetent employees.[21]

4.28

The duty includes a specific duty to provide a safe system of work.[22] There are two aspects to this, namely the devising of a system and its operation. Even if the system itself is safe a negligent failure to operate the system, whether by the employee, another employee or an independent contractor, may place an employer in breach of his duty. Thus the duty to provide a safe system of work may require the employer to instruct employees on procedures and supervise their implementation.[23] Reasonable care in respect of the provision of a safe system of work can extend to accounting for the fact that employees may be inadvertent or become heedless of the risks, particularly where they are encountered on a regular basis. This will involve taking reasonable steps, not only to instruct employees on safety procedures, but also to ensure that the procedures are followed. The duty requires an employer to act reasonably and prudently taking positive thought for the safety of its employees in the context of what is both known and ought reasonably to be known.[24]

4.29

2. Who is an employee?

A vexed question is, who is an employee? The Explanatory Notes, in dealing with s 3(3) of the Act, which provides that the existence of a duty of care in a particular case is a matter of law for the judge to decide, describe how: 'If considering whether a corporation owes a duty of care as employer, the judge will need to decide whether the victim was an employee of the corporation. The questions of fact that the judge will need to consider will generally be uncontroversial.'

4.30

Section 25 of the Act, the interpretation provision, offers a definition of employee, aimed as providing a key to the meaning of employer, namely:

4.31

'employee' means an individual who works under a contract of employment or apprenticeship (whether express or implied and, if express, whether oral or in writing), and related expressions are to be construed accordingly;

The status of a worker as employee or independent contractor may prove to be far from uncontroversial. The ambit of a duty of care owed to an independent contractor,

4.32

---

[20] *General Cleaning Contractors Ltd v Christmas* [1953] AC 180.
[21] In *Hudson v Ridge Manufacturing Co. Ltd* [1957] 2 QB 348 the plaintiff was injured by an employee with a reputation for persistently engaging in practical jokes, his employer was held to be in breach of his duty for having failed to take any steps to stop the activities of the recalcitrant employee.
[22] *Wilsons and Clyde Coal Co. Ltd v English* [1938] AC 57 at 84 clarified in *McDermid v Nash Dredging and Reclamation Co. Ltd* [1987] AC 906—Lord Hailsham at page 910.
[23] *McDermid v Nash Dredging and Reclamation Co. Ltd* [1987] 2 All ER 878, HL and see *General Cleaning Contractors Ltd v Christmas* [1953] AC 180; *Wilson v Tyneside Window Cleaning* [1958] 2 QB 110.
[24] *Heyes v Pilkington Glass Ltd* [1998] PIQR 103.

as opposed to an employee, in respect of a system of work, may also prove both to be a difficult question of law and fact in some cases.

4.33 It is simple to state how an employee is someone who works under a contract of service, in contrast to an independent contractor who works under a contract for service. Both the Health and Safety at Work etc. Act 1974, s 53(1) and Employment Rights Act 1996, s 230, provide (in a similar manner to s 25 of the Act) definitions of employee related to the existence of a contract of employment.

4.34 In *Lee Ting Sang v Chung Chi-Keung* [1990] 2 AC 374, Lord Griffiths, when delivering the judgment of the Privy Council, described the question of what was the appropriate common law test by which to determine whether a workman was working as an employee or as an independent contractor as one which, 'has proved to be a most elusive question', and how, 'despite a plethora of authorities the courts have not been able to devise a single test that will conclusively point to the distinction in all cases.'[25]

4.35 The House of Lords confirmed that the determination of the question whether there is a contract of employment is one of fact and law in *Carmichael v National Power plc* [1999] ICR 1226, opining how the question could only be an issue of law if all the terms of the contract were contained in documents which required to be construed.

4.36 Various tests have been described in a variety of cases, the perspective of each of which has differed. In some, the question has been whether a worker was liable for tax or national insurance, whilst in others, it has been in the context of the breach of an employer's statutory duties in respect of health and safety; whether there was a succession of pieces of work which might arguably be linked to form one employment under an 'umbrella' arrangement; whether the choice between employee or independent contractor masked the fact that the essential contract with which the case was concerned was not one of service or for services, but of a different character altogether or whether there had been continuity of employment for the purposes of claiming employment rights against an alleged employer.

(a) *The control test*

4.37 The judgment of MacKenna J in *Ready Mixed Concrete Ltd v Minister of Pension and National Insurance* [1968] 2 QB 497 at 515 contains the nearest to a classic definition of a contract of service:

A contract of service exists if these three conditions are fulfilled:
i) the servant agrees that, in consideration of a wage or other remuneration, he will provide his own work and skill in the performance of some service for his master,
ii) he agrees, expressly or impliedly, that in the performance of that service he will be subject to the other's control in a sufficient degree to make that other master,
iii) the other provisions of the contract are consistent with its being a contract of service.

---

[25] At p 382.

C. Work, the Duty Owed to Employees and Other Workers: s 2(1)(a)

The 'control test' has remained central to the determination of the issue of employment in civil cases and has been described by the Court of Appeal as 'the paramount test'.[26] However, it is only one of a cluster of tests adopted by courts, including the 'organizational test', the 'economic reality test', the 'mutuality of obligation' and the 'multiple test'.

4.38

The 'control test' stems from the concept of master and servant and involves the notion that a 'servant is a person subject to the command of his master as to the manner in which he shall do his work'.[27] In *Lane v Shire Roofing Co.* [1995] IRLR 493, the Court of Appeal said that in the context of safety at work, there was a real public interest in recognizing the employer/employee relationship. Lord Justice Henry described how a great many relationships which are in truth 'master and servant', and thus 'employer and employee', are, to the advantage of both parties, dressed up as self-employment, and that courts must look to the realities.

4.39

(b) *Agency workers*
Many recent cases have considered the position of agency workers.[28] Agency workers usually have a contract with the agency through whom they secure work, which is unlikely to be a contract of employment. The person for whom they work, the 'end-user', usually has a contract with the agency for the supply of the services of the agency worker, which the agency worker is not party to. Because the agency worker has no contract with, he cannot be an employee of, the end-user. Thus, on any conventional analysis, agency workers are employees of no-one; in both *Franks v Reuters Ltd* [2003] EWCA Civ 417, [2003] ICR 1166, CA and *Brook Street Bureau (UK) Ltd v Dacas* [2004] EWCA Civ 217, [2004] ICR 1437 the possibility that a contract might be implied between the agency worker and the end user, by virtue of having provided the services integrally for the organization over a long period of time, was raised as a potential common law answer. In *Dacas* it was suggested that the agency and end-user might jointly be the employer. The approach taken in *Dacas* was endorsed by the Court of Appeal in *Cable & Wireless plc v Muscat* [2006] EWCA Civ 220.

4.40

The 'agency' cases are all ones in which the agency worker has sought to assert employment rights of the kind conferred by the Employment Rights Act 1996. Where the issue is the existence of a duty of care in respect of safety, it is suggested that a court is unlikely to hold that an end-user's obligations to agency workers

4.41

---

[26] *Interlink Express Parcels Ltd v Night Trunkers Ltd* [2001] IRLR 224 CA.
[27] *Yewens v Noakes* (1880) 6 QBD 530.
[28] See *Garrard v A E Southey & Co. and Standard Telephones and Cables Ltd* [1952] 2 QB *Hewlett Packard v O'Murphy* [2002] IRLR 4, EAT; *Montgomery v Johnson Underwood Ltd* [2001] EWCA Civ 318, [2001] IRLR 269; *Franks v Reuters Ltd* [2003] EWCA Civ 417, [2003] ICR 1166, CA; *Stephenson v Delphi Diesel Systems Ltd* [2003] ICR 471; *Brook Street Bureau (UK) Ltd v Dacas* [2004] EWCA Civ 217, [2004] ICR 1437, CA. *Motorola Ltd v Davidson* [2001] IRLR 4, EAT.

working for it are different from the obligations owed simultaneously to direct employees of the business.

3. Non-employee workers

4.42 Traditionally, the duties owed by an employer to an employee have not extended to independent contractors[29] but under the general law of negligence, a duty of care similar to that owed by an employer to employees has been found to be owed by an undertaking to persons not in its employment, through the operation of forseeability and proximity, where the undertaking has assumed a responsibility for a worker. There are two broad categories in this regard: workers subject to another's factual control or supervision, and workers practically involved with another's activities. Duties analogous to those owed by employers to employees have been found to exist in relationships characterized by factual or legal control.[30] The reasons for imposing a duty of care on a non-employer analogous to that owed by an employer are stronger where an undertaking controls a worker and other workers or operations where he works and, in such circumstances no deliberate, voluntary acceptance of responsibility is required.[31]

4. Distinguishing vicarious liability

4.43 Another difficulty posed by this area in relation to a relevant duty of care under the Act stems from the close inter-relationship between the primary duty to provide competent employees and a safe system of work (a potential relevant duty of care) and the vicarious liability an employer has in respect of the defaults of an employee arising in the course of his employment (not being a relevant duty of care). In many civil negligence authorities, courts have not had to grapple with the limits of the primary duty, the defendant being liable in any event as a result of vicarious responsibility for the acts or defaults of his employee.

5. Statutory health and safety duties

4.44 There is a considerable body of health and safety regulations made pursuant to the Health and Safety at Work etc. Act 1974. These provisions create a host of work related duties, many stemming from European directives, upon different classes of person and involve differing standards and qualifications; some duties are absolute, some are qualified by 'reasonable practicability' others by different standards.

---

[29] *Jones v Minton Construction Ltd* (1973) 15 KIR 309.
[30] See *Morris v Breaveglen* [1997] EWCA Civ 1662 and *Nelhams v Sandells Maintenance Ltd and Gillespie (UK) Ltd* [1996] PIQR P 52, CA.
[31] *Smith v Eric S Bush (a firm)* [1990] 1 AC 831, HL at 862 per Lord Griffiths.

C. Work, the Duty Owed to Employees and Other Workers: s 2(1)(a)

Breach of statutory duty is an entirely separate tort from an action in negligence and the statutory duties are not relevant duties of care. The existence of a statutory duty owed by an organization to a class of persons including the alleged victim of an offence of corporate manslaughter will perhaps inevitably place the organization in a proximate relationship with the victim capable of founding a relevant duty of care. The statutory duty will inform the nature and standard of any common law duty of care, which will remain one to take reasonable care. What is reasonable will be informed by what is required by an organization through the operation of the statute. The subtleties of this have been somewhat lost in a number of the Court of Appeal individual gross negligence manslaughter authorities but the Act correctly recognizes this position in s 8 by providing that, in deciding whether there has been a gross breach of a relevant duty of care, a jury must consider, 'whether the evidence shows that the organisation failed to comply with any health and safety legislation that relates to the alleged breach'.[32]   4.45

The Construction (Design and Management) Regulations 2007 create a duty, in relation to construction sites, upon a principal contractor in respect of the health and safety of all workers, including sub-contractors and their employees. It is not the statutory duty that creates a common law duty of care, rather this establishes a relationship of proximity and informs the nature of any duty of care owed. Even prior to these Regulations being enacted, it has been held that an undertaking in the position of main contractor or simply the site owner which is co-ordinating the activities of sub-contractors, was liable for failure to allocate safety responsibilities when the operations of one sub-contractor endangered the workmen of another.[33]   4.46

6. *Volenti non fit injuria*

The doctrine of voluntary assumption of risk, *volenti non fit injuria*, held that a worker who knew of the risks involved in work, yet continued in his employment, had assumed the risk himself, thereby absolving the employer from any responsibility. In *Smith v Baker* [1891] AC 325 the House of Lords recognized that this was a fiction and that economic realities compel most people to accept the risks of their employment, removing the essential voluntary element. Subsequent cases stressed how an employee's knowledge of the existence of a danger does not in itself amount to consent to run the risk.[34]   4.47

In any event, s 2(6)(b) provides that for the purposes of the Act, 'any such rule that has the effect of preventing a duty of care from being owed to a person by reason of his acceptance of a risk of harm' is to be disregarded.   4.48

---

[32] See paras 6.64–6.68.
[33] See *Kealey v Heard* [1983] 1 WLR 573: *Wheeler v Copas* [1981] 3 All ER 405 and *Makepeace v Evans Brothers (Reading) (a firm)* [2001] ICR 241.
[34] See, eg, *Baker v James Bros & Sons Ltd* [1921] 2 KB 674; *Williams v Birmingham Battery and Metal Co.* [1899] 2 QB 338.

D. THE DUTY AS AN OCCUPIER OF PREMISES: s 2(1)(b)

4.49 Section 2(1)(b) of the Act provides that a duty owed by an organization under the law of negligence as occupier of premises is a relevant duty of care for the purposes of an offence under the Act.

4.50 Premises is defined, by s 25 of the Act, to be a term which 'includes land, buildings and moveable structures'.

4.51 Section 2(7) of the Act provides that the Occupiers' Liability Acts 1957 and 1984 and the Defective Premises Act 1972 and equivalent Scottish and Northern Irish legislation are included in, 'the law of negligence.'

4.52 The Occupiers' Liability Acts define the content of an occupier's duty only, the common law continues to define by whom and to whom the duty is owed. Thus the Acts do not define who is an occupier and the term 'occupier' has been described as no more than a convenient label for the kind of relationship which gives rise to a duty of care,[35] with the decisive factor being control. Control can exist with or without complete physical possession of the premises.[36] A landlord of tenanted premises does not owe a duty as occupier, although he may owe a duty pursuant to the Defective Premises Act 1972.

4.53 Lord Denning's opinion in *Wheat v Lacon & Co. Ltd* [1966] AC 552 contains a detailed consideration of who is an occupier of premises. In that case the House of Lords held that there was nothing to prevent two or more persons from being occupiers of the same premises if they shared control.[37] In *Ferguson v Welsh* [1987] 1 WLR 1553, Lord Goff suggested that it is equally possible for an entrant to be a lawful visitor of only one such occupier.

4.54 The Occupiers' liability Act 1957, s 1(3)(a) provides that the Act's provisions apply in relation to an occupier of premises and his visitors, 'in like manner and to the like extent as the principles applicable at common law to an occupier of premises and his invitees or licensees would apply, to regulate:—(a) the obligations of a person occupying or having control over any fixed or moveable structure, including any vessel, vehicle or aircraft.'

4.55 Thus in *Bunker v Charles Brand & Sons Ltd* [1969] 2 QB 480, the premises in question was a tunnel boring machine.

4.56 Any determination by a judge of the existence of a relevant duty of care under the Act in respect of an organization arising from its occupation of premises will depend upon an assessment of the facts relating to the nature and extent of its occupation and the control exercised by the organization over the premises.

---

[35] *Wheat v Lacon & Co. Ltd* [1966] 1 QB 335, 366, per Diplock LJ.
[36] See *Robertson v Riley* [1989] 2 All ER 474 and *Harris v Birkenhead Corporation* [1975] 1 WLR.
[37] See *AMF International v Magnet Bowling Ltd and another* [1968] 1 WLR 1028.

D. The Duty as an Occupier of Premises: s 2(1)(b)

1. The nature of the duty under the Occupiers' Liability Act 1957: the common duty of care

The Occupiers' Liability Act 1957 created a single category of 'lawful visitors' to whom an occupier owes the 'common duty of care'. The section defines the extent of the duty but the common law dictates who is a lawful visitor: namely, 'contractors' ie those entering pursuant to a contract, invitees and licensees. Pursuant to the Occupiers' Liability Act 1957, s 2(6), those, 'who enter premises for any purpose in the exercise of a right conferred by law' are also lawful visitors. A number of decisions relating to 'implied licences' to enter date from a time prior to the existence of any duty owed to trespassers.[38] Another source of difficulty stems from cases concerned with permissions limited by time, space, purpose of entry or given through agents/employees. 4.57

Section 2 provides: 4.58

1) An occupier of premises owes the same duty, the 'common duty of care', to all his visitors, except in so far as he is free to and does extend, restrict, modify or exclude his duty to any visitor or visitors by agreement or otherwise.
2) The common duty of care is a duty to take such care as in all the circumstances of the case is reasonable to see that the visitor will be reasonably safe in using the premises for the purposes for which he is invited or permitted by the occupier to be there.

The Occupiers' Liability Act 1957, s 2(5) provides that this duty, 'does not impose on an occupier any obligation to a visitor in respect of risks willingly accepted as his by the visitor (the question whether a risk was so accepted to be decided on the same principles as in other cases in which one person owes a duty of care to another)'. This statutory limitation seems to have escaped the provisions of Corporate Manslaughter and Corporate Homicide Act 2007, s 2(6), which appears only to disregard the application of any such common law rule for the purposes of determining the existence of a duty of care under the Act.[39] 4.59

Sections 2(3) and 2(4) of the Occupiers' Liability Act 1957 make provisions concerning child visitors, warnings to visitors of risk, and the employment of independent contractors who create danger: these provisions are relevant to discharge or breach of such a duty, not whether the duty of care existed or was owed to a particular person. 4.60

Section 2(1) of the Unfair Contract Terms Act 1977 provides that in cases of personal injury or death it is not possible to exclude liability resulting from the negligence of an occupier of 'business' premises.[40] Negligence is defined by the Unfair 4.61

---

[38] See, eg, *Lowery v Walker* [1911] AC 10.
[39] See paras 4.14, 4.16–4.19.
[40] Unfair Contract Terms Act 1977, s 1(3): 'business liability' means liability for breach of obligations or duties arising from either things done by a person 'in the course of business' or 'from the occupation of premises used for business purposes of the occupier'.

Contract Terms Act 1977, s 1(1)(c) to include the breach of the common duty of care under the Occupiers' Liability Act 1957.

2. The Occupiers' Liability Act 1984

4.62 The Occupiers' Liability Act 1984 provides for a duty, pursuant to s 1(4), upon an occupier of premises to 'persons other than his visitors',[41] 'to take such care as is reasonable in all the circumstances'.[42] Section 1(3) of the 1984 Act provides that the duty will arise if three requirements are satisfied:

- the defendant must be *'aware* of the danger' or if he 'has reasonable grounds to believe that it exists' (s 1(3)(a));
- the defendant must *'know'* or have 'reasonable grounds to believe that the entrant is in the vicinity of the danger or that he may come into the vicinity of the danger' (s 1(3)(b));
- thereafter, 'the risk is one against which, in all the circumstances of the case, he may reasonably be expected to offer the other some protection' (s 1(3)(c)).

4.63 The first two criteria, contained in the Occupiers' Liability Act 1984, ss 1(3)(a) and (b), appear capable of being subjective or objective. In *White v St Albans City and District Council*[43] the Court of Appeal held that an occupier who had taken measures to keep the public off his dangerous premises should not, by that reason alone, be deemed to have reason to believe that persons were likely to be in the vicinity of the danger for the purposes of s 1(3)(b) of the 1984 Act. Rather, the answer should be made to depend on all the facts of the case, including the state of the land. In *Swain v Buri* [1996] PIQR P442, it was held that the words 'have reasonable grounds to believe', in s 1(3)(b) of the 1984 Act, must be taken to refer to 'actual knowledge of the facts that would lead a reasonable man to expect the presence of a trespasser;' the court added that mere culpable ignorance, or constructive knowledge, was insufficient.

4.64 The Occupiers' Liability Act 1984, s 1(6), provides that no duty under the section, 'is owed to any person in respect of risks willingly accepted as his by that person (the question whether a risk was so accepted to be decided on the same principles as in other cases in which one person owes a duty of care to another)'. As with the 1957 Act, this statutory limitation appears to have escaped the provisions of s 2(6) of the Corporate Manslaughter and Corporate Homicide Act 2007, which disregard the application of any such common law rule.[44]

---

[41] Occupiers' Liability Act 1984, s 1(1)(a).
[42] The Countryside and Rights of Way Act 2000, makes special provision in respect of 'authorised ramblers' and the Occupiers' Liability Act 1984.
[43] *The Times*, 12 March 1990
[44] See paras 4.14, 4.16–4.19.

E. Duties Owed 'In Connection with' Various Activities: s 2(1)(c)

Unlike the 1957 Act, The Occupiers' Liability Act 1984 makes no reference to the question of whether an occupier can exclude or restrict his potential liability under the Act.   4.65

E. DUTIES OWED 'IN CONNECTION WITH' VARIOUS ACTIVITIES: s 2(1)(c)

Sections 2(1)(c)(i) to (iv) of the Act provide for a disparate collection of activities, some of which are relatively narrow and others of which are extremely wide, in connection with which a relevant of duty of care can arise.   4.66

1. The supply by the organization of goods or services

Section 2(1)(c)(i) provides that 'relevant duty of care', in relation to an organization, includes a duty owed by it under the law of negligence in connection with the supply by the organization of goods and services (whether for consideration or not).   4.67

During debates in both Houses of Parliament the Government explained how in respect of this subsection in particular and the relevant duty of care in general, the word 'provision' in relation to goods and services had been deliberately omitted: 4.68

> the term 'providing' covers a potentially wider range of activity and could include many situations in which no duty of care is owed. For example, it would extend to circumstances in which a service was provided to the public at large, such as when local authorities were working to cut crime. No duty of care is owed in that respect, nor is the activity being supplied.[45]

It appears the word 'supply' is intended to convey a relationship of proximity between the supplying organization and the deceased victim. The decided cases concerned with the extent of the tort of negligence arising from the supply of goods or services have grappled with the issue of proximity of supplier to injured party.   4.69

(a) *The supply of goods*

The common law duty of care in respect of the supply of defective goods is far more limited than remedies offered under contract and through the operation of statute, which are outwith the relevant duty of care under the Act. A purchaser of goods will have the benefit of implied terms as to the quality and fitness for purpose of the goods and services under the Sale of Goods Act 1979, s 14; the Supply of Goods and Services Act 1982, s 4 as amended by the Sale and Supply of Goods Act 1994, which in the case of 'consumer' transactions cannot be excluded, pursuant to the Unfair Contract Terms Act 1977, s 6. Such liability is strict, not being fault based on the part of the supplier. The Consumer Protection Act 1987 created an extensive strict liability in respect of defective goods. Most civil actions for damages following the   4.70

---

[45] *Official Report*, House of Commons Standing Committee B (24/10/06) Col 96.

4.71 Under the common law, the manufacturer's duty identified in *Donoghue v Stevenson* [1932] AC 562 has been given a broad interpretation. 'Products' are not limited to food and drink, but include almost any item capable of causing damage[46] and the 'ultimate consumer' appears to include anyone foreseeably harmed by the defective product not just a particular purchaser.[47] The class of potential defendants is wider than manufacturers and includes repairers, assemblers and suppliers of goods where the circumstances are that such an organization should reasonably have inspected the goods[48] or tested them. If a danger in respect of goods becomes apparent (or ought to have been discovered) then the manufacturer's duty of care extends to take reasonable steps to either warn users of a danger learnt following manufacture or recall the defective products[49] which gave rise to the injury.

supply of defective goods or services have been pursued under remedies provided by one or more of these statutes, which have not replaced the common law nor been included into the definition of the law of negligence under the Act. These statutes do not create relevant duties of care under the Act.

(b) *The supply of services*

4.72 A 'relevant duty of care' under the Act in connection with the supply of services by an organization to a person poses a number of potential difficulties. The first relates to the importance of distinguishing between vicarious liability for the negligence of an organization's employee providing that service (not a relevant duty of care) and a primary duty owed by the organization. A duty of care is owed by the provider of a service to a person whom may reasonably forseeably suffer physical harm through the performance of that service. The standard of care is of the reasonably skilled and experienced provider of such a service. Civil actions for negligence focus largely on the vicarious liability of an organization employing a service provider: it being a far more straightforward matter to establish negligence on the part of the individual employee service provider and unnecessary to do more.

4.73 The primary duty owed by an organization employing a service provider may, depending on the circumstances, extend to a duty to take reasonable care in the provision of sufficient competent adequately trained and properly supervised staff who work to a appropriate safe system of work: similar matters to that in relation to the duty of care owed by an employer to workers.[50] The test for the existence such a relevant duty of care under the Act will involve the general considerations of forseeability of harm and proximity discussed above at paras 3.46–3.53.

---

[46] See underpants (*Grant v Australian Knitting Mills Ltd* [1936] AC 85); motor cars *(Herschtal v Stewart & Arden Ltd* [1940] 1 KB 155); hair dye *(Watson v Buckley, Osborne Garrett & Co. Ltd* [1940] 1 All ER 174); lifts *(Haseldine v C. A. Daw & Son Ltd* [1941] 2 KB 343); and chemicals *(Vacwell Engineering Co. Ltd v BDH Chemicals Ltd* [1971] 1 QB 88).
[47] Eg *Stennett v Hancock* [1939] 2 All ER 578.
[48] See *Kubach v Hollands* [1937] 3 All ER 907 and *Andrews v Hopkinson* [1957] 1 QB 229.
[49] *Hobbs (Farms) Ltd v Baxenden Chemical Co. Ltd* [1992] 1 Lloyd's Rep 54.
[50] See paras 4.20–4.48.

E. Duties Owed 'In Connection with' Various Activities: s 2(1)(c)

4.74 Sections 4 to 7 of the Act are concerned with limiting the extent of this category of relevant duty of care in relation to public bodies, the Crown, the military and emergency services. This is considered at paras 5.41–5.88.

2. The carrying on by the organization of any construction or maintenance operations

4.75 Section 2(1)(c)(ii) of the Act provides that 'relevant duty of care', in relation to an organization, includes a duty owed by it under the law of negligence in connection with the carrying on by the organization of any construction or maintenance operations.

4.76 Section 2(7) provides that 'construction or maintenance operations' means operations of any of the following descriptions:

a) construction, installation, alteration, extension, improvement, repair, maintenance, decoration, cleaning, demolition or dismantling of—
   i) any building or structure,
   ii) anything else that forms, or is to form, part of the land, or
   iii) any plant, vehicle or other thing;
b) operations that form an integral part of, or are preparatory to, or are for rendering complete, any operations within paragraph (a)'.

4.77 The Explanatory Notes lump this subsection and that in 2(1)(c)(iv)i together with an explanation that states:

When constructing or maintaining buildings, infrastructure or vehicles etc or when using plant or vehicles etc. In many circumstances, duties of care owed, for example, to ensure that adequate safety precautions are taken when repairing a road or in maintaining the safety of vehicles etc will be duties owed by an organization in relation to the supply of a service or because it is operating commercially. But that may not be apt to cover public sector bodies in all such circumstances. These categories ensure that no lacuna is left in this respect.[51]

4.78 Thus the intention is to ensure that the activities of public bodies (which are otherwise subject to various exclusions contained within ss 3 to 6[52]), when connected with construction or maintenance are subject to relevant duties of care created by proximity and forseeability of harm.

4.79 Both the extended meaning of construction and the term maintenance encompass a very broad range of activities and situations.

(a) Construction

4.80 A number of health and safety regulations create statutory duties upon persons involved in construction to a wider group than merely employees. In particular the Construction (Design and Management) Regulations 2007. These statutory duties

---

[51] Corporate Manslaughter and Corporate Homicide Bill [HL 19], Explanatory Notes para 22.
[52] See paras 5.01–5.88.

create relationships of proximity from which a common law duty of care can arise. Such duties of care equally may be classed as falling within the categories under s 2(1)(a), 2(1)(c)(i) or s 2(1)(c)(iii) of the Act.

4.81 The Building Act 1984 included a provision in s 38 creating civil liability for a breach of building regulations, although that part of the section remains to be brought into force. How such matters have affected the relationship of proximity in a common law duty of care appears to be a very difficult question of law and fact.

4.82 The extent of the duty of care owed by an organization that constructs a defective building is far from straightforward.[53] It is clear that an organization involved in construction will owe a resultant duty of care to a third party, be that third party the owner, occupier, visitor or passer-by of the premises, in relation to a latent defect that causes a victim to suffer physical injury.[54] This is the most likely duty to form the basis for a 'relevant duty of care' under the Act. Beyond this the extent of duties of care arising in connection to construction is more difficult.

4.83 Under the common law, any person who did work on land was under a duty of care at the time when he did the work, but if he subsequently sold or let the premises on which he did the work, his potential liability for breach of that duty came to an end. The transaction of sales or letting alone conferred this immunity. The Defective Premises Act 1972, s 3(1) abolished this immunity[55] by providing that:

> where work of construction, repair, maintenance or demolition or any other work is done on or in relation to premises, any duty of care owed, because of the doing of the work, to persons who might reasonably be expected to be affected by defects in the state of the premises created by the doing of the work shall not be abated by the subsequent disposal of the premises by the person who owed the duty.

4.84 Section 1(1) of the Defective Premises 1972 Act provides that:

> A person taking on work or in connection with the provision of a dwelling...owes a duty: *(a)* if the dwelling is provided to the order of any person, to that person; and *(b)* without prejudice to paragraph *(a)* above, to every person who acquires an interest (whether legal or equitable) in the dwelling, to see that the work which he takes on is done in a workmanlike or, as the case may be, professional manner, with proper materials and so that as regards that work the dwelling will be fit for habitation when completed.

4.85 The duty applies only to dwellings[56] and is owed to those commissioning the work and anyone who subsequently acquires a legal or equitable interest in the land.

---

[53] See *Dutton v Bognor Regis UDC* [1972] 1 QB 373, approved in the subsequently doubted House of Lords decision in *Anns v Merton London Borough Council* [1978] AC 728. See more recent cases of *Murphy v Brentwood DC* [1991] 1 AC 398 and *Targett v Torfaen BC* [1992] 3 All ER 27.

[54] See the opinions in *Murphy v Brentwood DC* [1991] 1 AC 398. If the occupier of the property becomes aware of the defect before injury is caused then, at that stage, the defect ceases to be latent and, according to Lord Keith, it is 'the latency of the defect which constitutes the mischief' (at 464).

[55] However, Defective Premises Act 1972, s 3(2) specifies the situations when the section does not apply.

[56] Originally dwellings covered by an 'approved scheme' (the National House Builders Protection Scheme) were excluded from the application of Defective Premises Act 1972, s 1.

E. Duties Owed 'In Connection with' Various Activities: s 2(1)(c)

The term, 'taking on work' would appear to include not only builders, but architects, engineers, surveyors and subcontractors. (The extent to which it applies to local authorities is even more uncertain.)[57]

The ambit of the defence pursuant to Defective Premises Act 1972, s 1(2) represents another uncertainty. This provides that no breach occurs if the defendant agreed to do the work in accordance with instructions given by the other party (for whom he is doing the work) but does not apply if the defendant owes a duty to warn the other party of any defects in the instructions. 4.86

(b) *Maintenance*

An organization undertaking maintenance work will owe a duty of care in relation to those persons in a proximate relationship to it who could reasonably forseeably suffer personal injury as a result of the manner in which it carries out such maintenance operations—the same is true of the other activities listed in the definition of 'construction or maintenance operations' in s 2(7) of the Act. However, 'a duty arising in connection with. . .maintenance operations' is a term that has particular significance. 4.87

Firstly, the resultant duty of care placed on landlords of tenanted property who are under a duty to maintain the premises will be encompassed by this category and be potentially, a 'relevant duty of care' under the Act. Where premises are let under a tenancy which puts on the landlord an obligation to the tenant for the maintenance or repair of the premises, the landlord owes to all persons who might reasonably be expected to be affected by defects in the state of the premises a duty to take such care as is reasonable in all the circumstances to see that they are reasonably safe from personal injury or from damage to their property caused by a relevant defect. By the Defective Premises Act 1972, s 4(1), the duty is owed to all those 'who might reasonably be expected to be affected' by the defects in the premises and this includes tenants, visitors, neighbours, users of the highway and even trespassers. 4.88

Liability is imposed only for damage due to 'a relevant defect', which Defective Premises Act 1972, s 4(3) defines as: 4.89

A defect in the state of the premises existing at or after the material time and arising from, or continuing because of, an act or omission by the landlord which constitutes or would, if he had had notice of the defect, have constituted a failure by him to carry out his obligation to the tenant for the maintenance or repair of the premises.

Importantly, liability is not dependent on knowledge of the defect in question; further, the duty cannot be excluded or restricted. 4.90

In respect of maintenance operations, the second area of significance relates to the extent of a duty of care owed by a public authority under a statutory duty to 'maintain'. This has proved an area of great uncertainty and has been the subject of 4.91

---

[57] *Murphy v Brentwood DC* [1991] 1 AC 398.

two House of Lords authorities in recent years.[58] It may fall within the exclusion of a relevant duty of care founded upon an 'exclusively public function', contained in s 3 of the Act.[59]

3. The carrying on by the organization of any other activity on a commercial basis

4.92 Section 2(1)(c)(iii) of the Act provides that 'relevant duty of care', in relation to an organization, includes a duty owed by it under the law of negligence in connection with the carrying on by the organization of any other activity on a commercial basis.

4.93 The Explanatory Notes[60] describe how the inclusion of this category is intended to ensure, 'that activities that are not the supply of goods and services but which are still performed by companies and others commercially, such as farming or mining, are covered by the offence.'

4.94 The use of the term, 'any *other* activity' suggests that the subsection applies to an activity that does not fall within any other of provided categories of relevant duty of care.

4.95 The term 'commercial basis' is not defined by the Act. It appears in a variety of statutes, mostly employed as part of a phrase, 'commercial basis and with a view to the realisation of profits'.[61] It has not provided a foundation in decided cases for distinguishing circumstances in which a duty of care existed in the law of negligence. It is difficult to envisage any activity that an organization would engage in on a commercial basis, even in farming or mining, that could result in a 'relevant duty of care' under the Act but which was not related to the employment or control of workers, the occupation of premises, the supply of goods or services or the keeping or use of plant, machinery or 'other thing'.

4.96 Whether such commercial activities would involve a relevant duty of care owed to a deceased victim could only be determined through the factors of forseeability of harm and proximity. If the purpose of these categories is truly to assist investigators and prosecutors in readily identifying circumstances in which a duty of care existed without recourse to a detailed consideration of the law of negligence[62] then this category does little to achieve this.

4. The use or keeping by the organization of any plant, vehicle, or other thing

4.97 Section 2(1)(c)(iv) of the Act provides that 'relevant duty of care', in relation to an organization, includes a duty owed by it under the law of negligence in

---

[58] *Stovin v Wise* [1996] AC 923; *Gorringe v Calderdale Metropolitan Borough Council* [2004] UKHL 15, [2004] 1 WLR 1057.
[59] See paras 5.12–5.31.
[60] Corporate Manslaughter and Corporate Homicide Bill [HL 19], Explanatory Notes para 22.
[61] Eg Income and Corporation Taxes Act 1988, ss 53, 297, 384; Finance Act 1988, Sch 6, para 1.
[62] See *Hansard*, HL Grand Committee, Column 184 (15 January 2007).

connection with the use or keeping by the organization of any plant, vehicle, or other thing.

This extremely wide category is apparently there to sweep up a relevant activity undertaken by a public body that falls through the net of supplying goods or services or of any duty arising in respect of a commercial activity.[63] Thus the category is concerned with a duty of care arising from the keeping or use of anything by an organization. Notwithstanding that the Parliamentary explanation for these categories is to assist investigators and prosecutors in determining when a relevant duty of care will arise without recourse to the detailed law of negligence,[64] it will only be through the application of the tests of forseeability of harm, proximity and the reasonableness/justice of the situation that a determination can be made as to whether such keeping or use created a relevant duty of care owed to the deceased alleged victim. 4.98

F. THE 'CUSTODY' DUTY OF CARE: s 2(1)(d)

The addition of s 2(1)(d) resulted from a long and hard campaign in the House of Lords, principally fought by Lord Ramsbotham, that saw the Act 'ping-pong' between the two Houses until the deadline for a passage of the Act had nearly passed. The last-minute compromise that allowed the Act to be granted Royal Assent was the inclusion of the duty but with a particular clause concerning how it should come into force: s 27(2) requires the duty to be brought into force only by an order of the Secretary of State through a statutory instrument approved by a resolution of each House of Parliament. 4.99

1. Potential commencement

On 23 July 2007, in the House of Lords during the final stages of the 'ping-pong' process that finally resulted in the inclusion of the duty set out in s 2(1)(d), Baroness Ashton of Upholland, on behalf of the Government, described how, 'In providing for custody to be an integral part of the Bill, the Government are starting a clear process towards extending the offence to custody.'[65] However, she went on quote how the Secretary of State for Justice had suggested that he considered a delay of between five and seven years before implementation of the duty would be necessary to permit the police and the Prison Service to 'have time to understand fully the extent of these obligations and take steps to implement them'[66] and to otherwise avoid them becoming 'risk averse'. 4.100

---

[63] Corporate Manslaughter and Corporate Homicide Bill [HL 19], Explanatory Notes para 22.
[64] See *Hansard*, HL Grand Committee, Column 184 (15 January 2007).
[65] *Hansard*, HL Column 556 (23 July 2007).
[66] *Hansard*, HC Column 333 (18 July 2007).

4.101 Baroness Ashton of Upholland went on to state:

> Concerns have been raised that that sort of timetable does not provide the necessary impetus to take matters forward, and the Government are prepared to recognise and to respond to those concerns. For that reason, I give noble Lords an assurance that the sort of timetable that the Government will aim for will be the three-year period from commencement...[67]

4.102 Thus, with a proposed date for commencement of the Act being 6 April 2008, moves to bring the 'custody' duty appear promised to occur in 2010.

2. The relevant duty

4.103 The Act provides that a relevant duty of care in relation to an organization includes a duty owed by it under the law of negligence that is within s 2(1)(d), namely:

> (d) a duty owed to a person who, by reason of being a person within subsection (2), is someone for whose safety the organisation is responsible.

4.104 Subsection (2) provides:

> (2) A person is within this subsection if—
> (a) he is detained at a custodial institution or in a custody area at a court or police station;
> (b) he is detained at a removal centre or short-term holding facility;
> (c) he is being transported in a vehicle, or being held in any premises, in pursuance of prison escort arrangements or immigration escort arrangements;
> (d) he is living in secure accommodation in which he has been placed;
> (e) he is a detained patient.

4.105 Section 2(7) provides various definitions of the terms within subsection (2):

> '**custodial institution**' means a prison, a young offender institution, a secure training centre, a young offenders institution, a young offenders centre, a juvenile justice centre or a remand centre;
> '**detained patient**' means—
> (a) a person who is detained in any premises under—
>   (i) Part 2 or 3 of the Mental Health Act 1983 (c. 20) ('the 1983 Act'), or
>   (ii) Part 2 or 3 of the Mental Health (Northern Ireland) Order 1986 (SI 1986/595 (NI 4)) ('the 1986 Order');
> (b) a person who (otherwise than by reason of being detained as mentioned in paragraph (a)) is deemed to be in legal custody by—
>   (i) section 137 of the 1983 Act,
>   (ii) Article 131 of the 1986 Order, or
>   (iii) article 11 of the Mental Health (Care and Treatment) (Scotland) Act 2003 (Consequential Provisions) Order 2005 (SI 2005/2078);

---

[67] *Hansard*, HL Column 556 (23 July 2007).

F. The 'Custody' Duty of Care: s 2(1)(d)

(c) a person who is detained in any premises, or is otherwise in custody, under the Mental Health (Care and Treatment) (Scotland) Act 2003 (asp 13) or Part 6 of the Criminal Procedure (Scotland) Act 1995 (c. 46) or who is detained in a hospital under section 200 of that Act of 1995;

'**immigration escort arrangements**' means arrangements made under section 156 of the Immigration and Asylum Act 1999 (c. 33);

'**prison escort arrangements**' means arrangements made under section 80 of the Criminal Justice Act 1991 (c. 53) or under section 102 or 118 of the Criminal Justice and Public Order Act 1994 (c. 33);

'**removal centre**' and '**short-term holding facility**' have the meaning given by section 147 of the Immigration and Asylum Act 1999;

'**secure accommodation**' means accommodation, not consisting of or forming part of a custodial institution, provided for the purpose of restricting the liberty of persons under the age of 18.

4.106   In short, the scope of the duty defined by ss 2(1)(d) and 2(2) extends to that owed to all persons subject to compulsory detention that is, custody, remand, detention pursuant to immigration controls, secure accommodation, being transported during such detention and in respect of compulsory detention under the Mental Health Act 1983.

(a) *Detention outside of s 2(2)*

4.107   'Prison' is not defined and appears as a term within the meaning of 'custodial institution': the sole remaining military prison in the United Kingdom is known as the Military Corrective Training Centre and appears to fall out of the definition of 'custodial institution'.

4.108   The detention facilities used by Her Majesty's Revenue and Customs would also appear to fall outside the definition of 'custodial institution'.

(b) *The power to amend the categories of detained person in s 2(2)*

4.109   Section 23 of the Act provides:

(1) The Secretary of State may by order amend section 2(2) to make it include any category of person (not already included) who—
   (a) is required by virtue of a statutory provision to remain or reside on particular premises, or
   (b) is otherwise subject to a restriction of his liberty.
(2) An order under this section may make any amendment to this Act that is incidental or supplemental to, or consequential on, an amendment made by virtue of subsection (1).
(3) An order under this section is subject to affirmative resolution procedure.

4.110   Thus, categories of detained person can be added to s 2(2) through the same process as is required to bring the 'custody' duty into force, namely an order of the Secretary of State through a statutory instrument affirmed by a vote of both Houses of Parliament.[68]

---

[68] CMCHA, s 24 and para 4.99.

3. The nature of the common law duty

4.111 While the Act defines the scope of the duty, being that owed to all persons subject to compulsory detention, the nature of the duty is simply defined as the duty owed under the law of negligence by the organization to such a person as, 'someone for whose safety the organisation is responsible.'

4.112 The nature and extent of this duty of care under the common law of negligence is uncertain and has featured in a number of appellate decisions. Such duties of care of uncertain ambit were intended by the Government to be excluded from the Act through the operation of ss 3–7.[69] Indeed, the very terms of s 3(2), which excludes any relevant duty of care owed in respect of an 'exclusively public function', as originally proposed appeared designed principally with the exclusion of custody and detention in mind. If and when s 1(2)(d), the 'custody' duty, is brought into force so will the full provisions of s 3(2), which contains a clause placing 'custody' outwith the limitation of an exclusively public function.[70]

4.113 It is established that an organization responsible for the detention of a person owes that person a duty to take reasonable care in respect of his health and safety. The difficulty arises in defining what that duty extends to. Two issues that have featured regularly in cause célèbres are suicides and the deaths of detainees at the hands of other detainees. In respect of the former, the duty to take reasonable care undoubtedly encompasses a duty to take reasonable steps to prevent a person from committing suicide, if that person is known to be a suicide risk. In respect of the latter, whilst a number of such deaths at the hands of other prisoners have resulted in appellate decisions[71] concerning the scope of an inquiry and inquest required in such circumstances, none has resulted in judicial consideration of the scope of the duty of care to prevent such harm arising.

(a) Suicide/self harm

4.114 In *Kirkham v Chief Constable of the Greater Manchester Police* [1990] 2 QB 283, damages were awarded to the widow of a prisoner who had committed suicide shortly after being handed over to the prison authorities from police custody. The police knew that he was a suicide risk and that he had made recent attempts to commit suicide but did not communicate that information to the prison authorities. The Court of Appeal upheld the decision of the trial judge that the responsibilities, which the police assumed towards the deceased when they took him into custody and handed him over to the prison authorities, included

---

[69] See paras 5.01–5.88.
[70] See paras 5.12–5.19.
[71] See *R (on the application of Amin) v Secretary of State for the Home Department* (HL) [2003] 4 All ER 1264.

F. The 'Custody' Duty of Care: s 2(1)(d)

an obligation to pass on the information that he was a suicide risk. Lloyd LJ found:

> So I would be inclined to hold that where a man of sound mind commits suicide, his estate would be unable to maintain an action against the hospital or prison authorities, as the case might be. *Volenti non fit injuria* would provide them with a complete defence...[72]

The House of Lords, in *Reeves v Commissioner of Police of the Metropolis* [2000] 1 AC 360, again considered a case in which the deceased was known to be a suicide risk. He had been brought to the police station shortly after midday having tried to kill himself in the cell at the magistrates' court. He was examined by a doctor, who, whilst concluding that he was not suffering from any mental illness or other mental disturbance, considered him to be a suicide risk and left instructions that he should be observed frequently. Within 25 minutes of his being returned to his cell after being examined by the doctor, he had managed to hang himself. 4.115

The House of Lords was not concerned directly with the question of the scope of any a duty of care to take reasonable steps to prevent a person from committing suicide whilst in custody, for it was conceded that such a duty was owed to a person who was a known suicide risk. The direct concern was the question of whether or not there was any defence, given that a breach of that duty was also conceded. It was held, by a majority, that none of the true defences to the claim applied, namely *novus actus interveniens*, and *volenti non fit injuria*, but concluded that the deceased's suicide constituted 'fault' for the purposes of the doctrine of contributory negligence and apportioned responsibility 50-50. 4.116

The doctrine of *novus actus interveniens*, or new intervening event, impacts upon causation and not either the existence of a duty of care or whether such a duty has been breached. Unlike *volenti non fit injuria*, the operation of which is precluded by s 2(6) of the Act, *novus actus interveniens* and the issue of whether there has been a superseding intervening act is relevant to causation which remains a matter for the jury in any prosecution for an offence of corporate manslaughter. 4.117

In *Orange v Chief Constable of West Yorkshire Police* [2002] QB 347, the Court of Appeal reviewed the authorities before finding that the scope of the duty of the police to take reasonable care for the health and safety of a person in their custody had to be considered in the context of an increased risk of suicide amongst those in custody as against those in the community, and in this regard recognizing that those on remand or convicted prisoners were at significantly increased risk. However, the Court found that suicide was not a foreseeable risk in relation to every prisoner; rather that the increased risk of suicide amongst prisoners gave rise to an obligation, within the custodian's general duty of care for the prisoner's health and safety, to take reasonable steps to identify whether or not a prisoner presented a suicide risk. Furthermore, that the obligation to take reasonable care to prevent a prisoner from 4.118

---

[72] [1990] 2 QB 283, at p 290.

taking his own life deliberately only arose where the custodian knew or ought to have known that the individual prisoner presented a suicide risk.

4.119 Finally, in *Vellino v Chief Constable of Greater Manchester* [2002] 3 All ER 78, the Court of Appeal was concerned with injuries arising from an escape attempt. The claimant lived in a second floor flat, where he was frequently arrested. Often, when the police came to arrest the claimant, he would seek to evade arrest by jumping from the windows of his flat to the ground floor below. His propensity for escaping by that method, apparently, was very well known to the police. In September 1994 the claimant was arrested at the flat. Almost immediately afterwards, he jumped from a window of the flat and injured himself, fracturing his skull, and suffering severe brain damage and tetraplegia.

4.120 The claimant commenced proceedings for negligence against the police. The Court held that escaping from custody was a sufficiently serious criminal offence to attract the operation of the *ex turpi causa* principle, and in those circumstances the police did not owe an arrested person a duty to take care that he was not injured in a foreseeable attempt to escape police custody.

4.121 Section 2(6) of the Act excludes the operation of the principle of *ex turpi causa* from 'preventing a duty of care from being owed'.[73]

---

[73] See paras 4.14–4.16.

5

THE RELEVANT DUTY OF CARE III: THE EXEMPTIONS IN SECTIONS 3–7

A.	Overview	5.01
B.	Public Policy Decisions, Exclusively Public Functions, and Statutory Inspections	5.07
	1. Public authorities	5.08
	2. Public policy: s 3(1)	5.09
	3. Exclusively public functions: s 3(2)	5.12
	4. Public policy and public functions: relevant common law principles	5.20
	5. Summary of the effect of ss 3(1) and 3(2)	5.35
	6. Statutory inspections: s 3(3)	5.37
C.	Military Activities	5.41
	1. The armed forces	5.41
	2. Exemption for military 'operations': ss 4(1) and 4(2)	5.42
	3. Exemption for special forces: ss 12(3) and 12(4)	5.48
D.	Policing and Law Enforcement	5.49
	1. Police forces	5.49
	2. Exemption for policing 'operations': ss 5(1) and 5(2)	5.50
	3. The exemption for all other policing and law enforcement activity: s 5(3)	5.60
E.	Emergencies	5.65
	1. The exemption created by s 6	5.65
	2. The definition of 'emergency circumstances'	5.67
	3. The effect of the exemption in s 6	5.73
	4. The common law duty of care and emergency response	5.78
	5. Rescue at sea: ss 6(5) and 6(6)	5.82
F.	Child Protection and Probation Functions	5.84
	1. Child protection: ss 7(1) and 7(2)	5.84
	2. Probation functions: s 7(3)	5.86
	3. The effect of s 7	5.87

5. The Relevant Duty of Care III

A. OVERVIEW

5.01 Section 1(4) provides that for the purposes of the Act 'relevant duty of care' has the meaning given to by s 2, 'read with sections 3 to 7'. Section 2(3) further provides that the meaning of 'relevant duty of care' contained within s 2(1) is subject to ss 3–7.

5.02 To be a relevant duty of care, a duty must be one owed by an organization under the law of negligence[1] and be of a kind that falls within the categorization set out in s 2(2) of the Act.[2]

5.03 Sections 3–7 create a series of activities and circumstances exempt from being capable of founding a relevant duty of care for the offence. The sections are variously concerned with:

- public policy and exclusively public functions (s 3);
- military activities (s 4);
- policing and law enforcement (s 5);
- emergencies (s 6); and
- child and probation services (s 7).

5.04 A number of other provisions in ss 11–13, concerned variously with the application of the Act to Crown bodies, police forces and the armed forces, impact upon the effect of ss 3–7.

5.05 Each of the provisions contained within ss 3–7 of the Act is intended to limit the scope and circumstances in which a judge may find the existence of a relevant duty of care.

5.06 A number of the provisions within ss 3–7 do no more than particularize an existing common law limitation on the circumstances in which a duty of care can arise, others confirm that an activity does not fall within the categories of relevant duty of care particularized in s 2(1), whilst a number provide what can be viewed as a clear limitation in relation to developing, difficult or 'novel' circumstances[3] where a duty might otherwise be held to arise under the law of negligence.

B. PUBLIC POLICY DECISIONS, EXCLUSIVELY PUBLIC FUNCTIONS, AND STATUTORY INSPECTIONS

5.07 Section 3 of the Act is intended to exclude from the ambit of a relevant duty of care, any duty of care owed in respect of a decision as to public policy, in respect of anything done in the exercise of an exclusively public function and in respect of statutory inspections.

---

[1] See paras 3.01–3.56.
[2] Paras 4.01–4.121.
[3] See *Caparo Industries v Dickman* [1990] 1 All ER 568 and para 3.52.

B. Public Policy Decisions, Exclusively Public Functions, and Statutory Inspections

1. Public authorities

5.08 A public authority, pursuant to s 25 of the Act, has the same meaning as in Human Rights Act 1998, s 6, excluding the provisions of ss Human Rights Act 1998, s 6(3)(a) and 6(4) which are to be disregarded. Thus a public authority, for the purposes of the offence, includes, 'any person certain of whose functions are functions of a public nature'[4] but not any court or tribunal nor the House of Parliament.[5] The Human Rights Act 1998 does not define 'functions of a public nature' and the Act does not further define 'public policy'.

2. Public policy: s 3(1)

5.09 Section 3(1) provides that any duty of care owed by a public authority in respect of a decision as to matters of public policy (including in particular the allocation of public resources or the weighing of competing public interests) is not a 'relevant duty of care'.

5.10 As the Explanatory Notes[6] describe:

At present, the law of negligence recognises that some decisions taken by public bodies are not justiciable, in other words, are not susceptible to review in the courts. This is because they involve decisions involving competing public priorities or other questions of public policy. This might, for example, include decisions by Primary Care Trusts about the funding of particular treatments. A recent example in which the courts declined to find a duty of care on this basis related to whether the Department of Health owed a duty of care to issue interim advice about the safety of a particular drug. In many circumstances, these sorts of issues will not arise in respect of matters covered by the specified categories of duty. . .And basing the offence on the duty of care should mean that the offence would not apply to these sorts of decision in any event.

5.11 The Explanatory Notes continue by claiming that s 3(1) simply confirms, 'that deaths alleged to have been caused by such decisions will not come within the scope of the offence'.

3. Exclusively public functions: s 3(2)

5.12 Section 3(2) provides that any duty of care in respect of things done in the exercise of an exclusively public function is not a relevant duty of care unless it falls within s 2(1)(a), (b) or (d), namely a duty owed to employees or those working for an organization,[7] a duty as occupier of premises[8] or a duty owed by an organization to a person in custody or detention.[9]

---

[4] Human Rights Act 1998, s 6(3)(b).
[5] Human Rights Act 1998, ss 6(3)(a) and 6(4).
[6] Corporate Manslaughter and Corporate Homicide Bill [HL 19], Explanatory Notes para 25.
[7] See paras 4.20–4.48.
[8] See paras 4.49–4.65.
[9] See paras 4.99–4.121.

5.13 By s 3(4), 'exclusively public function' is defined to mean a function that falls within the prerogative of the Crown or is, by its nature, exercisable only with authority conferred by the exercise of that prerogative, or by or under a statutory provision.

5.14 In many circumstances, functions of this nature would not fall within the categories of relevant duty set out in s 2(1). However, some public functions would amount to the supply of goods or services or be performed commercially, particularly if performed by the private sector on behalf of the State, and thus be otherwise capable of founding a relevant duty of care.

5.15 A number of arguably 'exclusively public functions' have founded some of the more difficult negligence cases which resulted in appellate authorities. The concept of an 'exclusively public function' is not one that is derived from any of these authorities or the law of negligence. However, the nature and existence of common law duties of care flowing from the exercise of such prerogative powers and from statutory provisions has been at the heart of the issues in these cases. It appears that the section aims to remove this uncertain area entirely from the scope of the Act. Far from removing the uncertainty, the section may have created fresh difficulty with the identification with certainty of an 'exclusively public function'.

5.16 The original intention behind this provision was to ensure that all such functions, but particularly duties of care arising from 'custody', fell out of the ambit of the Act. 'Custody' became the battleground between the Houses of Commons and Lords, with the latter eventually winning a compromise whereby 'custody' became a 'relevant duty of care' in the Act[10] but the provision so doing could only be brought into force by affirmative resolution of both Houses.[11] Thus 'custody' is now within the Act as a relevant duty of care and 'custody' is outwith the limitation on exclusively public functions founding a relevant duty of care.

5.17 The Explanatory Notes, in relation to 'Exclusively public functions', demonstrate the centrality of 'custody' to the original proposed clause and the difficulty in identifying other activities as certainly falling within the definition:

> The test covers both functions falling within the prerogative of the Crown (for example, where the Government provides services in a civil emergency) and *types* of activity that by their nature require a statutory or prerogative basis, in other words, that cannot be independently performed by private bodies. This looks at the nature of the activity involved. It therefore would not cover an activity simply because it was one that required a licence or took place on a statutory basis. Rather, the *nature* of the activity involved must be one that requires a particular legal basis, for example, functions relating to the custody of prisoners (the function of lawfully detaining someone requiring a statutory basis).[12]

5.18 According to the Explanatory Notes,[13] 'This test is not confined to Crown or other public bodies but also excludes any organisation (public or otherwise)

---

[10] CMCHA, s 2(1)(d).
[11] CMCHA, s 27(2).
[12] Corporate Manslaughter and Corporate Homicide Bill [HL 19], Explanatory Notes para 27.
[13] ibid para 26.

B. Public Policy Decisions, Exclusively Public Functions, and Statutory Inspections

performing that particular type of function'. The section appears intended to exclude a function exercisable only with statutory authority (or under the prerogative) but not exclude activities simply because they were provided under a statute.

Would a commercially operating organization being paid to carry out a statutory function during a civil emergency be covered by this exclusion? Presumably, yes. Thus, for example, however negligently a contractor disposed of infected animal remains the contractor had slaughtered through the exercise of statutory powers during an infectious disease outbreak, where a death resulted through cross infection with humans, would the contractor be out of the reach of the Act? 5.19

4. Public policy and public functions: relevant common law principles

The ambit of the exclusion from the common law of negligence for decisions involving public policy and in relation to the exercise of discretion, statutory duty and statutory power has been the subject of a number of appellate authorities. 5.20

(a) *Public bodies as defendants*

Prior to the passing of the Crown Proceedings Act 1947 the Crown enjoyed a general immunity in negligence, but since that time and pursuant to that Act, the Crown can be sued in negligence for the actions of its servants and agents. Outside the Crown Proceedings Act 1947, the Crown continues to be immune. The CMCHA 2007, s 11 provides that the Government bodies listed in Sch 1 and any corporation acting as servant to the Crown, 'is to be treated as owing whatever duties of care it would owe if it were a corporation that was not a servant or agent of the Crown'. Section 11(4) further provides, that 'for the purposes of sections 2 to 7 anything done purportedly by a department or other body listed in Sch 1, although in law by the Crown or by the holder of a particular office, is to be treated as done by the department or other body itself.' 5.21

Local government authorities, health authorities and other bodies with public responsibilities enjoy no general immunity from negligence actions and the starting point under the common law is that a public body is subject the general law of tort in the same way as a trading company or a private individual. However, an act or decision that is invalid is subject to judicial review and does not for that reason become civilly actionable in damages. 5.22

(b) *The Prerogative, statutory powers, statutory duties and discretion*

The functions of public bodies are carried out pursuant to statues or, especially in the case of central government, the Prerogative. Usually, these give an element of discretion as to how the function shall be performed and as to what resources shall be devoted to them. This discretion has been reflected by the law when such a body has been sued, so that such public bodies can be said to have been treated differently by the courts to corporations or other private individuals for the purposes of the duty of care in negligence. 5.23

5.24   Under the common law, no difficulty has arisen in relation to the liability of a public body in respect of foreseeable physical injury or similar harm brought about by a positive act. The contentious civil negligence cases involving public bodies mostly relate to situations in which the damage caused either does not involve physical harm to the person or arises from an omission/failure to act.

5.25   Bodies whose power derives from statute will not incur liability in negligence merely for failing to perform a duty imposed upon them by legislation, still less for failing to exercise a statutory power or discretion. The existence of a common law duty of care must be independently established. An action for breach of a statutory duty, where it is available, is not part of the law of negligence. The statutory duty does not give rise to a duty of care and there is no tort of 'negligent performance of a statutory duty' As Scott LJ described in *Gorringe v Calderdale Metropolitan Borough Council* [2004] UKHL 15, [2004] 1 WLR 1057 a common law duty of care cannot 'grow parasitically out of a statutory duty not intended to be owed to individuals.'[14]

5.26   Many of these issues were considered by the House of Lords in *Stovin v Wise* [1996] AC 923. In that case, S had been injured in an accident at a dangerous junction caused by the negligence of W and recovered damages against W. W had then sought a contribution from Norfolk CC, the highway authority. Under the Highways Act 1980, there was a civilly actionable statutory duty to maintain the highway which concerned the state of repair of the roadway whereas the danger at the junction arose from poor visibility. The authority had a statutory power under the Highways Act 1980 to require the removal of an obstruction. A year before the accident, the authority had decided to remove the obstruction itself but had not taken any action thereafter.

5.27   The statute gave rise to no liability and a majority of the House of Lords found that its breach could not be the basis of a liability at common law: Lord Hoffman described, as a position of 'uncompromising orthodoxy',[15] that:

> although a public authority may be under a public duty, enforceable by mandamus, to give proper consideration to the question whether it should exercise a power, this duty cannot be equated with, or regarded as a foundation for imposing a duty of care on the public authority in relation to the exercise of the power. Mandamus will compel proper consideration of the authority of its discretion, but that is all.[16]

5.28   In *Gorringe v Calderdale Metropolitan Borough Council*,[17] the House of Lords was concerned with another case of failure to improve the highway (on this occasion, by not erecting warning signs). Steyn LJ described how the subject of negligence and statutory duties and powers was one 'of great complexity and very much an evolving area of the law'.[18] The Court went further than it had in *Stovin v Wise*,[19] where the

---

[14] [2004] 1 WLR 1057, at p 1078C.
[15] [1996] AC 923 at 951.
[16] ibid.
[17] [2004] UKHL 15, [2004] 1 WLR 1057.
[18] [2004] 1 WLR 1057, at p 1059D.
[19] [1996] AC 923.

B. Public Policy Decisions, Exclusively Public Functions, and Statutory Inspections

possibility had been left open that there might somewhere be a statutory power or public duty which generated a common law duty. In *Gorringe*,[20] it was held that the existence of a broad public duty did not generate a common law duty of care and thus a private law right of action. A common law duty to act could not be imposed upon a local authority based solely on the existence of a broad public law duty. In this context, Rodgers LJ described how, 'even if it would have been wholly unreasonable for the council not to provide an additional sign, this does not mean that they were in breach of a common law duty to do so.'[21]

However, the reasoned opinions in *Gorringe*[22] make clear that where a public body has negligently performed an act, albeit one carried out pursuant to a statutory power or duty, it may nevertheless be in breach of a duty of care. As Lord Hoffman explained, the Judicial Committee was, 'not concerned with cases in which public authorities have actually done acts or entered into relationships or undertaken responsibilities which give rise to a common law duty of care. In such cases the fact that the public authority acted pursuant to a statutory power or public duty does not necessarily negative the existence of a duty.'[23]

Lord Hoffman went on to explain how, in such circumstances, 'the duty rests upon a solid, orthodox common law foundation and the question is not whether it is created by the statute but whether the terms of the statute (for example, in requiring a particular thing to be done or conferring a discretion) are sufficient to exclude it.'

Steyn LJ, adopting similar reasoning, referred to four House of Lords decisions[24] as having been 'milestones in the evolution of this branch of the law' that had 'helped to clarify the correct approach, without answering all the questions.'[25] In his opinion, with a case framed in negligence, against the background of a statutory duty or power, a basic question is whether the statute excludes a private law remedy?'

(c) *Policy*
In one of Steyn LJ's four milestone authorities, *X and others (minors) v Bedfordshire CC* [1995] 3 All ER 353, Browne-Wilkinson LJ described how a duty of care would not arise where it involved a court entering into areas of policy which are not properly 'justiciable' nor interfere with decisions involving policy as opposed to the operation of services and activities. Thus true 'policy' decisions are non-justiciable in a private law action for negligence but 'operational' decisions are more likely to lead to liability, though still contain elements of discretion in some cases. The line

---

[20] [2004] UKHL 15, [2004] 1 WLR 1057.
[21] [2004] 1 WLR 1057, at p 1084E.
[22] [2004] UKHL 15, [2004] 1 WLR 1057.
[23] [2004] 1 WLR 1057, at p 1068G.
[24] *X and others (minors) v Bedfordshire CC*, [1995] 3 All ER 353, [1995] 2 AC 633, *Stovin v Wise (Norfolk CC, third party)* [1996] 3 All ER 801, [1996] AC 923, *Barrett v Enfield LBC* [1999] 3 All ER 193, [2001] 2 AC 550 and *Phelps v Hillingdon London BC* [2000] 4 All ER 504, [2001] 2 AC 619.
[25] [2004] UKHL 15, [2004] 1 WLR 1057 at para 2.

between the two categories cannot be sharply drawn, as the decision to do an operational act may easily involve and result from a policy decision.[26]

5.33 As was identified by Dyson LJ in *Carty v London Borough of Croydon* [2005] 2All ER 517, most of the discussion in the cases concerning such issues has been directed to the question of whether a public authority is vicariously liable for the negligence of its employees and not to direct liability for a breach of a duty of care.[27] He cited how in *Phelps v London Borough of Hillingdon* [2000] 4 All ER 504, [2001] 2 AC 619, Lord Slynn had identified that was that a direct claim would be likely to be based on decisions which were heavily policy-laden, and they were likely to be non-justiciable on that ground.[28]

5.34 However, in the much earlier House of Lords authority of in *Home Office v Dorset Yacht Co. Ltd* [1970] 2 All ER 294, [1970] AC 1004 it was held that there was no ground in public policy for granting complete immunity from liability in negligence to the Home Office or its officers; that the statutory powers and discretions of the Home Office in connection with the rehabilitation of young offenders were not sufficient to exclude liability for a breach of their common law duty of care which arose from their bringing some young offenders to an island and leaving them unsupervised when it was reasonably foreseeable that they would cause damage if they tried to escape. The fact that something was done in pursuance of statutory authority did not warrant its being done unreasonably so that avoidable damage was negligently caused.

5. Summary of the effect of ss 3(1) and 3(2)

5.35 In summary, whilst ss 3(1) and 3(2) attempt to remove all decisions as to public policy, the exercise of prerogative powers and statutory functions from forming the basis of a relevant duty of care, the manner in which they do so is different from the approach of the common law of negligence. There may be situations in which ss 3(1) and 3(2) do not preclude public functions or activities that amount to the exercise of statutory powers from founding a relevant duty of care; in such situations, recourse to common law authorities will be necessary to divine whether a duty of care is owed under the law of negligence and thereafter whether such duty falls within the categorization of relevant duty of care within s 2(1).

5.36 Pure public policy decisions are not justiciable in negligence and courts may find public policy reasons for not imposing a duty of care on bodies carrying out a public function. However, the exemption afforded by the Act in relation to exclusively public function is absolute but only in respect of functions that can only be performed by prerogative or statutory power; the approach of the common law of negligence is not focused on the exclusive nature of the power that founds the activity,

---

[26] *Barrett v Enfield LBC* [2001] 2 AC 550 at 571, per Slynn LJ.
[27] [2005] 2 All ER 517 at [36].
[28] [2000] 4 All ER 504 at 522, [2001] 2 AC 619 at 658.

B. Public Policy Decisions, Exclusively Public Functions, and Statutory Inspections

but rather whether the particular exercise of the power has created a situation of proximity, where foreseeable damage has been caused, and whether it is just and reasonable to impose such a duty or whether there are public policy reasons for not imposing a duty: that the activity flows from the exercise of a statutory duty or power does not either create or preclude the foundation of a common law duty of care.

6. Statutory inspections: s 3(3)

5.37 Section 3(3) provides that any duty of care owed by a public authority in respect of inspections carried out in the exercise of a statutory function is not a 'relevant duty of care unless it falls within s 2(1)(a) or (b), namely a duty owed to employees or those working for an organization,[29] a duty as occupier of premises.[30] By s 3(4), 'statutory function' means a function conferred by or under a statutory provision.

5.38 This exemption is intended to cover regulatory activities to ensure compliance with statutory standards, such as inspection activities by the health and safety enforcing authorities. Whilst the Explanatory Notes[31] state how it is unlikely that such bodies would owe relevant duties of care under the Act, the Notes go on to suggest that the purpose of the subsection is because otherwise it would be possible that the carrying out of an inspection might involve the use of equipment and thus fall within the relevant duty of care in s 2(1)(c)(iv).[32] However, it would appear that such inspections would squarely fall within the exclusion of 'exclusively public function' contained in s 3(2).[33]

5.39 Furthermore, unlike the exemption for 'exclusively public functions' in s 3(2), the exclusion in s 3(3) only extends to public authorities and not any other organization undertaking such a statutory inspection: there are now many commercial organizations carrying out statutory inspections in various fields.

5.40 There are a number of common law civil negligence cases concerned with the liability of inspectors and regulatory bodies, both statutory and otherwise. In general, the approach of the courts has been to limit the range of matters concerning which negligence actions may be brought against such bodies, finding the existence of no duty of care, in part, because to so find would be to divert such bodies from the efficient performance of their duties.[34] However in two cases involving physical harm the Court of Appeal has found the existence and breach of a duty of care.[35]

---

[29] See paras 4.20–4.48.
[30] See paras 4.49–4.65.
[31] Corporate Manslaughter and Corporate Homicide Bill [HL 19], Explanatory Notes para 28.
[32] See paras 4.97–4.98.
[33] See paras 5.12–5.32.
[34] The leading House of Lords authority is *Marc Rich & Co. and others, AG v Bishop's Rock Marine Co. Ltd and others, The Nicholas H* [1996] AC 211.
[35] *Perrett v Collins* [1998] 2 Lloyd's Rep 255; *Watson v British Boxing Board of Control* [2001] QB 1134.

C. MILITARY ACTIVITIES

1. The armed forces

5.41 By s 12 of the Act, 'the armed forces' is deemed to mean any of the naval, military or air forces of the Crown raised under the law of the United Kingdom; s 12 further provides that for the purposes of s 2 and a relevant duty of care, a person who is a member of the armed forces is to be treated as employed by the Ministry of Defence.[36]

2. Exemption for military 'operations': ss 4(1) and 4(2)

5.42 Section 4 of the Act provides a series of limitations on the potential scope of a relevant duty of care in relation to military activities by the armed forces and specifically in respect of certain 'operations', namely those, 'including peacekeeping operations and operations for dealing with terrorism, civil unrest or serious public disorder, in the course of which members of the armed forces come under attack or face the threat of attack or violent resistance'.[37]

5.43 Section 4 provides that any duty of care owed by the Ministry of Defence in respect of:

(a) such operations;
(b) activities carried on in preparation for, or directly in support of, such operations; or
(c) training of a hazardous nature, or training carried out in a hazardous way, which it is considered needs to be carried out, or carried out in that way, in order to improve or maintain the effectiveness of the armed forces with respect to such operations, is not a 'relevant duty of care'.

5.44 A wide range of operational military activities will be exclusively public functions and thus be excluded from possibly founding a relevant duty of care by s 3(2).[38] However, that exemption does not relate to an organization's duties as employer or occupier. Importantly, the exemption in s 4(1) does extend to the duties owed as employer to employees and to workers and to duties arising from the occupation of premises.

5.45 The scope of the definition of 'operations', which includes those involving 'the threat of attack or violent resistance' would extend to activities and training in connection with combat, peace keeping and civil disorder: thus, this would appear to be a blanket exemption as far as military activities are concerned.

5.46 The test which s 4(1)(c) employs for hazardous training 'with respect to such operations' is that 'which it is considered needs to be carried out': the subsection

---

[36] CMCHA, s 12(2).
[37] CMCHA, s 4(2).
[38] See paras 5.12–5.32.

does not specify by whom it must be considered to be needed but presumably this must be the Ministry of Defence. At what level and by what means such consideration is to be expressed appears to be left to a judge to divine, should the issue arise, as part of his consideration of whether a relevant duty of care was owed, pursuant to s 2(5).[39]

5.47 The law of negligence already recognizes that the military authorities will rarely owe a duty of care in circumstances related to hostile activities.[40] In *Mulcahy v Ministry of Defence* [1996] QB 732 the Court of Appeal held that the military could not be liable for the negligence of a member of the armed forces under battle conditions and it appears that training and preparation attract the same exemption, based upon public policy. In such circumstances, no duty is owed to soldiers, civilians or to property.

3. Exemption for special forces: ss 12(3) and 12(4)

5.48 Sections 12(3) and (4) place the activities of the special forces outside the scope of the Act. The special forces is defined to mean those units of the armed forces the maintenance of whose capabilities is the responsibility of the Director of Special Forces or which are for the time being subject to the operational command of that Director. The exemption provided by s 12(3) is total and provides that, 'Any duty of care owed by the Ministry of Defence in respect of activities carried on by members of the special forces is not a 'relevant duty of care'.

D. POLICING AND LAW ENFORCEMENT

1. Police forces

5.49 A police force is an organization, pursuant to s 1(2)(c),[41] which is subject to the Act and which can commit the offence of corporate manslaughter. Section 13 of the Act defines the term 'police force' and makes specific provision for the application of the Act to police forces.[42]

2. Exemption for policing 'operations': ss 5(1) and 5(2)

5.50 Section 5 of the Act provides a series of limitations on the potential scope of a relevant duty of care owed by a public authority, including a police force, in relation to policing and law enforcement.

---

[39] See paras 3.10–3.33.
[40] See further Crown Proceedings (Armed Forces) Act 1987 and *Matthews v Ministry of Defence* [2003] 2 WLR 435.
[41] See para 2.51.
[42] See paras 2.52–2.56.

5.51 Firstly the limitation extends to certain policing 'operations', specifically those defined by s 5(2) that:

(a) are operations for dealing with terrorism, civil unrest or serious disorder,
(b) involve the carrying on of policing or law-enforcement activities, and
(c) officers or employees of the public authority in question come under attack, or face the threat of attack or violent resistance, in the course of the operations.

5.52 Section 5(1) provides that any duty of care owed by a public authority in respect of:

(a) such operations,
(b) activities carried on in preparation for, or directly in support of, such operations, or
(c) training of a hazardous nature, or training carried out in a hazardous way, which it is considered needs to be carried out, or carried out in that way, in order to improve or maintain the effectiveness of officers or employees of the public authority with respect to such operations is not a relevant duty of care for the purposes of the offence.

5.53 Thus, this wide exemption from a relevant duty of care, including one owed as employer to employees or workers and as occupier of premises, extends to a police force or any other public body with responsibility for policing (eg the police authority), but is available in limited circumstances: specifically, operations dealing with terrorism, civil unrest or serious disorder in which officers or employees come under attack or the threat of attack; or where the authority in question is preparing for or supporting such operations; or where it is carrying on training with respect to such operations.

5.54 The Explanatory Notes[43] describe how this section, 'reflects the approach adopted in the existing law of negligence, which has already recognised that the policing of violent disorder where the police come under attack or the threat of attack will not give rise to liability on the part of an employer'.

5.55 The position of the common law of negligence is not quite as straightforward as the Notes suggest and s 5(1), by exempting all potential relevant duties of care, particularly those owed as employer to employees, appears to provide a wider exemption than the common law.

(a) *The common law of negligence and policing violent events*

5.56 One line of decided cases has been founded upon claims against Chief Constables in respect of vicarious liability for the allegedly negligent acts of a police officer. In *Hughes v National Union of Mineworkers* [1991] 4 All ER 278, May J struck out as disclosing no cause of action a claim by a police officer who was injured while policing the miners' strike and who alleged that the police officer in charge had deployed

---

[43] Corporate Manslaughter and Corporate Homicide Bill [HL 19], Explanatory Notes para 31.

his officers negligently. May J held 'as a matter of public policy, if senior police officers charged with the task of deploying what may or may not be an adequate force of officers to control serious public disorder are to be potentially liable to individual officers under their command if those individuals are injured by attacks from rioters, that would be significantly detrimental to the control of public order.'

However, there have been a number of actions brought by injured officers alleging negligence against fellow officers in failing to adequately assist or protect them, in some a duty of care has been found to have been breached, founded upon an assumption of responsibility which has thereafter been negligently performed.[44]

5.57

Another line of cases[45] does establish that, subject to public policy, a chief constable owes duties to police officers analogous to those owed to an employee by an employer. In *Waters v Commissioner of Police for the Metropolis* [2000] 1 WLR 1607, it was recognized that an established public policy existed for not imposing a duty of care upon the police in relation to the investigation and suppression of crime. However, the House of Lords also recognized that in the context of a claim put forward on the basis of a breach of duty by a chief constable as employer, there were competing public interests and that in balancing the relevant considerations of public policy, a court should put into the balance in favour of the claimant police officer the fact that it is ordinarily the duty of an employer to take reasonable care to devise and operate a safe system of work.

5.58

Mullaney v Chief Constable of West Midlands Police [2001] EWCA Civ 700, was such a case where the Court of Appeal found that the Chief Constable had been in breach of his duty as an employer, to take reasonable care to devise and operate a safe system of work, in circumstances where a police officer was injured in a violent incident.

5.59

3. The exemption for all other policing and law enforcement activity: s 5(3)

Section 5(3) creates a further exemption by providing that any duty of care owed by a public authority in respect of all other policing or law enforcement activities is not a 'relevant duty of care' unless it falls within s 2(1)(a), (b) or (d) namely a duty owed as employer to employees or those working for an organization,[46] a duty as occupier of premises[47] or a duty owed by an organization to a person in custody or detention.[48]

5.60

---

[44] *Costello v Chief Constable of Northumbria Police* [1999] 1 All ER 550,(CA); *Mullaney v Chief Constable of West Midlands Police* [2001] EWCA Civ 700 (paras [25] to [43] of the judgment provide a review of the relevant authorities).
[45] See *Waters v Commissioner of Police for the Metropolis* [2000] 1 WLR 1607, at 1610.
[46] See paras 4.20–4.48.
[47] See paras 4.49–4.65.
[48] See paras 4.99–4.121.

5. The Relevant Duty of Care III

5.61 Section 5(4) defines 'policing or law-enforcement activities' to include:

(a) activities carried on in the exercise of functions that are—
   (i) functions of police forces, or
   (ii) functions of the same or a similar nature exercisable by public authorities other than police forces;
(b) activities carried on in the exercise of functions of constables employed by a public authority;
(c) activities carried on in the exercise of functions exercisable under Chapter 4 of Part 2 of the Serious Organised Crime and Police Act 2005 (c.15) (protection of witnesses and other persons);
(d) activities carried on to enforce any provision contained in or made under the Immigration Acts.

5.62 Thus, s 5(3) takes all policing and law enforcement activity, other than that already subject to the blanket exemption relating to certain policing 'operations' created by s 5(2),[49] out of the scope of a relevant duty of care unless the activity falls within the duties owed to employees and workers as an employer or owed as an occupier of premises. 'Custody' will not be an activity subject to the exemption if and when an Order bringing the 'custody' duty within the Act is brought into force.[50] The effect of the exemption is to exclude all other circumstances where the pursuit of law enforcement activities has resulted in a fatality to a member of the public.

5.63 In any event, many if not all such activities will not fall within the categorization of relevant duties of care in s 2(1) and/or would amount to exclusively public functions exempt through the operation of s 3(2).[51] Thus, this exemption goes beyond that afforded to the police under the common law of negligence,[52] the scope and extent of which was recently reconsidered by the House of Lords in *Brooks v Metropolitan Police Commissioner & others* [2005] 2 All ER 489.

5.64 Furthermore, the exemption is not confined to police forces and extends to other bodies operating similar functions and to other law enforcement activity. Therefore it will cover the activities of HM Revenue and Customs when conducting investigations and the activities of traffic officers. It also extends to the enforcement of immigration law, for example where the immigration authorities are taking action to arrest, detain or deport an immigration offender

---

[49] See para 5.51.
[50] See paras 4.99–4.121.
[51] See paras 5.12–5.32.
[52] See *Hill v Chief Constable of West Yorkshire* [1989] 1 AC 53; *Alcock v Chief Constable of South Yorkshire Police* [1992] 1 AC 310, [1991] 4 All ER 907; *Alexandrou v Oxford* [1993] 4 All ER 328; *Ancell v McDermott* [1993] 4 All ER 355; *Swinney v Chief Constable of Northumbria Police* [1997] QB464; *Brooks v Metropolitan Police Commissioner & others* [2005] 2 All ER 489 (HL).

E. EMERGENCIES

1. The exemption created by s 6

5.65 Section 6 is concerned with limiting the scope of any duty of care arising from responding to an emergency, with s 6(1) providing that, 'Any duty of care owed by an organisation within subsection (2) in respect of the way in which it responds to emergency circumstances is not a 'relevant duty of care' unless it falls within section 2(1)(a) [a duty owed to employees or those working for an organization[53]] or 2(1)(b) [a duty as occupier of premises[54]]'.

5.66 The organizations within subsection (2) are:
(a) a fire and rescue authority in England and Wales;
(b) a fire and rescue authority or joint fire and rescue board in Scotland;
(c) the Northern Ireland Fire and Rescue Service Board;
(d) any other organization providing a service of responding to emergency circumstances either—
   (i) in pursuance of arrangements made with an organization within paragraph (a), (b) or (c), or
   (ii) (if not in pursuance of such arrangements) otherwise than on a commercial basis;
(e) a relevant NHS body;[55]
(f) an organization providing ambulance services in pursuance of arrangements—
   (i) made by, or at the request of, a relevant NHS body, or
   (ii) made with the Secretary of State or with the Welsh Ministers;
(g) an organization providing services for the transport of organs, blood, equipment or personnel in pursuance of arrangements of the kind mentioned in paragraph (f);
(h) an organization providing a rescue service;
(i) the armed forces.

2. The definition of 'emergency circumstances'

5.67 By subsection (7), 'emergency circumstances' is defined to mean circumstances that are present or imminent and—
(a) are causing, or are likely to cause, serious harm or a worsening of such harm, or
(b) are likely to cause the death of a person.

---

[53] See paras 4.20–4.48.
[54] See paras 4.49–4.65.
[55] Defined by s 6(8) to mean:
  (a) a Strategic Health Authority, Primary Care Trust, NHS trust, Special Health Authority or NHS foundation trust in England;
  (b) a Local Health Board, NHS trust or Special Health Authority in Wales;
  (c) a Health Board or Special Health Board in Scotland, or the Common Services Agency for the Scottish Health Service;
  (d) a Health and Social Services trust or Health and Social Services Board in Northern Ireland.

5.68   The term 'serious harm' is further defined to mean:

(a) serious injury to or the serious illness (including mental illness) of a person;
(b) serious harm to the environment (including the life and health of plants and animals);
(c) serious harm to any building or other property.

5.69   Section 6(8) provides that a reference in the section to emergency circumstances includes a reference to circumstances that are believed to be emergency circumstances.

(a) *Medical treatment*

5.70   By s 6(3), the provision of medical treatment is outwith the wide exclusion on the circumstances in which a relevant duty of care may arise in dealing with emergency circumstances and thus capable of founding a relevant duty of care. The subsection provides that for these purposes, the way in which an organization responds to emergency circumstances does not include the way in which—

(a) medical treatment is carried out, or
(b) decisions within subsection (4) are made.

5.71   Subsection (4) is concerned with 'decisions as to the carrying out of medical treatment, other than decisions as to the order in which persons are to be given such treatment'.

5.72   'Medical treatment' is defined to include any treatment or procedure of a medical or similar nature.[56]

3. The effect of the exemption in s 6

5.73   Thus, the effect of s 6 is to provide that the offence does not apply to the emergency service, and some others, when responding to emergencies. The section does not exclude the duties such organizations owe as employers to employees and workers or as occupiers of premises nor to the duties that arise which do not relate to the way in which a body responds to an emergency.

5.74   Emergency circumstances are defined in terms of those that are life-threatening or which are causing, or threaten to cause, serious injury or illness or serious harm to the environment or buildings or other property. However, the exemption does not extend to medical treatment itself, or decisions about this (other than decisions that establish the priority for treating patients).

5.75   The effect of exemption is intended to exclude from the offence matters such as the timeliness of a response to an emergency, the level of response and the effectiveness of the way in which the emergency is tackled. In any event, this is an uncertain area of the common law of negligence.

5.76   If medical treatment was not excluded from the 'emergency' exemption, then most, if not all, the activities undertaken in accident and emergency departments of

---

[56] CMCHA, s 6(8).

E. Emergencies

hospitals and a significant part of other activity undertaken by NHS bodies would be outwith the scope of the Act. Thus the exclusion of medical treatment from the 'emergency' exemption places the organization and management of medical services and the resultant standard of care within the ambit of the offence.

However, it potentially places more than this as the foundation for a relevant duty of care: medical treatment is widely defined under the Act[57] and may be undertaken by a wide variety of organizations, not just medical personnel, during 'emergency circumstances' (eg the giving of oxygen therapy or the provision of CPR by fire or police officers). Such activity may amount to the provision of a service and thus be an activity capable of founding a relevant duty of care. The circumstances necessary to place such persons under a duty of care is within an area of uncertainty of common law negligence.

5.77

4. The common law duty of care and emergency response

The general position under the common law is that no person is under duty to come to the rescue of a member of the public and that includes the rescue services (and, by extension, the providers of medical services). If a rescue is undertaken, such persons can only be liable for making matters worse than they would otherwise have been, or for undertaking an assumption of responsibility to act. Similarly, the standard of care when acting in emergency circumstances, whilst still that of reasonable care, is one that takes account of the emergency circumstances: a 'wrong' decision, especially one taken in such circumstances, may not necessarily be a negligent one.

5.78

In *Capital and Counties plc v Hampshire CC* [1997] 2 All ER 865, [1997] QB 1004 the Court of Appeal held that a fire service is not under a common law duty of care to answer a call for assistance. Furthermore, that by taking control of fire fighting operations, a senior fire officer is not to be seen as undertaking a voluntary assumption of responsibility to the owner of the premises on fire, whether or not the owner in fact relies upon the fire brigade. It was held that simply by attending the fire and conducting fire fighting operations a fire service does not, other than in exceptional circumstances, create or increase the danger. Thus, it was held that a fire service does not enter into a sufficiently proximate relationship with the owner or occupier of premises such as to become subject to a duty of care merely by attending and fighting the fire, notwithstanding that the senior officer actually assumes control of the fire fighting operations. The court also considered whether it was just, fair and reasonable to impose a duty of care, asking the question whether a fire service should have the benefit of immunity as a matter of public policy. It was concluded that no immunity should exist in cases where by its own positive action a fire service had created or increased the danger. In one of the three consolidated appeals before the court, where the defendants negligently turned off sprinklers which were at that

5.79

---

[57] CMCHA, s 6(8); para 5.72.

stage containing the fire and they by their positive act exacerbated the fire so that it rapidly spread, a duty of care was established.

5.80 In *OLL Ltd v Secretary of State for Transport* [1997] 3 All ER 897, it was held that there was no obvious distinction between the fire brigade responding to a fire where lives were at risk and the coastguard responding to an emergency at sea and, on that basis, the coastguard owed no duty of care to respond to an emergency call, nor, if they did respond, would they be liable if their response was negligent, unless such negligence amounted to a positive act which directly caused greater injury than would have occurred if they had not intervened at all. Moreover, it was found in that case that the coastguard did not owe any duty of care in cases where they misdirected other rescuers outside their own service.

5.81 However, in *Kent v Griffiths* [2000] 2 All ER 474, the claimant had suffered an asthma attack at home, her doctor called for an ambulance and was assured that it was on its way. In fact the ambulance did not arrive until much later and the claimant suffered an avoidable respiratory arrest. The doctor gave evidence that if she had been informed of the likely delay she would have had the claimant driven to hospital by other means. The Court of Appeal found that a duty of care was owed as a result of the acceptance, following the telephone call, that an ambulance would be despatched. The Court emphasised that it was not concerned with a situation where a decision had been taken by the public body about the allocation of limited resources, nor with a case where, with the benefit of hindsight, a 'wrong' decision had been taken in an emergency on the basis of limited information. The Court of Appeal distinguished the cases of the fire service and the police apparently on the basis that in such cases the duty had been owed to the public at large, and not an identified claimant.

5. Rescue at sea: ss 6(5) and 6(6)

5.82 Sections 6(5) and 6(6) provide that any duty of care owed in respect of the carrying out, or attempted carrying out, of a rescue operation at sea in emergency circumstances is not a 'relevant duty of care' unless it falls within s 2(1)(a) [a duty owed to employees or those working for an organization[58]] or 2(1)(b) [a duty as occupier of premises[59]].

5.83 Section 6(6) further provides that any duty of care owed in respect of action taken in order to comply with a direction under Merchant Shipping Act 1995, Sch 3A (safety directions) or Sch 3, para 4 (action in lieu of direction) is not a 'relevant duty of care' unless it falls within s 2(1)(a), a duty owed to employees or those working for an organization,[60] or 2(1)(b), a duty as occupier of premises.[61]

---

[58] See paras 4.20–4.48.
[59] See paras 4.49–4.65.
[60] See paras 4.20–4.48.
[61] See paras 4.49–4.65.

F. CHILD PROTECTION AND PROBATION FUNCTIONS

1. Child protection: ss 7(1) and 7(2)

Section 7 provides that any duty of care owed by a local authority or other public body in relation to the exercise of functions to protect children from harm or in relation to the activities of probation services (or equivalent bodies in Scotland and Northern Ireland) will not be a relevant duty of care for the purposes of the offence, unless it falls within s 2(1)(a), (b) or (d) namely a duty owed as employer to employees or those working for an organization,[62] a duty as occupier of premises[63] or a duty owed by an organization to a person in custody or detention (if and when the 'custody duty', s 2(1)(d) is brought into force).[64]

Section 7(2) achieves this in respect of child protection by application to any duty of care 'that a local authority or other public authority owes in respect of the exercise by it of functions conferred by or under—

(a) Parts 4 and 5 of the Children Act 1989,
(b) Part 2 of the Children (Scotland) Act 1995, or
(c) Parts 5 and 6 of the Children (Northern Ireland) Order 1995 (SI 1995/755 (NI 2)).

2. Probation functions: s 7(3)

Section 7(3) provides that any duty of care will not be a relevant duty of care for the purposes of the Act that a local probation board or other public authority owes in respect of the exercise by it of functions conferred by or under—

(a) Chapter 1 of Part 1 of the Criminal Justice and Court Services Act 2000,
(b) s 27 of the Social Work (Scotland) Act 1968, or
(c) Art 4 of the Probation Board (Northern Ireland) Order 1982 (SI 1982/713 (NI 10)).

3. The effect of s 7

It would appear that the exclusion in s 3(2) of 'exclusively public functions' from forming the subject of a relevant duty of care achieves the same result as s 7, in that such child protection and probation functions are exercisable only by authority conferred by statutory provision. The motivation for the inclusion of s 7 in the Act is to ensure that these functions, whose exercise in a number of *cause célèbres* has been publicly identified with the cause of a death, remain conclusively outwith the ambit of the Act. In particular, such concern arises from the exercise (or the failure to exercise)

5.84

5.85

5.86

5.87

---

[62] See paras 4.20–4.48.
[63] See paras 4.49–4.65.
[64] See paras 4.91–4.121.

5. The Relevant Duty of Care III

powers to take a child into care, the supervision of offenders and the provision of accommodation in approved premises for offenders.

5.88 Whilst it is very unlikely that the common law of negligence would impose a duty of care towards members of the public in respect of the supervision of offenders, the same cannot be said with certainty about an identifiable child victim of a public authority negligent in its particular exercise of child protection in that child's case.[65] In any event, the section clearly and unambiguously places any such duty of care outwith the scope of the offence.

---

[65] See the approach of the Court of Appeal in *Carty v Croydon LBC* [2005] 2 All ER 517.

6
COMMITTING THE OFFENCE: CAUSATION AND BREACH OF DUTY

A.	Overview	6.01
B.	Management Failure, Breach, and Senior Management	6.07
C.	The Way in which the Organization's Activities are Managed or Organized Caused the Death: s 1(1)(a)	6.10
	1. 'The way its activities are managed or organised'	6.12
	2. Causation	6.21
	3. Causation and 'management failure': summary of position and principles	6.41
D.	'The Way in which its Activities are Managed or Organised' Amounted to a Gross Breach of that Relevant Duty of Care: s 1(1)(b)	6.46
	1. The definition of gross breach	6.47
E.	Gross Breach: the Jury Factors in s 8	6.59
	1. Health and safety legislation: s 8(2)	6.64
	2. Health and safety duties and offences	6.78
	3. Specific factors which the jury may take into account: s 8(3)	6.105
F.	The Senior Management Requirement	6.117
	1. The criticism of the 'senior management' requirement	6.121
	2. The Government's view of the 'senior management' requirement	6.124
	3. The test for 'senior management'	6.128
	4. A substantial element of the breach	6.148
	5. Summary: the meaning of the 'senior management' requirement	6.157

A. OVERVIEW

6.01 An organization subject to the Act that owed a deceased person a relevant duty of care, will commit the offence of corporate manslaughter where:

- 'the way in which its activities are managed or organised' caused a person's death (s 1(1)(a));
- 'the way in which its activities are managed or organised' amounted to a gross breach of that relevant duty of care (s 1(1)(b)), and:
- 'the way in which its activities are managed or organised' by its senior management is a substantial element in the breach (s 1(3)).

6.02 'Gross' breach has a particular meaning under the Act, namely where the conduct alleged to amount to a breach of that duty falls far below what can reasonably be expected of the organization in the circumstances (s 1 (4)(c)).

6.03 Section 8 provides factors that the jury must take account when assessing 'gross' breach, factors that the jury may take into account and how the jury may have regard to any other matters they consider relevant.

6.04 A factor the jury must consider is whether the evidence shows that the organization failed to comply with any health and safety legislation that relates to the alleged breach of relevant duty of care, and if so, how serious that failure was and how much of a risk of death it posed.

6.05 A jury may consider the extent to which the evidence shows that there were 'attitudes, policies, systems or accepted practices within the organization' that were likely to have encouraged or produced tolerance of any such failure to comply with any health and safety legislation. The jury may also have regard to any health and safety guidance that relates to the alleged breach.

6.06 The 'senior management' requirement, whereby an organization is only guilty of an offence if the way its activities are managed or organized by its senior management is a substantial element in the gross breach, rests upon a definition of 'senior management' in s 1(4)(c). That definition incorporates the term 'significant role' in relation to the making of decisions about how, or the actual managing or organizing of, the whole or 'a substantial part' of its activities. Both 'significant' and 'substantial' are adjectives capable of more than one meaning; the Act provides no guidance as to the meaning of any of these terms nor what factors a jury should consider in relation to what amounts to a 'substantial part' of an organization's activities or a 'substantial element' of a breach.

B. MANAGEMENT FAILURE, BREACH, AND SENIOR MANAGEMENT

6.07 Section 1(1) of the Act provides:

(1) An organisation to which this section applies is guilty of an offence if the way in which its activities are managed or organised—
  (a) causes a person's death, and

C. The Way in which the Organization's Activities are Managed

(b) amounts to a gross breach of a relevant duty of care owed by the organisation to the deceased.

Section 1(3) provides: 6.08

(3) An organisation is guilty of an offence under this section only if the way in which its activities are managed or organised by its senior management is a substantial element in the breach referred to in subsection (1).

On its face, the multi-layered and complex approach to the drafting of s 1 has the apparent effect of separating breach of the relevant duty of care from cause of death of the person to whom the duty was owed. However, each of the three elements identified above is founded upon the way the organization's activities are managed or organized. 6.09

C. THE WAY IN WHICH THE ORGANIZATION'S ACTIVITIES ARE MANAGED OR ORGANIZED CAUSED THE DEATH: s 1(1)(a)

'Causation' under the common law offence of manslaughter by gross negligence, which will continue to apply to individuals and organizations not subject to the Act, requires no more than proof that a gross breach of a duty of care owed by a defendant caused the death of the deceased. 6.10

The offence of corporate manslaughter requires, pursuant to s 1(1)(a), that the way in which an organization's activities were managed or organized (described in the Explanatory Notes as the 'management failure'), caused the victim's death. The Explanatory Notes[1] describe how, 'The usual principles of causation in the criminal law will apply to determine this question. This means that the management failure need not have been the sole cause of death; it need only be a cause (although intervening acts may break the chain of causation in certain circumstances).' 6.11

1. 'The way its activities are managed or organised'

Neither the Act nor the Explanatory Notes provide guidance as to the interpretation or meaning of the phrase 'the way its activities are managed or organised'. 6.12

The view of the Government was that, 'The intention is for the new offence to capture failings in the strategic management of activities where there were inadequate systems or practices in the organization as a whole'[2] and that 'while the word "managed" is probably sufficient to cover all the kinds of behaviour that we are concerned about, there is a possibility that, for example, the way a process for carrying out an activity was designed would not be considered the management of 6.13

---

[1] Corporate Manslaughter and Corporate Homicide Bill [HL 19], Explanatory Notes para 15.
[2] *Hansard,* HL Grand Committee, Column 138, per Lord Bassam of Brighton (11 January 2007).

that activity the way a process for carrying out an activity was designed would not be considered the management of that activity. We are trying to ensure that we capture that properly. We would not want gross failures to ensure a safe working environment to be exempt from the Bill because the word "management" was interpreted too narrowly.'[3]

6.14 The genesis of the phrase, 'the way its activities are managed or organised' was the Law Commission's report and recommendations concerning the reform of involuntary manslaughter. Back in 1996, the Law Commission had proposed 'that there should be a special offence of corporate killing,'[4] that would broadly correspond to a new proposed offence of killing by gross carelessness, which together would replace the common law of gross negligence manslaughter. The Law Commission further recommended:

> that, for the purposes of the corporate offence, a death should be regarded as having been caused by the conduct of a corporation if it is caused by a failure, in the way in which the corporation's activities are managed or organised, to ensure the health and safety of persons employed in or affected by those activities.[5]

6.15 The basis for the Law Commission's proposal was founded upon a rejection of the creation of an offence incorporating vicarious liability, aggregation or a radically new corporate regime[6] in favour of one founded upon the scope of the common law duty of care owed by an employer to provide a safe system of work.[7] This non-delegable duty, the Law Commission proposed to use, 'as a model for the duty of every corporation to all those (not just employees) who may be affected by the corporation's activities'.[8]

6.16 With this proposal, 'there would be no need to identify the controlling officers of the company. The question would be whether there had been a management failure, rather than, as at present, whether there was blameworthy conduct on the part of any individual or group of individuals which should be attributed to the company'.[9]

6.17 (a) *'Way'*

Thus, the Law Commission's proposal was an offence based upon 'the way in which the corporation's activities were managed or organised fails to ensure the health and safety of persons employed in or affected by those activities': that was the management failure which had to be a cause of a person's death.

---

[3] *Hansard*, HL Grand Committee, Column 138, per Lord Bassam of Brighton (11 January 2007).
[4] *Legislating the Criminal Code: Involuntary Manslaughter* (Law Com No 237, 1996) (HC 171) para 8.35.
[5] ibid 8.35.
[6] ibid 7.28–7.37.
[7] See paras 4.20–4.48 for the common law duty of care of an employer in respect of 'system of work' which is a relevant duty under the Act.
[8] *Legislating the Criminal Code: Involuntary Manslaughter* (Law Com No 237, 1996) (HC 171) 8.10.
[9] ibid 8.20.

C. The Way in which the Organization's Activities are Managed

In s 1(1)(a) of the Act, in relation to an organization, 'the way in which its activities are managed or organised' must be shown to have caused a death. 'Way' is a term that appears broad enough to encompass decisions and acts or even inactivity: the *Oxford Dictionary of English* defines 'way' as 'a method, style, or manner of doing something'. Section 1(1)(a) of the Act does not require proof that this 'way' was 'unlawful', in the sense of being in breach of any duty, or even 'wrongful', simply that it caused the death. (Section 1(1)(b) does require that this 'way' amounts to a gross breach of the relevant duty of care.)

6.18

Employees at every level but the most junior in very many organizations are described as 'managers'. To a greater or lesser extent what is undertaken by each can be styled as the management or organization of activities: at the lower end, decisions about which employee is to perform a task or even what type of ladder should be used to change a light bulb would appear capable of being held to be the way activities are managed or organized. As the *Guide to the Corporate Manslaughter and Corporate Homicide Act 2007* states:

6.19

The offence is concerned with the way in which activities were managed or organised. This represents a new approach to establishing corporate liability for manslaughter/culpable homicide and does not require the prosecution to establish failure on the part of particular individuals or managers. It is instead concerned with how an activity was being managed and the adequacy of those arrangements.[10]

Perhaps the list of factors in s 8(3)(a)[11] that collectively are intended to encapsulate 'organizational culture' may have relevance to the 'way its activities are managed or organised', being 'attitudes, policies, systems or accepted practices within the organization'.

6.20

2. Causation

The Law Commission Report described how, in relation to management failure, the issue would always be a question of fact for a jury to decide, but how 'there will be some cases in which the jury will have to draw a somewhat fine line between an employee's "casual" negligence and a management failure. Such cases abound in the field of employer's liability.'[12]

6.21

(a) The Law Commission and causation
The Law Commission considered that, 'To a large extent this will involve the application of the ordinary principles of causation, as in any other homicide offence. If, for example, the jury are not satisfied beyond reasonable doubt that the death

6.22

---

[10] *Guide to the Corporate Manslaughter and Corporate Homicide Act 2007* (Ministry of Justice) October 2007, p 12.
[11] See paras 6.102–6.106.
[12] *Legislating the Criminal Code: Involuntary Manslaughter* (Law Com No 237, 1996) (HC 171) 8.36.

would not have occurred had it not been for the management failure, the offence will not be proved.'[13]

6.23   The Law Commission's report continued thereafter in the following way:

> However, we think that the scope for any defence of a 'break in the chain of causation' should be very limited. . . It does not, in our view, follow that the employee's conduct should in itself absolve the *corporation* from liability, because the management failure may have consisted in a failure to take precautions against the very kind of error that in fact occurred. . . The company's fault lies in its failure to anticipate the foreseeable negligence of its employee, and any consequence of such negligence should therefore be treated as a consequence of the company's fault.[14]

6.24   However, according to the Law Commission, it was 'not clear how far the ordinary law of causation takes account of this reasoning' and thus that there was 'a danger that, without more, the application of the ordinary rules of causation would in many cases result in a management failure being treated as a "stage already set", and hence not linked in law to the death.'[15]

6.25   As a result, The Law Commission recommended that the inclusion of 'an express provision to the effect that in this kind of situation the management failure may be *a* cause of the death, even if the *immediate* cause is the act or omission of an individual.'[16]

6.26   Despite the subsequent recommendations of the Joint Committees on Home Affairs and Work and Pensions (the Joint Committees) in their First Report[17] in response to the Government's draft Bill in 2005, which echoed those made by the Law Commission in this regard, this 'express provision' concerning causation did not find a place in the Act. The justification offered by the Government, was that as a result of the decision of the House of Lords in *Environmental Agency (formerly National Rivers Authority) v Empress Cars (Abertillery) Ltd* [1999] 2 AC 22, [1998] 1 All ER 481 the law of causation had moved on, so that 'only abnormal and extraordinary events will break the causal chain'.[18]

(b) *The usual principles of causation in the criminal law*

6.27   The 'usual principles of causation in the criminal law'[19] provide that a defendant's act need not be the sole, or principal cause of death, but only that it must have

---

[13] *Legislating the Criminal Code: Involuntary Manslaughter* (Law Com 237, 1996) (HC 171) 8.36.
[14] ibid 8.37.
[15] ibid 8.38.
[16] ibid 8.39.
[17] First Joint Report from the Home Affairs and Work and Pensions Committees Session 2005–06 (HC540).
[18] ibid para 94.
[19] Corporate Manslaughter and Corporate Homicide Bill [HL 19], Explanatory Notes, para 15.

C. The Way in which the Organization's Activities are Managed

contributed significantly to the death.[20] Put another way, the defendant's act must be proved to have been a substantial cause of the death.[21]

(c) *Environmental Agency (formerly National Rivers Authority) v Empress Cars (Abertillery) Ltd*

Environmental Agency (formerly National Rivers Authority) v Empress Cars (Abertillery) Ltd,[22] concerned the meaning of 'cause' in the Water Resources Act 1991, s 85(1), which creates an offence of causing pollution. In the House of Lords, the single opinion was given by Lord Hoffman, who considered the meaning of the concept of causation and summarized the outcome of that discussion in five propositions.[23]

6.28

Those propositions included how, in a prosecution for a breach of Water Resources Act 1991, s 85(1), it did not need to be proved against a defendant that he did something which was the immediate cause of the pollution, for example, maintaining tanks, lagoons or sewage systems full of noxious liquid would be sufficient, even if the immediate cause of the pollution was the lack of maintenance, a natural event or the act of a third party.

6.29

In the context of considering the nature of causation, Lord Hoffman stated:

6.30

The first point to emphasise is that common sense answers to questions of causation will differ according to the purpose for which the question is asked. Questions of causation often arise for the purpose of attributing responsibility to someone, for example, so as to blame him for something which has happened or to make him guilty of an offence or liable in damages. In such cases, the answer will depend upon the rule by which responsibility is being attributed.[24]

Lord Hoffman went on to explain how, 'one cannot give a common sense answer to a question of causation for the purpose of attributing responsibility under some rule without knowing the purpose and scope of the rule. Does the rule impose a duty which requires one to guard against, or makes one responsible for, the deliberate acts of third persons? If so, it will be correct to say, when loss is caused by the act of such a third person, that it was caused by the breach of duty.'[25]

6.31

In the context of pollution, Lord Hoffman described how, if the defendant did something which produced a situation in which the polluting matter could escape but a necessary condition of the actual polluting event which happened was also the act of a third party or a natural event, the issue to be resolved was whether that act or event should be regarded as a normal fact of life or something extraordinary. If it was in the general run of things a matter of ordinary occurrence, it would not negative the causal effect of the defendant's acts, even if it was not foreseeable that it would happen to that particular defendant or take that particular form. If it could

6.32

---

[20] See *R v Curley* 2 Cr App R 96 at 109.
[21] See *R v Cato* [1976] 62 Cr App R 41 at 46.
[22] [1999] 2 AC 22, [1998] 1 All ER 481.
[23] [1998] 1 All ER 481 at 492–3.
[24] ibid at 486.
[25] ibid at 488.

be regarded as something extraordinary, it would be open to a tribunal of fact to hold that the defendant had not caused the consequence. According to Lord Hoffman, the distinction between ordinary and extraordinary was one of fact and degree.

(d) Novus actus interveniens/*new intervening act*

6.33 The traditional, common law approach to causation involves the principal of *novus actus interveniens*, or new intervening act, namely:

> The new intervening act (*novus actus interveniens*) of a responsible actor, who had full knowledge of what he is doing, and is not subject to mistake or pressure, will normally operate to relieve the defendant of liability for a further consequence, because it makes the consequence too remote. . . What a person does (if he has reached adult years, is of sound mind and is not acting under mistake, intimidation or other similar pressure) is his own responsibility, and is not regarded as having been caused by other people.[26]

6.34 The extent to which Lord Hoffman's opinion in *Empress Cars (Abertillery) Ltd*,[27] has moved the law of causation on from this traditional approach, so that 'only abnormal and extraordinary events will break the causal chain' is a matter of debate.

6.35 The supply of a fatal dosage of drugs in a syringe by a fellow drug user to another who then self injects has founded a series of unlawful act manslaughter cases in which the issue of 'causation' has featured heavily. In the most recent of these cases, *Kennedy No 2* [2005] 2 Cr App R 23, the Lord Chief Justice appeared to restrict the application of the interpretation of causation in *Empress Cars (Abertillery) Ltd*,[28] as 'very much concerned with the context in which the issue arose for decision'[29] in that case and suggested that such an interpretation may apply in a 'statutory context'.[30]

(e) *Analysing 'management failure' in terms of causation*

6.36 However, analysing the 'rule', in the manner suggested by Lord Hoffman as necessary for resolving causation, namely, for the purpose of attributing responsibility, would suggest the imposition of 'a duty which requires one to guard against, or makes one responsible for, the deliberate acts of third persons':[31] the 'rule' in s 1(1) is, in relation to an organization, 'the way it manages or organises its activities' caused the death. This test, originated by the Law Commission, was founded upon the wide non-delegable duty upon an employer in respect the system of work of

---

[26] *Textbook of Criminal Law* (Glanville Williams) (2nd edn., 1983), p 391, quoted in [2005] Crim LR 819, at p 823. See also *R v Latif* [1996] 2 Cr App R 92, at 104.
[27] [1999] 2 AC 22, [1998] 1 All ER 481.
[28] [1999] 2 AC 22, [1998] 1 All ER 481.
[29] [2005] 2 Cr App R 23 at para 39.
[30] [2005] 2 Cr App R 23 at paras 40 and 42.
[31] *Empress Cars (Abertillery) Ltd* [1999] 2 AC 22 at p 31E, [1998] 1 All ER 481 at 488H.

C. The Way in which the Organization's Activities are Managed

those under his control, including responsibility for the manner in which such persons could be anticipated to behave.

(f) *Contributory negligence*

The doctrine of contributory negligence can be viewed as deriving from *novus actus* 6.37 *interveniens*, or new intervening event. In negligence, where a claimant has failed to exercise reasonable care for his own safety and this has contributed to the damage he has suffered, then a court can reduce the amount of damages it awards accordingly.

The present law is contained in the Law Reform (Contributory Negligence) Act 6.38 1945, s 1(1) of which provides:

> (1) Where any person suffers damage as the result partly of his own fault and partly of the fault of any other person or persons, a claim in respect of that damage shall not be defeated by reason of the fault of the person suffering the damage, but the damages recoverable in respect thereof shall be reduced to such extent as the court thinks just and equitable having regard to the claimant's share in the responsibility for the damage.

By Law Reform (Contributory Negligence) Act 1945, s 4, 'fault' means negli- 6.39 gence, breach of statutory duty or other act or omission which gives rise to a liability in tort or would, apart from the Act, give rise to the defence of contributory negligence.

As with the existing common law offence of individual gross negligence man- 6.40 slaughter,[32] contributory negligence on the part of a deceased cannot amount to a 'defence' to a charge of corporate manslaughter under the Act. The relevant issue, in respect of corporate manslaughter, is whether the way in which the organization managed or organized its affairs can be shown to have caused death and to have amounted to a gross breach of a relevant duty of care: contributory negligence on the part of the deceased may be relevant to whether the way the organization managed or organized its affairs was a substantial cause of death; it may be also be relevant to whether the way the organization managed or organized its affairs amounted to a gross breach of a relevant duty.

3. Causation and 'management failure': summary of position and principles

Proof that the way an organization managed or organized its activities caused the 6.41 death is an element required to be proved by the prosecution in charge of corporate manslaughter, pursuant to s 1(1)(a) of the Act. 'Way' appears broad enough to encompass decisions, acts or even inactivity and omission; 'way' means 'a method, style, or manner of doing something'. Section 1(1)(a) of the Act does not require proof that this 'way' was 'unlawful', simply that it caused the death. Whether the way an organization managed or organized its activities caused a death is an issue of

---

[32] *R v Swindall and Osbourne* (1846) 2 C & K 230; *R v Dant* (1865) L & C 567; *R v Hutchinson* (1864) 9 Cox 555; *R v Jones* (1870) 11 Cox 544; and *R v Kew and Jackson* (1872) 12 Cox 355.

fact for a jury. Determination of this will be based upon the 'usual principles of causation in criminal law'.[33]

6.42 The staring point is the principle that a defendant's management failure must be proved to have been a substantial cause of the death, but not the sole or even principal cause.

6.43 The phrase 'the way it organized or managed its activities' used in s 1(1) is derived from the 1996 Law Commission's recommendations. That was founded upon the notion of the non-delegable duty upon an employer in respect of the provision of a safe system of work that is the concept of responsibility for systems, which include provision for and anticipation of the way in which work will be undertaken.[34]

6.44 The opinion of Lord Hoffman in *Empress Cars (Abertillery) Ltd*[35] established that in respect of some 'rules' or criminal offences, third party acts or a natural event will break the chain of causation only if they are 'extraordinary'. This development of the principles of causation has been the subject of criticism and may not be of universal application.

6.45 It remains to be seen how management failure and causation of death will be treated by courts. The issue is one of fact for a jury but analysis of the 'rule', in the manner suggested by Lord Hoffman in *Empress Cars (Abertillery) Ltd*,[36] suggests responsibility for third party acts where these fall within the ambit of 'system': resolution may revolve around issues of management control and what should have been anticipated.

D. 'THE WAY IN WHICH ITS ACTIVITIES ARE MANAGED OR ORGANISED' AMOUNTED TO A GROSS BREACH OF THAT RELEVANT DUTY OF CARE: s 1(1)(b)

6.46 Following on from proof that the way in which an organization's activities were managed or organized caused a person's death, (s 1(1)(a)), is the requirement, created by s 1(1)(b), that the way in which its activities are managed or organized, 'amounts to a gross breach of a relevant duty of care owed by the organization to the deceased'.

1. The definition of gross breach

6.47 Section 1(4)(b) provides that, 'a breach of a duty of care by an organisation is a "gross" breach if the conduct alleged to amount to a breach of that duty falls far below what can reasonably be expected of the organisation in the circumstances'.

---

[33] Corporate Manslaughter and Corporate Homicide Bill [HL 19], Explanatory Notes, para 15.
[34] See paras 4.20–4.48 for the common law duty of care of an employer in respect of 'system of work' which is a relevant duty under the Act.
[35] [1999] 2 AC 22, [1998] 1 All ER 481.
[36] ibid.

D. Gross Breach of that Relevant Duty of Care: s 1(1)(b)

This definition is borrowed from the recommendations of the Law Commission in their 1996 proposals for an offence of corporate killing by gross carelessness. 6.48

The Government described the test in the following terms[37] 6.49

> Corporate manslaughter is indeed a grave criminal offence and so we believe should be targeted at only the most serious corporate failings. We have therefore retained the high threshold of a 'gross' breach for the offence. This threshold is in line with the current law of manslaughter and reflects the Law Commission's proposals of behaviour falling far below what could reasonably be expected (which the Government and Committees accept is an appropriate way of defining this test).

This test involves the determination of two questions by the jury: 6.50

- What was reasonably expected of the organization in the circumstances? and
- Did the conduct of the organization, the way in which its activities were managed or organized, fall far below that standard?

Directing the jury upon and defining the existence of a relevant duty of care, may necessarily involve the trial judge directing the jury as to the answer, at least in part, to the first question 6.51

(a) *Gross breach and common law manslaughter*

The existing common law offence of gross negligence manslaughter, which will continue to be applicable to organizations not subject to the Act and to individuals, employs the same term, 'gross', and the direction[38] to the jury is derived from the speech of Lord Mackay in *R v Adomako* [1995] 1 AC 171, where he described: 6.52

> The jury will have to consider whether the extent to which the defendant's conduct departed from the proper standard of care incumbent upon him, involving as it must have done a risk of death... was such that it should be judged criminal. It is true that to a certain extent this involves an element of circularity, but in this branch of the law I do not believe that is fatal to its being correct as a test of how far conduct must depart from accepted standards to be characterised as criminal. This is necessarily a question of degree and an attempt to specify that degree more closely is I think likely to achieve only a spurious precision. The essence of the matter, which is supremely a jury question, is whether, having regard to the risk of death involved, the conduct of the defendant was so bad in all the circumstances as to amount in their judgment to a criminal act or omission.

(b) *Breach and the standard of care in negligence*

In negligence, breach of a duty of care is concerned with whether the defendant was careless, in the sense of failing to conform to the standard of care applicable to him. The level at which the standard is set is a question of law, but one that is framed in general terms. In *Hazell v British Transport Commission* [1958] 1 WLR 169, at 171, 6.53

---

[37] The Government Reply to the First Joint Report from the Home Affairs and Work and Pensions Committees Session 2005–06 (Cm 6755), p 16.

[38] See *R v Misra and Srivastava* [2005] 1 Cr App R 21 and *R v Yaqoob* [2005] EWCA Crim 1269, [2005] All ER (D) 109 (Aug).

Pearson J described how, 'the basic rule is that negligence consists in doing something which a reasonable man would not have done in that situation or omitting to do something which a reasonable man would have done in that situation, and I approach with scepticism any suggestion that there is any other rule of law, properly so called, in any of these cases'.

6.54 Thus, this objective standard remains whatever the defendant or situation: professional defendants or those with a specialist skill are governed by the standard of care of a normal person of their occupation or specialism. In *Bolam v Friern Barnet Hospital* [1957] 1 WLR 582, at 586, it was said that 'the test is the standard of the ordinary skilled man exercising and professing to have that special skill'.

(c) *Conduct, 'way' and breach of a relevant duty of care*

6.55 The effect of ss1(1)(b) and 1(4)(b), is to require that the way in which an organization's activities are managed or organised' must be proved to have been 'conduct that amounts to a breach of that duty falls far below what can reasonably be expected of the organization in the circumstances.'

6.56 As is set out above at paras, 'way' is a term that appears broad enough to encompass decisions, acts or even inactivity and omission.

6.57 However, resolution of whether there has been 'conduct that amounts to a breach of that duty' depends to a very large part on the relevant duty of care identified by the judge as existing and having been owed to the deceased.

6.58 Section 2(6) provides that the existence of a relevant duty of care is matter of law to be decided by the judge, who must decide all facts necessary to make that determination.[39] It appears that at the close of the case, in summing up to the jury, the judge will direct the jury as to the existence of the relevant duty of care owed by the organization. This will involve identifying what the relevant duty of care was and may involve identifying to what it extended. In effect, this may involve directing the jury that the organization owed a duty of care to take a step or act in some way in respect of which the evidence clearly reveals the organization did not so do.

E. GROSS BREACH: THE JURY FACTORS IN s 8

6.59 Section 8 contains a list of factors for a jury to take into account when considering the issue of 'gross' breach. The Government stressed how these factors, 'are not conditions that must be satisfied before a conviction can be secured but simply factors to assist the jury's consideration. As such, it would not be necessary for the prosecution to prove or adduce evidence on all or indeed any of them, although they are intended to highlight particularly relevant considerations.'[40]

---

[39] See paras 3.10–3.33.
[40] The Government Reply to the First Joint Report from the Home Affairs and Work and Pensions Committees Session 2005–06 (Cm 6755), p 16.

E. Gross Breach: the Jury Factors in s 8

Sections 8 is entitled, 'Factors for Jury' and the section applies where: 6.60

(a) it is established that an organisation owed a relevant duty of care to a person, and
(b) it falls to the jury to decide whether there was a gross breach of that duty.[41]

The Explanatory Notes[42] claim that the purpose of these factors is 'To provide a clearer framework for assessing an organisation's culpability'. The Notes continue: 6.61

Thus in order to reach a determination upon the issue of 'gross' breach and whether the 'conduct alleged to amount to a breach of that duty falls far below what can reasonably be expected of the organization in the circumstances the jury must consider whether the evidence shows that the organization failed to comply with any health and safety legislation that relates to the breach.[43]

It is in this context that the jury must consider, 'how serious that failure was' and 'how much of a risk of death it posed', echoing the elements of the direction in respect of a defendant's conduct for gross breach under the common law for individual gross negligence manslaughter. 6.62

In addition the jury may consider further factors, set out in s 8(3), and thereafter, s 8(4) provides: 6.63

(4) This section does not prevent the jury from having regard to any other matters they consider relevant.

1. Health and safety legislation: s 8(2)

Section 8(2) provides: 6.64

(2) The jury must consider whether the evidence shows that the organisation failed to comply with any health and safety legislation that relates to the alleged breach, and if so—
   (a) how serious that failure was;
   (b) how much of a risk of death it posed

Section 25 defines 'health and safety legislation' to mean any statutory provision dealing with health and safety matters, including in particular provision contained in the Health and Safety at Work etc. Act 1974 (HSWA).[44] 6.65

Previously, on indictments alleging common law gross negligence manslaughter against a company, breaches of health and safety legislation and in particular of the employers' duties under ss 2 and 3 of the Health and Safety at Work etc. Act 1974 were alleged in addition or as alternatives. In light of the drafting of CMCHA, s 8(2), such breaches of health and safety legislation are likely to feature on indictments in addition to corporate. Furthermore, juries may be invited to consider such counts alleging health and safety breaches prior to deliberating on the corporate 6.66

---

[41] CMCHA, s 8(1).
[42] Corporate Manslaughter and Corporate Homicide Bill [HL 19], Explanatory Notes, para 39.
[43] ibid.
[44] Or the Health and Safety at Work (Northern Ireland) Order (SI 1978/1039 (NI9)).

6. Committing the Offence

manslaughter allegation and to view any such breaches as being a failure to comply with health and safety legislation that relates to the alleged breach of the relevant duty of care for corporate manslaughter, pursuant to s 8(2).

(a) *Health and safety legislation that relates to the breach*

6.67 Section 8(2) requires a jury to consider only a failure to comply with health and safety legislation, 'that relates to the alleged breach' of the relevant duty of care. Neither the general duties under the Health and Safety at Work etc. Act 1974 (HSWA) nor the various provisions within health and safety regulations created pursuant to HSWA, s 15, found a relevant duty of care. These statutory duties are different to duties of care and harm is not required for breach to occur.

6.68 How such a failure must 'relate' is not defined and whether it relates to the relevant breach of duty of care will, like all considerations under s 8, be a matter for the jury. Such relationship may arise from the activity that caused the harm, for example a licensed activity such as asbestos removal,[45] a regulated operation such as mechanical lifting,[46] or a proscribed activity such as working from height without suitable precautions,[47] from the identity or function of the deceased, for example as employee at work or as a non-employee provided with premises as a workplace,[48] and from the status of the defendant, for example as employer,[49] person in control of premises, licence holder, or principal contractor of a construction project.[50]

(b) *'How serious the failure was': s 8(2)(a)*

6.69 Breach of the general duties under HSWA, ss 2–6 is a criminal offence, pursuant to HSWA, s 33(1)(a), punishable by way of a maximum fine of £20,000 in the Magistrates Court and unlimited fine in the Crown Court; breach of a health and safety regulation is a criminal offence, pursuant to s 33(1)(c), punishable by way of a maximum fine of Level 5 (currently £5,000) in the Magistrates' Court and unlimited fine in the Crown Court.[51]

6.70 The duties are not drafted in a way that provides a hierarchy of seriousness in respect of their breach. Thus, the jury's determination of how serious a failure to comply with any health and safety legislation will not be assisted by any specific provision within the legislation.

6.71 The Court of Appeal, in *R v Howe & Son (Engineers) Ltd* [1999] 2 Cr App R (S) 37, gave guidance on the approach to be adopted when assessing culpability of

---

[45] Control of Asbestos Regulations 2006.
[46] Lifting Operations and Lifting Equipment Regulations 1998.
[47] Work at Heights Regulations 2005.
[48] Health and Safety at Work etc. Act 1974 , s 4.
[49] Health and Safety at Work etc. Act 1974 , ss 2 and 3.
[50] Construction (Design and Management) Regulations 2007.
[51] Pursuant to the remarkably complicated provisions of HSWA s 33(3)(b)(i) and (4), in the Crown Court the offence can attract a sentence of imprisonment of up to two years in certain circumstances.

E. Gross Breach: the Jury Factors in s 8

health and safety offences, while acknowledging how the circumstances of individual cases would vary almost infinitely. Scott-Baker LJ described how, 'Failures to fulfil the general duties under the Act are particularly serious' before identifying the following relevant features:

(a) How far short the defendant fell from the relevant safety standard, thus with the general duties, how far the defendant fell short of doing what was reasonably practicable.
(b) Whether death or serous injury resulted from the breach. The court conceded that it is often a matter of chance whether death or serious injury results from even a serious breach
(c) Whether the defendant deliberately profited from a failure to take necessary health and safety measures or run a risk to save money. If so, it will be a seriously aggravating feature.
(d) The degree of risk and the extent of the danger created by the offence.
(e) The extent of the breach—whether it was an isolated incident, or whether it had been continuing for a period of time.
(f) A failure to heed warnings is another aggravating factor.

6.72 In terms of the application of these features as a means of assessing the seriousness of a failure by a jury for the purposes of CMCHA, s 8(2)(a) the most relevant would appear to be a), d), e) and f).

6.73 The *Howe* feature, c), whether the defendant deliberately profited from a failure or ran a risk to save money featured in the draft Bill as a separate factor for a jury's consideration.[52] However, during proceeding before the Joint Committees,[53] the Government formed the opinion that this was a matter more appropriately 'dealt with in terms of its impact on sentencing rather than its impact on the criminal behaviour itself'.[54]

6.74 In the event, the determination by a jury of how serious a failure to comply with any health and safety legislation is will be likely to be founded upon competing submissions by the prosecution and defence and a collective view based on the factual circumstances presented in court.

(c) 'How much of a risk of death it posed': s 8(2)(b)

6.75 It appears anomalous that for 'gross' breach in corporate manslaughter a jury must consider how much of a risk of death was posed by any failure to comply with health and safety legislation that relates to the breach of duty, rather than how much of a risk of death was posed by the breach of the duty, as is the position with common law gross negligence manslaughter.

---

[52] Clause 3(2)(b)(iii).
[53] Joint Home Affairs and Work and Pensions Committee, para 193.
[54] First Joint Report from the Home Affairs and Work and Pensions Committees Session 2005–06. Minutes of Evidence (HC-540-III) Vol III, Q 577.

6.76 Depending upon the health and safety provision and the breach of duty of care to which it relates, there may be no risk of death involved in the one yet a significant risk of death involved in the other. The very nature of a relevant duty of care in negligence involves the consideration of the 'risk of death': the forseeability of physical harm is a determiner of the existence of a duty of care.[55]

6.77 Bearing in mind both how s 8(4) provides that the jury are not prevented from having regard to any other matters they consider relevant and how central the issue of 'risk of death' is to 'gross' breach under the common law, it is anticipated that judges may continue to direct juries, in respect of 'gross' breach for corporate manslaughter, to consider the 'risk of death' posed by the defendant's conduct.

2. Health and safety duties and offences

6.78 It appears from the drafting of s 8(2) that it is intended that health and safety legislation will play a central part in a jury's consideration of 'gross' breach. Part of the reason why the Government resisted calls for the offence of corporate manslaughter to be based upon breach of the duties under HSWA, was because of the their near absolute nature: the broad definition of risk, namely the possibility of danger,[56] and the high standard, with a reverse burden, of doing all that was reasonably practicable means that an organization may often be in breach of one of these duties without 'fault', in the sense of having acted in anyway negligently. Thus breach of a duty under the HSWA would not have provided a 'fault' threshold on which to found the offence of corporate manslaughter.

6.79 A further reason is that the duties HSWA, ss 2 and 3, fall upon employers alone:[57] there are many organizations, including commercial companies, that have very substantial undertakings yet employ no one: many group companies have a single service company which employs all employees for the group; many companies rely upon agency workers or contractors to carry out the company's undertaking. Thus a corporate manslaughter offence founded upon these duties would not have had universal application across range of organizations which now it has been applied to.

6.80 Similarly, the duty under HSWA, s 4, in relation to premises, is very limited in its application (relating to non-domestic premises provided to non-employees as a workplace by a person in the course of an undertaking); HSWA, s 6 provides an onerous duty but its extent is limited largely to articles for use at work.

(a) *The nature of health and safety legislation.*

6.81 While the definition of 'health and safety legislation' in s 25 is intentionally wide so as to be 'any statutory provision dealing with health and safety matters' and thus not

---

[55] See para 3.43–3.44.
[56] See *R v Board of Trustees of Science Museum* [1993] 3 All ER 853 CA.
[57] And the self employed, by HSWA, s 3(2).

E. Gross Breach: the Jury Factors in s 8

limited to the HSWA and health and safety regulations made pursuant to this Act, nonetheless, these provisions are the principal source of such legislation

(b) *The general duties under HSWA*

The major provisions of HSWA are the general duties contained in ss 2–6. These are duties placed on persons, whether human, corporate or unincorporate, by virtue of their status as employer, self-employed, person in control of premises or supplier of articles. In law, the employer cannot 'delegate' the performance of these duties to another party, be it a manager, another employee or even a different organization. The duty remains at all times upon the employer who will remain liable for a failure. Vicarious liability plays no part in the operation of these duties. 6.82

By HSWA, s 33(1)(a), breach of one of these general duties is an 'either-way' criminal offence, punishable in the Crown Court by a fine without limit. 6.83

HSWA, s 2(1) imposes a wide general duty upon employers to ensure the safety of their employees at work; section 3(1) imposes a wide general duty upon employers to conduct their undertaking so as to ensure the safety of those not in their employment who may be thereby affected. These two general duties, while modelled on the common law duty of care that an employer owes to an employee in respect of his health and safety, have been interpreted as imposing both a higher and a different standard upon the employer. 6.84

Breach of the ss 2 and 3 duties is not dependent upon proof of harm or damage nor do the duties give rise to civil liability,[58] but only to a more strict criminal liability. The protective intent of the HSWA is paramount and cannot be defeated by arguments that civil liability would not arise in negligence. 6.85

An employer will have failed to ensure health and safety if there can be shown to exist a risk to health and safety or welfare. Risk bears its ordinary meaning of denoting the possibility of danger rather than actual danger.[59] 6.86

Some operations are inherently dangerous so that the possibility of danger cannot be entirely removed. HSWA recognizes this by qualifying these duties. The duties impose a strict liability subject only to the qualification of 'reasonable practicability' requiring an employer to take every reasonably practicable step to prevent or minimize the possibility of danger: the duty is not aimed at preventing or proscribing work that is or may be dangerous, rather in ensuring that all reasonable precautions are taken to minimize the risk posed by such work. 6.87

By HSWA, s 40, in any proceedings for a health and safety offence under HSWA, the defendant is under the burden to show that he took all reasonably practicable steps. Reasonably practicable is narrower than physically possible: An assessment must be made by the employer in which the degree of risk is placed on one side of the scale and the sacrifice involved in any of the steps necessary for minimizing or 6.88

---

[58] HSWA s 47(1)(a) provides that nothing in the Act shall be construed as conferring a right of action in any civil proceedings in respect of any failure to comply with any duty imposed by ss 2 to 7.
[59] *R v Board of Trustees of Science Museum* [1993] 3 All ER 853, CA.

6. Committing the Offence

averting the risk, whether in money, time or trouble, is placed on the other. If the there was a great disproportion between any of them—the risk being insignificant in comparison to the sacrifice involved—then an employer can demonstrate that the step was not reasonably practicable.

6.89 In a series of cases commencing in the late 1990s and culminating in the recent Court of Appeal decision in *R v HTM Ltd* [2006] EWCA Crim 1156, the courts have considered the nature of the statutory duties imposed by HSWA, ss 2 and 3. Although in the first of these cases, *R v British Steel* [1995] 1 WLR 1356, the actual issue before the courts was whether employers were in breach of their duties through the act or omission of a junior employee—that is whether the identification doctrine or vicarious liability had any place when considering the general duties—they naturally fell to considering the ambit and scope of reasonable practicability. Indeed, in the later cases it became key to the understanding of how the duties applied in practice. In general terms, in the early judgments the duties were interpreted in onerous and restrictive terms, and the scope of any defence limited, in the later cases a relaxation of approach appears to have occurred.

6.90 The current position of the duties under HSWA ss 2 and 3 can be summarized in the following way: an employer must show that all reasonably practicable steps were taken by him, or on his behalf. The duty cannot be delegated to any person, be they manager, employee or independent contractor. Should there be a failure to take all reasonably practicable steps by the employer, or on his behalf, then the employer will remain liable unless he can show that the only failing was by the person doing the work and all of the following applied: he had the appropriate skill and instruction; safe systems of work had been laid down; he had been subject to adequate supervision; he had been provided with safe plant and equipment for the proper performance of the work.

6.91 Section 4 of HSWA is a complex structured provision that creates an absolute duty to ensure that premises which are made available for use by non-employees are safe. The duty is owed by all those who have a degree of control over the relevant premises or of the relevant plant or substance. This duty is very different to that at common law and under the Occupiers Liability Acts, which is a relevant duty of care under CMCHA, s 2(1)(b).[60]

6.92 The duty under HSWA, s 4 is owed 'in relation to' non-employees who use non-domestic premises made available to them as a place of work, by any person who has, to any extent, control of such premises. HSWA s 4(4) provides that any reference to a person having control of any premises or matter is a reference to a person having control of the premises or matter in connection with the carrying on by him of a trade, business or other undertaking (whether for profit or not). Such a person is under a duty to take such measures as it is reasonable for a person in his position to take to ensure that the relevant premises is or are safe and without risks to health, so far as is reasonably practicable.

---

[60] See paras 4.49–4.65.

E. Gross Breach: the Jury Factors in s 8

Section 6 of HSWA contains a series of interrelated and complex provisions which place duties on designers, importers, manufacturers and suppliers in respect of safety relating to specific aspects of the use of articles for work, fairground equipment and substances. HSWA s 53(1) defines 'article for use at work' to mean, any plant designed for use or operation (whether exclusively or not) by persons at work, and any article designed for use as a component in any such plant. 6.93

(c) *Health and safety regulations*
In general terms, health and safety regulations are subordinate legislation created pursuant to HSWA, s 15. Currently, there are approximately 200 sets of regulations, which includes all those created to give effect to the health and safety Directives that emanated from Europe during the 1980s and 1990s. 6.94

The wealth of health and safety regulations place obligations upon those engaged in a wide range of activities in different capacities. Many of these regulations are drafted in absolute terms. Regulations imposing strict liability duties are not uncommon. Contravention of a health and safety regulation is an offence contrary to HSWA, s 33(1)(c). 6.95

Regulations fall into two categories: those with general application across all workplaces, and those addressed to specific hazards arising in particular industries or workplaces. Generally, the former tend to be drafted in 'goal-setting' terms, setting out what ought to be done, and not how it should be done; while the latter are often *prescriptive*, that is providing mandatory minimum requirements in relation to a specific matter. 6.96

The drafting of health and safety regulations has evolved over the past fifteen years. Many of the principal regulations were first enacted in 1992 and have since have been replaced with fresh provisions. Many regulations drafted post-1997 follow the same form, incorporating an express statutory defence that requires a defendant to show 'reasonable practicability' of steps taken and all 'due diligence', rather than qualifying the duty itself by the phrase 'so far as reasonably practicable'. Following the Court of Appeal's decision in *HTM Ltd*[61] the distinction between the first category of 'qualified' duties and the second category of post-1997 statutory defence duties is likely to prove important: the former will not be subject to the Management of Health and Safety at Work Regulations 1999, reg 21, whilst the latter will. 6.97

The Management of Health and Safety at Work Regulations 1999, reg 21 provides that provides that, 'Nothing in the relevant statutory provisions shall operate so as to afford an employer a defence in any criminal proceedings for a contravention of those provisions by reason of any act or default of (a) an employee of his'. Latham LJ, in *HTM Ltd*,[62] ruled in terms that the phrase 'reasonably practicable' was properly to be viewed as a qualification of the general duties in HSWA and not 6.98

---

[61] [2006] EWCA Crim 1156.
[62] ibid.

a defence, thus reg 21 had no application: the same with apply to such pre-1997 'qualified' duties in regulations.

6.99 A third category of health and safety regulations incorporate 'reasonable practicability' only as a qualification upon the standard of required measures.

6.100 The most important health and safety regulations of general application are the Management of Health and Safety at Work Regulations 1999 SI 1999/3242. By reg 3(1), every employer is obliged to make a suitable and sufficient assessment of the risks to the health and safety of his employees to which they are exposed while they are at work; and the risks to the health and safety of persons not in his employment arising out of or in connection with the conduct by him of his undertaking for the purpose of identifying the measures he needs to take to comply with the requirements and prohibitions imposed upon him by or under health and safety provisions.

(d) *Health and safety offences, s 8 and corporate manslaughter*

6.101 The following issues are apparent from the above consideration of the general duties under HSWA and health and safety regulations.

6.102 The key duties and regulations fall upon employers and are non-delegable. The Act has a number of provisions that deem an organization to be the employer for the purposes of the Act, these apply to:

- Departments or bodies listed in Sch 1 in respect of Crown employees (s 11(3));
- The Ministry of Defence in respect of members of the armed forces (s 12(2)); and
- Police forces in respect of police personnel (s 13(3))

6.103 In respect of prosecutions under health and safety legislation, great care is often required to be taken to identify the legal person who is an employer: many organizations have complex legal structures whereby a particular service company is the employer of all personnel across a group of companies. In such circumstances, that service company's 'activities' may be very limited and it may not be the organization that thereby owes relevant duties of care for the purposes of the Act. An organization that is not an employer will not owe the non-delegable statutory duties as employer and will not have 'failed to comply with health and safety legislation'.

6.104 In the context of a jury's consideration, pursuant to s 8(2), of whether the evidence shows that the organization failed to comply with any health and legislation, namely one of the general duties under HSWA or a health and safety regulation, unless a count alleging such an offence is on the indictment, it may be that no reverse burden, pursuant to HSWA, s40, can fall on the defendant: if so, then the prosecution will bear the burden of proving every element of an alleged failure to comply with health and safety legislation.

3. Specific factors which the jury may take into account: s 8(3)

6.105 Section 8(3) provides:

(3) The jury may also—
 (a) consider the extent to which the evidence shows that there were attitudes, policies, systems or accepted practices within the organisation that were likely to have

E. Gross Breach: the Jury Factors in s 8

encouraged any such failure as is mentioned in subsection (2), or to have produced tolerance of it;
(b) have regard to any health and safety guidance that relates to the alleged breach.

(a) *Attitudes, policies, systems and accepted policies*

This subsection owes it existence to the Joint Committees[63] and their representations to the Government concerning the draft Bill.[64] The Committees wanted the Government to abandon 'relevant duty of care' as the core of the offence, to rethink the 'senior management' requirement and to return to the Law Commission's 1996 proposal for an offence based on 'management failure'.[65] Part of the Government's argument was that 'management failure' by itself would cover failings within a company that occur at too low a level to be fairly associated with the company as a whole.[66]

6.106

In the event, the Joint Committees stated:

6.107

We suggest that juries be assisted in their task by being required to consider whether there has been a serious breach of health and safety legislation and guidance or other relevant legislation. In assessing this they could consider whether a corporate culture existed in the organisation that encouraged, tolerated or led to that management failure.

The Government's response to the Joint Committees stated, 'We are interested in this idea and the way in which it reinforces the concept of wider, corporate management failures and consider that such a factor may well have a useful role to play. However, we are not satisfied that it represents the whole answer.'[67]

6.108

The factors in s 8 were the result. The Committees notion of 'corporate culture' that encouraged or tolerated failures to comply with health and safety legislation has been translated into what can be styled 'organizational culture', defined through a list of indicators, and is a factor that the jury *may* take into account.

6.109

Of this list of indicators, 'policies' and 'systems' would appear to be the most significant; 'attitudes' and 'accepted practices' would appear to beg the question, by whom?

6.110

Perhaps the greatest effect of this provision will be upon those charged with investigating such alleged offences, who may, as a result, investigate the potential existence of such a corporate culture in every case.

6.111

---

[63] First Joint Report from the Home Affairs and Work and Pensions Committees Session 2005–06 (HC 540).
[64] Draft Corporate Manslaughter Bill (Cm 6497).
[65] First Joint Report from the Home Affairs and Work and Pensions Committees Session 2005–06 (H-540) paras 104, 123, 140, 199.
[66] The Government Reply to the First Joint Report from the Home Affairs and Work and Pensions Committees Session 2005–06 (Cm 6755), p 18.
[67] ibid.

(b) *Health and safety guidance*

6.112 The reasoning for the inclusion of health and safety guidance that relates to the alleged breach of the relevant duty of care as a factor that a jury may, as opposed to must, take into account when considering whether there was a gross breach is provided by the Explanatory Notes:

> Guidance does not provide an authoritative statement of required standards and therefore the jury is not required to consider the extent to which this is not complied with. However, where breaches of relevant health and safety duties are established, guidance may assist a jury in considering how serious this was.[68]

6.113 Health and safety guidance for the purposes of s 8 is defined by s 8(5) to mean 'any code, guidance, manual or similar publication that is concerned with health and safety matters and is made or issued (under a statutory provision or otherwise) by an authority responsible for the enforcement of any health and safety legislation'.

6.114 This is clearly wider than solely Approved Codes of Practice (ACOPs) and guidance issued by the Health and Safety Commission (HSC) and Health and Safety Executive (HSE), but these represent the most significant material that falls within the definition. By HSWA, s 16 the HSC is empowered to approve codes of practice with the consent of the appropriate Secretary of State. According to the HSE, ACOPs offer practical examples of good practice, and give advice on how to comply with the law. For example, they may provide a guide to what is reasonably practicable for a work activity within a particular industry.

6.115 Although such Codes of Practice do not themselves impose legally enforceable duties, HSWA s 17 provides that, while a failure on the part of any person to observe any provision of an approved code of practice shall not of itself render him liable to any civil or criminal proceedings, failure to comply with the provisions may be taken by a court in criminal proceedings as evidence of a failure to comply with the requirements of HSWA or of regulations to which the ACOP relates, unless it can be shown by the defendant that those requirements were complied with in some equally effective way.

6.116 The HSE publishes guidance on a range of subjects, its primary purpose being to assist in the understanding of and compliance with health and safety law. It is not compulsory to follow guidance.

F. THE SENIOR MANAGEMENT REQUIREMENT

6.117 Arguably the most controversial provision in the Act is s 1(3), which provides:

> (3) An organisation is guilty of an offence under this section only if the way in which its activities are managed or organised by its senior management is a substantial element in the breach referred to in subsection (1).

---

[68] Corporate Manslaughter and Corporate Homicide Bill [HL 19], Explanatory Notes, para 39.

F. The Senior Management Requirement

Thus, the way the organization's activities are managed or organized must be proved to have caused a person's death and to amount to a gross breach of a relevant duty of care owed by the organization to the deceased. Furthermore, the way those activities are managed or organized by senior management must be a substantial element in the gross breach.   6.118

This concept, of the role of an identifiable group as 'senior management' and such a role being a 'substantial element' in the breach, is entirely novel. Beyond a definition of who are senior managers in s 1(4)(c), neither the Act nor the Explanatory Notes give further clue as to the interpretation and application of this concept.   6.119

In October 2007, the Ministry of Justice published *A Guide to the Corporate Manslaughter and Corporate Homicide Act 2007*, but this provides little assistance save for noting: 6.120

> The Act does not require the prosecution to prove specific failings on the part of individual senior managers. It will be sufficient for a jury to consider that the senior management of the organisation collectively were not taking adequate care, and this was a substantial part of the organisation's failure.[69]

1. The criticism of the 'senior management' requirement

The Bill[70] originally proposed by the Government simply defined the offence as occurring where the way an organization's activities are managed or organized by its senior managers causes a death and amounts to a gross breach of a relevant duty of care. That proposal was the subject of much criticism and the Joint Committees recommended that the Government rethink the 'senior management' requirement.   6.121

The Joint Committees[71] had various concerns regarding the 'senior management' requirement, these included that: 6.122

- it would have the perverse effect of encouraging organizations to reduce the priority given to health and safety by delegation to avoid responsibility falling on senior managers
- as a result of it, the offence would simply broaden the identification doctrine into some form of aggregation of the conduct of senior managers. This would do little to address the problems that have plagued the common law offence in its application to companies.
- it would introduce additional legal argument about who is and who is not a 'senior manager'.
- that by aiming at senior management to catch larger organizations, it actually focuses on smaller organizations.

---

[69] *Guide to the Corporate Manslaughter and Corporate Homicide Act 2007* (Ministry of Justice) October 2007, p 14.
[70] Draft Corporate Manslaughter Bill (Cm 6497).
[71] First Joint Report from the Home Affairs and Work and Pensions Committees Session 2005–06 (HC-540), paras 130–169.

6.123 In response, the Government promised to revisit the issue of the 'senior management' requirement. In the event, the result was an unchanged definition of senior management and the requirement that, instead of the whole, the way the organization's activities are managed or organized by senior management must be a 'substantial element' of the gross breach of the relevant duty of care.

2. The Government's view of the 'senior management' requirement

6.124 Many of the concerns raised by the Joint Committees concerning the draft Bill where 'senior management's involvement was not qualified by the word 'substantial', were repeated in respect of the new test, now s 1(3) of the Act, namely, the way the organization's activities are managed or organized by senior management must be a substantial element of the gross breach of the relevant duty of care.

6.125 In answer to these concerns and in respect of management failure, Lord Bassam told the House of Lords in Grand Committee:

> In looking at how an activity was managed or organised by the organisation as a whole, the prosecution would have to examine how the activity was being managed at all levels, including the senior level. Without further amendment, we doubted that gross negligence would be found in the organisation overall unless there were failures at the senior level, but we were concerned that this was not clear in the Bill. The Law Commission noted that there would be a somewhat fine line between an employee's 'casual' negligence and a management failure. We were concerned that such a fine line was not acceptable in a criminal offence as serious as manslaughter, and that organisations should be clear about the circumstances in which the offence might bite. To address this, we put the requirement in the Bill that there was a failure at the senior level.[72]

6.126 The principal concern regarding the 'senior management' requirement was the concern that organizations could simply avoid potential liability by delegating responsibility for health and safety down from senior management. Lord Bassam dealt with this concern in the following way:

> The Government recognise the importance of health and safety being led from the top of organisations. . . At the same time, they do not want organisations to believe that no management of health and safety can be delegated. Appropriate delegation and appropriate supervision of such delegation is part of the proper management of health and safety. However, inappropriate delegation of health and safety responsibilities will not be a legitimate defence to a charge of gross negligence. The courts will be able to consider how the activity was managed at senior level, and if the answer is that those at senior level failed to manage health and safety appropriately in respect of the activity, that will be potent evidence of failures at that level.

6.127 In this context, the *Guide to the Corporate Manslaughter and Corporate Homicide Act 2007*, notes the existence of new guidance, entitled 'Leading health and safety: leadership actions for directors and board members', being drawn up jointly by the Health and Safety Commission and the Institute of Directors, which has now been published.

---

[72] *Hansard*, HL Grand Committee, Column 134 (11 January 2007).

F. The Senior Management Requirement

3. The test for 'senior management'

6.128 On its face, the definition of an organization's senior management under the Act has a far wider compass than merely those, under common law, who constituted the 'directing minds' of a company, which was effectively limited to a company's Board of Directors. The difficulty with the definition of 'senior management' is that it is constructed of terms that have no established meaning in either legislation or case law.

6.129 Section s 1(4)(c) provides:

(c) 'senior management', in relation to an organisation, means the persons who play significant roles in—
i) the making of decisions about how the whole or a substantial part of its activities are to be managed or organised, or
ii) the actual managing or organising of the whole or a substantial part of those activities.

6.130 Employees at every level but the most junior in very many organizations are described as 'managers'. To a greater or lesser extent each is likely to be involved in the 'actual managing or organising' of a part of the organization's activities if they do not additionally make decisions about the managing or organizing of those activities. At the lower end, decisions about which employee is to perform a task or even what type of ladder should be used to change a light bulb would appear capable of being held to be the making of decisions about how the organization's activities are to be managed or organized or to involve the actual managing or organising' of a part of the organization's activities.

6.131 Thus the terms 'significant roles' and the 'whole or a substantial part of its activities' are the key limitations that inform the meaning of 'senior management' in s 1(4)(c). Having posed the question, 'Who are an organisation's senior management?', the *Guide to the Corporate Manslaughter and Corporate Homicide Act 2007* answers in the following way:[73]

- These are the people who make significant decisions about the organisation, or substantial parts of it. This includes both those carrying out headquarters functions (for example, central financial or strategic roles or with central responsibility for, for example, health and safety) as well as those in senior operational management roles.
- Exactly who is a member of an organisation's senior management will depend on the nature and scale of an organisation's activities. Apart from directors and similar senior management positions, roles likely to be under consideration include regional managers in national organisations and the managers of different operational divisions.

---

[73] *Guide to the Corporate Manslaughter and Corporate Homicide Act 2007*, (Ministry of Justice) October 2007, p 13.

(a) *Significant roles*

6.132 What are significant roles? In *Lambeth London Borough Council v Grewal* 82 Cr App Rep 301; [1986] Crim LR 260, the Divisional Court was concerned with an appeal by way of case stated concerning the definition of 'sex shop'. The Local Government (Miscellaneous Provisions) Act 1982, Sch 3, para 4(1) defined 'sex shop' as meaning any premises used for a business which 'consisted to significant degree of selling. . . sex articles'.

6.133 In that case Mustill LJ, rejected the approach of holding that 'significant', in the context of that statutory instrument, was to be left to a court of trial to measure the facts against its own understanding of the word. Reference was made to the 'not wholly dissimilar word "substantial"', in respect of which it was said appellate courts 'have indeed set out to provide a gloss'.[74] In the opinion of Mustill LJ, leaving the meaning of words in ordinary speech deliberately without interpretation was 'most appropriate where the word under discussion has only one meaning or, at any rate, one meaning which is predominant over any other. Here, it seems to me that "significant" does have more than one shade of meaning, and I believe that the appellate court must identify the meaning which it is intended to have in the context of the 1982 Act'.

6.134 The judgment rejected the notion that the meaning of 'significant' could be arrived at by assuming that it was the obverse of 'insignificant'. Mustill LJ said:

In the result, I would express my opinion as follows. The word 'significant' has more than one meaning. It is capable, in some contexts, of meaning 'more than trifling'. It does not have this meaning in the present context.

6.135 A similar approach, of rejecting 'insignificant' as a means to defining 'significant', was adopted by Potter LJ in *Ramsden v Secretary of State for Work and Pensions* [2203] EWCA Civ 32, in an appeal from a decision of the Social Security Commissioner which concerned the meaning of 'significant portion of the day' in Social Security (Contributions Benefits) Act 1992, s 72(1)(a)(i).

6.136 Potter LJ described how he did 'not find such a method of definition of real assistance' and that, 'If resort is to be had to the dictionary', the words of definition in the *Concise Oxford Dictionary* that provided a more helpful guide to the meaning of the word 'significant' in the context of that statute were: 'of considerable amount or effect or importance'.

6.137 In relation to the term 'significant roles' in the definition of senior management in s 1(3) of the Act it appears that the word 'significant' does have more than one potential meaning: 'something more than trivial or trifling' is very different to 'of considerable amount or effect or importance'. It remains to be seen whether a trial judge when directing a jury will treat the word as one not requiring further definition or guidance, being a word in ordinary English use; if not, in the context of a

---

[74] At p 306.

F. The Senior Management Requirement

statute creating criminal liability, the meaning 'of considerable amount or effect or importance' would appear to be appropriate, being the construction most favourable to the defendant.

(b) *'Whole or a substantial part of its activities'*

As was noted by Mustill LJ, 'substantial' is a word which the appellate courts have 'set out to provide a gloss'.[75] Some years later, this time giving the leading speech in the House of Lords case of *South Yorkshire Transport Ltd and another v Monopolies and Mergers Commission and another* [1993] 1 All ER 289 [HL], a case concerned with the interpretation of the words 'substantial part' in the phrase 'in the United Kingdom, or in a substantial part of the United Kingdom' in Fair Trading Act 1973, s 64(1)(a)(3), Mustill LJ stated:

6.138

no recourse need be made to dictionaries to establish that 'substantial' accommodates a wide range of meanings. At one extreme there is 'not trifling'. At the other, there is 'nearly complete', as where someone says that he is in substantial agreement with what has just been said. In between, there exist many shades of meaning, drawing colour from their context.

Mustill LJ could not accept that 'substantial' can never mean 'more than de minimis', but in the context of the statute he was satisfied that 'the word does indeed lie further up the spectrum than that.' However, he added, 'To say how far up is another matter. The courts have repeatedly warned against the dangers of taking an inherently imprecise word, and by redefining it thrusting on it a spurious degree of precision. I will try to avoid such an error.'

6.139

In the event, in the context of 'substantial part', Mustill LJ held that various factors were relevant and he provided the formulation that this conveyed 'of such size, character and importance'.[76]

6.140

However, in a criminal context, the word 'substantial' appears in the phrase 'substantial impairment of mental responsibility', which is the test of diminished responsibility in Homicide Act 1957, s 2(1) and whether a defendant has established he was suffering from such substantial impairment is an issue for a jury to resolve.

6.141

In *R v Lloyd* (1966) 50 Cr App R 61, the Court of Appeal was concerned with an appeal based upon the adequacy of the summing up of Ashworth J. The Court approved directions as to the word 'substantial' to the effect that the jury should approach the word in a broad common sense way and the following:

6.142

I am not going to try to find a parallel for the word 'substantial'. You are the judge, but your own common sense will tell you what it means. This far I will go. Substantial need not be totally impaired, so to speak, destroyed altogether. At the other end of the scale substantial does not mean trivial or minimal. It is something in between and Parliament has left it to you and other juries to say on the evidence, was the mental responsibility impaired, and, if so, was it substantially impaired?

---

[75] At p 306.
[76] At p 307.

6.143 Subsequently, in *R v Egan* (1992) 95 Cr App R 278, the Court indicated that guidance as to the meaning of 'substantial' should be explicitly provided for a jury by using one or other of these two meanings, that is i) the jury should approach the word in a broad commonsense way, or 2) that the word meant more than trivial but less than total.

6.144 The definition of 'senior management' in s 1(4)(c) remains unchanged from the draft Bill that was scrutinized by the Joint Committees. The then Lord Chief Justice, Lord Woolf, provided a written memorandum to the Joint Committees highlighting this very issue and giving his opinion as to how:

> there may be some difficulty created by the word 'substantial', in the phrase 'substantial part of its activities'. Is it different from 'significant' (as in the phrase 'plays a significant role')? Does it mean major, or only 'more than trivial'? It may be thought inappropriate for judges to offer further definitions of their own when summing up if the word is incapable of further definition in the statute; but if they do not, it will be left to each jury to define the term themselves. . . The question of whether a business unit represents a substantial part of the organisation's activities does not involve a value judgment, and the answer should not vary from case to case in respect of broadly similar organisations. I cannot offer a definition myself, but this phrase warrants further scrutiny.[77]

6.145 During the debate in Grand Committee in the House of Lords, Lord Bassam described the Government's view that:

> 'substantial' is intended to convey a quantitative sense, so that the part of the organisation will be large. We think that using the word 'significant' runs the risk—I put it no higher than that—that high-profile areas of business will be given undue weight and that possibly large but otherwise lower-profile areas could be considered 'insignificant'.[78]

6.146 It would appear that 'substantial part of its activities' could convey such a part of the activities of the organization that can be described as more than trivial in terms of its scope, character and importance. Potentially relevant factors to this consideration can be identified, these would include, the number of staff employed, turnover or output generated, working space occupied and the importance in terms of the organization's reputation.

6.147 Whether a trial judge adopts any further direction to a jury beyond the words of the statute remains to be seen.

4. A substantial element of the breach

6.148 Section 1(3) requires that an organization is guilty of the offence of corporate manslaughter only if the way in which its activities are managed or organized by its senior management is a substantial element in the breach.

---

[77] First Joint Report from the Home Affairs and Work and Pensions Committees Session 2005–06. Minutes of Evidence (HC -540-II), Volume II, Ev 108.
[78] *Hansard*, HL, Grand Committee, Column 150 (11 January 2007).

F. The Senior Management Requirement

Thus, having defined senior management in terms of 'significant role' in the way in which a 'substantial part' of an organization's activities are managed or organized, the jury must go on to consider whether that role was a 'substantial element' in the gross breach of the relevant duty of care. 6.149

The common law offence of manslaughter by gross negligence in its application to corporations was undermined by two related problems: the identification doctrine provided that only the gross breach of an individual 'directing mind', and not the aggregated lesser failings of more than one such 'directing mind', could attach to the corporation;[79] secondly, at common law, directors and those who manage a company do not owe a duty of care to any third party by reason of holding such an office,[80] nor do they owe a duty of care in relation to the company's compliance with laws, certainly not such a duty of care in respect of the company's non-delegable statutory health and safety duties as employer,[81] and will only owe any duty of care as a result of some particular assumption or appointment of responsibility.[82] Thus while a company could only be grossly negligent through its directors, nonetheless proving the existence of a duty of care owed by such a director was very difficult. 6.150

The 'way' in which an organization's activities are managed or organized by its senior management, for the purposes of s 1(3), denotes neither individual responsibility nor something 'wrongful' or 'unlawful': for s 1(3), the prosecution is not required to prove a negligent act or omission by any one senior manager nor even that the aggregated acts amount to some failing of compliance with a duty. 6.151

The 'way' is a term that appears broad enough to encompass decisions, acts or even inactivity and indecision: the *Oxford Dictionary of English* defines 'way' as 'a method, style, or manner of doing something'. Presumably, the prosecution would seek to criticize or censure such an identified decision, act, inactivity or indecision on the part of senior management, perhaps by reference to the same factors as are set out in s 8 as being relevant to a jury's consideration of 'gross' breach, particularly the organization's duties under health and safety legislation and the indicators of an 'organizational culture' in s 8(3)(a),[83] but not necessarily so. 6.152

Of those indicators in s 8(3)(a), 'policies' and 'systems' referable to senior management would appear to be pertinent to senior management; borrowing the words used by s 8(3) it can be speculated that 'attitudes' and 'accepted practices' which senior management can be proven to have 'encouraged' or 'tolerated' would be significant. 6.153

---

[79] *Attorney-General's Reference* (No 1 of 1995) [1996] 2 Cr App R 320.
[80] *Performing Right Society Ltd v Ciryl Theatrical Syndicate Ltd* [1924] 1 KB 1 at 14; *Williams and another v Natural Life Health Foods Ltd and another* [1997] 1 BCLC 131 (CA); *Williams and Another v Natural Life Health Foods Ltd* (HL) [1998] 2 All ER 577.
[81] *Huckerby v Elliot* [1970] 1 ALL ER 189, DC; *R v P and another* [2007] All ER (D) 173 (Jul).
[82] *R v Great Western Trains Company Ltd* (unreported) Central Criminal Court, 30 June 1999, per Scott-Baker J; *Williams and Another v Natural Life Health Foods Ltd* (HL) [1998] 2 All ER 577.
[83] See paras 6.105–6.110.

6.154　This 'way' the organization's activities are managed or organized by its senior management must be shown to have been a 'substantial element' in the breach of the relevant duty of care; while, undeniably, the word has more than one meaning, 'substantial', in this context, would appear to be consistent with the meaning given in *R v Lloyd*,[84] in relation to 'substantial impairment', of being something more than trivial but less than complete.

6.155　An 'element' is defined in the *Oxford Dictionary of English* as an 'essential or characteristic part of something abstract'.

6.156　'Substantial element' may be another term that trial judges will not attempt to expand upon and leave to a jury's interpretation. The 'way' the organization's activities are managed or organized by its senior management must be proved to have had a direct relationship to the gross breach of the relevant duty of care: this 'way' must be more a 'substantial element' of what amounted to the organization's breach, in the sense of more than trivial in terms of its importance.

5. Summary: the meaning of the 'senior management' requirement

6.157　The 'senior management' requirement is constructed of a number of arguably nebulous terms; juries may be left to apply the relevant facts, as they find them, to the meaning of each of these terms, as they interpret them, using a 'commonsense' approach; alternatively, trial judges may attempt to give guidance as to the meaning of some, or all, of these terms.

6.158　The following represents an attempt to provide some expansion of the meaning of these terms:

- The senior management of an organization are those persons who play significant roles, (in the sense of a role of considerable effect or importance), in the either the making of decisions about how, or the actual managing or organizing of, the whole or a substantial part, (being such a part of the activities of the organization that can be described as more than trivial in terms of size).
- The 'way' the organization's activities are managed or organized by its senior management must be proved to have had a direct relationship to the gross breach of the relevant duty of care: this 'way' must be a substantial element in the organization's breach, in the sense of more than trivial in terms of importance.
- The 'way' in which an organization's activities are managed or organized by its senior management does not necessarily involve a negligent act or omission by any one senior manager nor even that the aggregated acts amount to some failure to comply with a duty; the 'way' suggests 'a method, style, or manner of doing something'.

---

[84] (1966) 50 Cr App R 61.

7
SENTENCE AND ORDERS UPON CONVICTION

A.	Overview	7.01
B.	Sentence by way of Fine	7.03
	1. The Sentencing Advisory Panel consultation paper	7.06
	2. Sentence in health and safety cases	7.18
	3. Sentencing public bodies and the 'public element'	7.29
	4. The means of the organization and relevant financial information	7.33
C.	Remedial Orders and Publicity Orders	7.44
	1. Remedial orders	7.45
	2. Publicity orders	7.53

A. OVERVIEW

7.01 The offence of corporate manslaughter is punishable by way of fine. The Sentencing Advisory Panel has been asked by the Sentencing Guidelines Council to produce advice on sentencing in respect of the offence. The Panel has produced a consultation paper and invited responses to be received by February 2008. It is anticipated that thereafter the Panel will publish advice on guidelines for use by sentencers to roughly coincide with the date of the Act coming into force, on 6 April 2008.

7.02 The Act also creates two powers that a sentencing judge may exercise to impose upon an organization convicted of the offence a remedial order, under s 9, and a publicity order, under s 10. Failure to comply with such an order is an offence punishable by way of fine.

B. SENTENCE BY WAY OF FINE

7.03 Section 1(6) of the Act provides that an organization that is guilty of corporate manslaughter 'is liable on conviction to a fine'.

7.04 On 15 November 2007 the Sentencing Advisory Panel published a consultation paper to which it invited responses to be received by February 2008. The consultation paper outlines both the offence of corporate manslaughter and existing offences under health and safety legislation, before turning to consider the factors which may influence an assessment of the seriousness of these offences.

7.05 In the consultation paper, the Panel notes how there are many similarities between the two types of offence and how the existing guidance on sentencing under health and safety law may provide a useful starting point for the approach to corporate manslaughter. However, according to the Panel, they are separate and distinct offences, and the paper draws attention to differences which may be relevant to sentencing.[1]

1. The Sentencing Advisory Panel consultation paper

7.06 The consultation paper sets out a proposed approach to sentencing for corporate manslaughter and for breaches of the Health and Safety at Work etc. Act 1974 (HSWA) resulting in death based upon an assessment of the seriousness of the offence. The paper suggests that the primary factor in assessing the seriousness of an offence of corporate manslaughter or of a HSWA offence that has resulted in death is the extent to which the conduct of the offender fell below the appropriate standard of care.

7.07 The Panel has devised a list of potential aggravating and mitigating features, based upon the approach of Scott-Baker LJ in *R v Howe & Sons (Engineers) Ltd* [1999] 2 Cr App R (S) 37. The paper suggests that the following aggravating or mitigating factors are relevant:

- aggravating factors increasing the level of harm:
  - more than one person killed
  - serious injury to one or more person(s)
- aggravating factors affecting the degree of culpability:
  - failure to act upon advice, cautions or warning from regulatory authorities
  - failure to heed relevant concerns of employees or others
  - carrying out operations without an appropriate licence
  - financial or other inappropriate motive
  - corporate culture encouraging or producing tolerance of breach of duty
- mitigating factor
  - employee acting outside authority or failing in duties
- offender mitigation
  - ready co-operation with authorities
  - good safety record.

---

[1] The consultation document is available at <http://www.sentencing-guidelines.gov.uk/>.

B. Sentence by Way of Fine

7.08 Concerning the potential mitigating factor of an employee acting outside the scope of his authority or failing in his duties, the consultation paper notes:

> If a death has resulted from the actions of a maverick employee acting outside authority, in most cases the offence of corporate manslaughter will not be made out. However, there may be convictions under the CMA where the immediate failure of an employee (whether or not the person who died) also contributed to the offence. In such a case the court will take the contributory conduct into consideration, but the fact that the offence involves a gross breach of the relevant duty of care suggests that any impact on sentence will be limited.[2]

7.09 The Panel suggests in the consultation document that the aims of the imposition of a fine should be:

- to reflect the serious concern at the loss of life
- to ensure future compliance with safety standards
- to eliminate financial benefit.

7.10 Of this last aim, the Panel noted how the recent Macrory review of regulatory penalties[3] recommended that these should aim to eliminate any financial gain or benefit resulting from non-compliance with safety standards on the basis that if the expected penalty cost does not outweigh the expected gain from the offence, an organization might choose to take the risk of being detected and prosecuted. The Panel's position was that while, in principle, it should not be cheaper to offend than to prevent the commission of an offence, however, eliminating any financial benefit from the offence is unlikely to be achievable in all circumstances. The consultation document suggests that a court should request details of any gain made from the offence if such information is available, but notes how it is unclear how profits made or costs that have been avoided, deferred or saved would be calculated.

7.11 In fulfilling these aims, the Panel notes that a court is obliged to have regard to both the seriousness of the offence and the financial circumstances of the offender. The Panel further comments on the widely held desire for a consistent method of calculating the fine to reflect the seriousness of the offence and the financial circumstances of the offender and the widely perceived lack of consistency in fines imposed in respect of health and safety offences. However, in the Panel's view, consistency of *approach* rather than *outcome* (ie quantum) is the aim, as the organization's ability to pay must be taken into account. As a result, the consultation document considers a number of methods that could be used to develop a consistent approach to the setting of financial penalties for such offences before expressing the Panel's provisional view: that annual turnover is the most appropriate measure of an organization's ability to pay a fine.

---

[2] Sentencing Advisory Panel, *Consultation Paper on Sentencing for Corporate Manslaughter* (November 2007) para 29.
[3] R Macrory, *Regulatory Justice; Making Sanctions Effective* (2006).

7. Sentence and Orders upon Conviction

7.12   The Panel proposes starting points and ranges expressed as percentages of annual turnover. It suggest that it would be for the prosecution to provide evidence of particularly high profitability if it considered the fine indicated by annual turnover to be too low, or for the offender to provide evidence of low liquidity if it considered the fine indicated by annual turnover to be too high.

7.13   The Panel's view is that a fine imposed for an offence under the CMCHA should be set at a level significantly higher than for an offence under the HSWA involving death. The Panel's provisional starting point for an offence of corporate manslaughter committed by a first time offender pleading not guilty is a fine amounting to 5 per cent of the offender's average annual turnover during the three years prior to sentencing. The proposal is that the court will then take into account any aggravating and/or mitigating factors, arriving at a fine which will normally fall within a range of 2.5 to 10 per cent of average annual turnover. Significant aggravating factors or previous convictions may take the fine beyond the range. The court will then consider any mitigation related to the offender (rather than the offence), which may take the fine below the range.

7.14   The Panel's provisional starting point for an offence under the HSWA involving death is a fine amounting to 2.5 per cent of average annual turnover during the three years prior to the offence. The Panel suggest that fine will normally fall within a range of 1 to 7.5 per cent of average annual turnover.

7.15   The consultation paper spells out that where the offender is a very large organization, the Panel's provisional approach would result in larger fines than have been imposed previously by the courts and suggests that a fine expressed as a percentage of average annual turnover is designed to have an equal economic impact on all sizes of organization, in order to reflect the seriousness of the offence even where the offender has large financial resources.

7.16   Under the Panel's proposed approach an offender should be required to provide comprehensive accounts for a three-year period, to enable the court to make an accurate assessment of its financial status. The consultation paper describes how this period will usually be the last three financial years, but the court should be alert to the possibility that the organization may try to rearrange its finances in order to receive a lower fine, particularly where several years have passed between the offence and the imposition of sentence. Where three years or more have passed in the interim, the court may also wish to examine accounts from a period prior to the offence. The consultation document adopts the suggestion that a financial pre-sentence report would be desirable in principle, but notes how it is unclear how and by whom such a report would be provided.

7.17   In respect of compensation, the Panel adopts the existing approach in HSWA cases, namely that the level of complexity surrounding the calculation of compensation is likely to be such that it is an issue best resolved outside the criminal proceedings. Thus the document notes that whilst a court is always under an obligation to consider whether a compensation order can be made, it is more likely that a court will decide to leave the issue to the civil court.

B. Sentence by Way of Fine

2. Sentence in health and safety cases

With the Panel's proposals being modelled upon the guidelines in health and safety cases, the approach of the courts is likely to be firmly based upon such existing principle. The 1999 guideline case of *R v Howe & Son (Engineers) Ltd* [1999] 2 Cr App R (S) 37 saw Scott Baker LJ provide an analysis of how fines in health and safety cases had been perceived as, and were, too low. The judgment in *Howe* articulates that a fine in a health and safety case should be large enough 'to bring the message home', not only to those who manage a company but also to its shareholders.[4] Scott Baker LJ then set out relevant factors, aggravating features and mitigating features which were to inform a judge's approach to fixing the level of fine in health and safety cases. Since that time, the *Howe* factors have been adopted as a basis for the approach to sentencing corporations in relation to other criminal offences, such as environmental offences.[5]

7.18

The Court of Appeal in *Howe*[6] stressed how there could be no tariff in respect of health and safety cases, because the facts and relevant features of individual cases will vary almost infinitely, and have subsequently commented how, for this reason, consistency of sentence across such cases may not be an aim of courts.[7] While this message was recently endorsed by the Lord Chief Justice,[8] nonetheless something approaching a tariff has undoubtedly crept in: in *R v Colthrop Board Mills Ltd* [2002] 2 Cr App R (S) 359. the Court noted:

7.19

It appears from the authorities that financial penalties of up to around half a million pounds are appropriate for cases which result in the death even of a single employee, and perhaps of the serious injury to such a single employee. We would not wish the sum of £500,000 to appear to be set in stone or to provide any sort of maximum limit for such cases. On the contrary, we anticipate that as time goes on and awareness of the importance of safety increases, that courts will uphold sums of that amount and even in excess of them in serious cases, whether or not they involve what could be described as major public disasters.[9]

However, the most decisive factor has proved to be the means of the offending corporation. Assessing the means of an organization, and how this should be done by a court has been another important feature of health and safety cases; with the Court of Appeal stressing how it is not possible to say that a fine should stand in any specific relationship with a turnover or net profit.[10] The approach proposed by the

7.20

---

[4] [1999] 2 Cr App R (S) 37 at 44.
[5] See *R v Milford Haven Port Authority* [2000] 2 Cr App R (S) 423.
[6] [1999] 2 Cr App R (S) 37.
[7] See *R v Jarvis* [2006] Cr App R (S) 44, at para 7; *R v Balfour Beatty Rail Infrastructure Services Ltd* [2006] EWCA Crim 1586, at para 23.
[8] See *R v Transco* [2006] EWCA Crim 838, at paras [22]–[24]; and *R v Balfour Beatty*.
[9] [2002] 2 Cr App R (S) 80 [22] .
[10] See *R v Howe & Son (Engineers) Ltd* [1999] 2 Cr App R (S) 37 and *Balfour Beatty Rail Infrastructure Services* [2006] EWCA Crim 1586.

Sentencing Advisory Panel in its consultation paper is for a starting point based upon a percentage of an organization's turnover.

(a) *The Howe factors*

7.21 The guideline factors identified by Scott-Baker LJ in *R v Howe & Son (Engineers) Ltd*[11] are set out below. A sentencing judge should consider:

(a) How far short the defendant fell from doing what was reasonably practicable.
(b) Whether death or serous injury resulted from the breach. Death resulting from any breach was to be regarded as an aggravating factor.
(c) Whether the defendant deliberately profited from a failure to take necessary health and safety measures or run a risk to save money. If so, it will be a seriously aggravating feature.
(d) The degree of risk and the extent of the danger created by the offence.
(e) The extent of the breach—whether it was an isolated incident, or whether it had been continuing for a period of time.
(f) A failure to heed warnings amounts to another aggravating factor.

7.22 Mitigating factors include: a prompt admission of responsibility and a timely plea of guilty; steps taken to remedy deficiencies after they were drawn to the defendant's attention; and a good safety record.

7.23 A conviction for corporate manslaughter would, by definition, involve the causing of a death (b), that the organization had fallen far below the standard expected in the circumstances (a) and the presence of a substantial degree of risk of death (d); however, it would appear, that factors (c), (e) and (f) would be matters a sentencing judge would asses and have regard to.

(b) *R v Balfour Beatty Rail Infrastructure Services Ltd and Transco Plc*

7.24 Both the *Balfour Beatty Rail Infrastructure Services Ltd* conviction and that of *Transco Plc* in Scotland for health and safety offences followed failed manslaughter by gross negligence allegations that foundered on the 'identification' doctrine. Both cases involved allegations of management failures having caused deaths.

7.25 In *R v Balfour Beatty Rail Infrastructure Services Ltd* [2006] EWCA Crim. 1586, the court was concerned with an appeal from the fine imposed upon the company by Mr Justice Mackay. The fine constituted £10 million, and £300,000 costs, for the breach of the duty to ensure the safety of persons affected by the employer's conduct of his undertaking, under the HSWA, s 3 duty. This had been an operating cause of the Hatfield rail disaster on 17 October 2000, in which 102 passengers were injured and four lost their lives. The court endorsed the sentencing judge's summary of the guidance taken from health and safety cases, which he had reduced to 13 propositions.[12]

---

[11] [1999] 2 Cr App R (S) 37.
[12] [2006] EWCA Crim. 1586, at para 22.

B. Sentence by Way of Fine

Many of the Lord Chief Justice's comments in that case are equally apposite to the offence of corporate manslaughter. In his judgment he referred to the objectives of sentencing, which are expressly set out in Criminal Justice Act 2003, 142, before considering the duty under HSWA 1974 , s 3, to ensure the safety of persons affected by an employer's conduct of his undertaking, stating: 7.26

> Knowledge that breach of this duty can result in a fine of sufficient size to impact on shareholders will provide a powerful incentive for management to comply with this duty. This is not to say that the fine must always be large enough to affect dividends or share price. But the fine must reflect both the degree of fault and the consequences so as to raise appropriate concern on the part of shareholders at what has occurred. Such an approach will satisfy the requirement that the sentence should act as a deterrent. It will also satisfy the requirement, which will rightly be reflected by public opinion, that a company should be punished for culpable failure to pay due regard for safety, and for the consequences of that failure.[13]

In the event, the Court reduced the fine to £7.5 million, not because it was wrong in principle but purely because of what was found to be the disparity between the sentence on the company and that imposed upon the co-defendant, Railtrack. 7.27

In *R v Transco Plc*, the company was fined a record £15 million, at the High Court of Justiciary in Edinburgh, after a jury found it guilty of an offence contrary to HWSA, s 3. The charge arose from an explosion caused by a leaking gas main which destroyed a family home, killing its two adult and two child occupants, in December 1999. The Sentencing Advisory Panel, in its consultation paper, notes how this represented 5 per cent of the company's after-tax profits and less than 1 per cent of annual turnover and thus had not necessarily provided an effective individual or general deterrent. 7.28

3. Sentencing public bodies and the 'public element'

With the increased potential for organizations responsible for public services to be liable in respect of corporate manslaughter, the approach of the Court of Appeal to the sentencing of 'public bodies' may prove highly relevant and appears to have been adopted in the consultation paper issued by the Sentencing Advisory Panel. 7.29

In *R v Milford Haven Port Authority* [2000] 2 Cr App R (S) 423, the Court of Appeal reduced a fine of £4million to £750,000. This was done for a number of different reasons. Among the submissions made, on behalf of the appellant, was that the status of the Port Authority, as a public trust port, was relevant to determining the appropriate level of fine. In argument, it was said that this was 'not because such bodies are subject to any lesser standard of duty or care in safety or environmental matters, but because the burden of paying the fine falls not on shareholders or directors or employees of the company but on either customers of the Port Authority... or the public on whose behalf the Port Authority carries out its operations.'[14] 7.30

---

[13] [2006] EWCA Crim 1586 at paras 42–3.
[14] [2000] 2 Cr App R (S) 423.

7.31   The Court of Appeal held that whereas it would be wrong to suggest that public bodies are immune from criminal penalties because they have no shareholders and the directors do not receive 'handsome annual bonuses', the sentencing judge does have to consider how any financial penalty will be paid, and the effect of a very substantial penalty on the proper performance by a statutory body was not something to be disregarded.[15]

7.32   The *Milford Haven* decision is to be viewed alongside, and contrasted with, *Jarvis Facilities Ltd* [2006] Cr App R (S) 44. In that case, the court said that it was entitled to take a more severe view of breaches of health and safety legislation where there is 'a significant public element'. The court observed:

> This is particularly so in cases (like the railway) where public safety is entrusted to companies in the work that they do...in our view public service cases will often be treated more seriously than those in which the breaches are confined within the private sector even where there is comparability between gravity of breach and economic strength of defendant.[16]

4. The means of the organization and relevant financial information

7.33   In *R v F Howe & Son (Engineers) Ltd* [1999] 2 Cr App R (S) 37, the court also gave guidance as to the financial information to be provided by a corporate defendant, for the purpose of sentencing:

> The starting point is its annual accounts. If a defendant company wishes to make any submission to the court about its inability to pay a fine, it should supply copies of its accounts and any other financial information on which it intends to rely in good time before the hearing both to the court and to the prosecution. This will give the prosecution the opportunity to assist the court should the court wish it. Usually, accounts need to be considered with some care to avoid reaching a superficial and perhaps erroneous conclusion. Where accounts or other financial information are deliberately not supplied, the court will be entitled to conclude that the company is in a position to pay any financial penalty it is minded to impose. Where the relevant information is provided late it may be desirable for sentence to be adjourned, if necessary at the defendant's expense, so as to avoid the risk of the court taking what it is told at face value and imposing an inadequate penalty.

7.34   However, in the case of *R v Transco Plc* [2006] EWCA Crim 838, the Court of Appeal clarified a particular issue. A court imposing a fine will always wish to have some information in relation to the means of the offender. It may not always be necessary, however, for the court to have detailed particulars of the financial position of a company when sentencing in health and safety cases, where it is made plain that the company's means are 'very substantial'.

7.35   Whilst Criminal Justice Act 2003, s 162 provides a court with a power to make a 'financial circumstances order', requiring a convicted person to provide such a

---

[15] [1999] 2 Cr App R (S) 37.
[16] [2006] Cr App R (S) 44 at para 11.

B. Sentence by Way of Fine

statement of his financial circumstances as the court may require, the provision applies only to an 'individual', being a term that does not include a company within its meaning and thus would not encompass an organization under the Act.[17]

7.36 While most of the organizations subject to the Act will prepare annual accounts of some form, there presently appears no power to compel production of the same to a sentencing court, other than the threat of treating the organization as having sufficient means to be able to pay whatever fine the court considers appropriate.

7.37 One of the recommendations of the Joint Committees was that courts should have a 'pre-sentence report' on a convicted company partly in order to have details of its financial status.[18] However, no provision was included in the Act as the Government's response was that it was, 'satisfied that the courts have sufficient authority to require this information from the parties involved in the case where necessary.'[19] The Sentencing Advisory Panel have now invited representations as to the benefit of adopting this course and the idea of the preparation of financial pre-sentence reports following conviction for an offence of corporate manslaughter.

7.38 The principle that the level of fine should be proportionate to the means of the offender is now formally enshrined by the Criminal Justice Act 2003 and was referred to during the judgment of the Lord Chief Justice, in the case of *R v Transco Plc*.[20]

7.39 Section 164 of the Criminal Justice Act 2003, provides:

Fixing of Fines
(1) Before fixing the amount of any fine to be imposed on an offender who is an individual, a court must inquire into his financial circumstances.
(2) The amount of any fine fixed by a court must be such as, in the opinion of the court, reflects the seriousness of the offence.
(3) In fixing the amount of any fine to be imposed on an offender (whether an individual or other person), a court must take into account the circumstances of the case including, among other things, the financial circumstances of the offender so far as they are known or appear to the court.
(4) Subsection (3) above applies whether taking into account the financial circumstances of the offender has the effect of increasing or reducing the amount of the fine.

7.40 However, in *Howe*,[21] whilst the Court acknowledged that generally a fine 'should not be so large as to imperil the earnings of employees or create a risk of bankruptcy', nonetheless it observed how 'there may be cases where the offences are so serious

---

[17] See para 2.33.
[18] First Joint Report from the Home Affairs and Work and Pensions Committees Session 2005–06 (HC540), para 268.
[19] The Government Reply to the First Joint Report from the Home Affairs and Work and Pensions Committees Session 2005–06 (Cm 6755), p 26.
[20] [2006] EWCA Crim 838 at para 25.
[21] [1999] 2 Cr App R (S) 37.

that the defendant ought not to be in business'.[22] It can be observed that a sentencing court may have more of a basis and justification for so finding following a conviction for corporate manslaughter.

(a) *Sentencing an organization that is part of a wider group*

7.41 It is common for companies to be connected to an organization that wholly owns its shares or be part of a wider group of wholly owned companies. A company's statutory accounts are now required to reveal the nature of group ownership and inter-group transactions, thus, to a large extent, revealing the economic realities of a subsidiary company's affairs.

7.42 The issue has frequently arisen in health and safety cases as to whether a court should it direct its punishment towards the single organization convicted of the offence, or towards the wider group or corporate structure.

7.43 Sentencing courts in health and safety cases have frequently looked beyond a defendant company, to the means of the wider corporate family. For example, in *R v Brintons Ltd*,[23] the Court of Appeal looked at the corporate group, of which the defendant company was a part, and took into account its annual turnover of some £91 million per year and in *R v Keltbray Ltd* [2000] 1 Cr App R (S) 132, where the Court considered group company profits.

C. REMEDIAL ORDERS AND PUBLICITY ORDERS

7.44 The Act creates two orders that a judge may impose upon an organization upon conviction of an organization for an offence of corporate manslaughter. A remedial order requiring the organization to take specified steps to remedy matters and a publicity order, requiring an organization to publicize details of its conviction.

1. Remedial orders

7.45 The power to make a remedial order under s 9 appears very similar to the power given to a judge by HWSA s 42, which provides that where a person is convicted of a health and safety offence and there appears to the court to be matters in respect of which he was convicted which it is in his power to remedy, the court may, in addition to, or instead of, imposing any punishment, order him, within such time as may be fixed by the order, to take such steps as may be specified in the order for remedying the matters.

7.46 This power has been rarely, if ever exercised, by a judge. This is for the reason that all such matters will have been remedied, in the usual course of events, during the course of any investigation. Remedy will have been secured either voluntarily, or

---

[22] At p 44.
[23] (CA 22 June 1999).

C. Remedial Orders and Publicity Orders

through the service upon the organization of improvement or prohibition notices (pursuant to HWSA ss 21 and 22) by a health and safety inspector.

The same would appear to be the position with the s 9 power to impose a remedial order, especially bearing in mind the likely passage of time between the commission of the offence and any conviction. 7.47

Section 9(1) provides that a court before which an organization is convicted of corporate manslaughter may make a remedial order requiring the organization to take specified steps to remedy: 7.48

(a) the gross breach of the relevant duty of care ('the relevant breach');
(b) any matter that appears to the court to have resulted from the relevant breach and to have been a cause of the death;
(c) any deficiency, as regards health and safety matters, in the organisation's policies, systems or practices of which the relevant breach appears to the court to be an indication.

A remedial order may be made only on an application by the prosecution specifying the terms of the proposed order.[24] Before making such an application, the prosecution is required to consult such enforcement authorities[25] (eg the Health and Safety Executive) as it considers appropriate having regard to the nature of the relevant breach.[26] 7.49

Any such order must be on such terms (whether those proposed or others) as the court considers appropriate having regard to any representations made, and any evidence adduced, in relation to that matter by the prosecution or on behalf of the organization.[27] 7.50

By s 9(4) a remedial order must specify a period within which the steps referred to in the order are to be taken and may require the organization to supply evidence that the steps have been taken, within a specified period, to any enforcement authority that was consulted by the prosecution. 7.51

By s 9(5), an organization that fails to comply with a remedial order is guilty of an indictable-only offence punishable by way of fine. 7.52

2. Publicity orders

The Hampton Review into regulation in the UK recommended that the Government establish a comprehensive review of regulators' penalty regimes. Following this recommendation, in November 2006, the final report of the Macrory Review of 7.53

---

[24] CMCHA, s 9(2).
[25] 'Enforcement Authority' is defined by s 25 to mean an authority responsible for the enforcement of any health and safety legislation, being defined by the same section as any statutory provision dealing with health and safety matters, including in particular provision contained in the Health and Safety at Work etc. Act 1974 or the Health and Safety at Work (Northern Ireland) Order 1978 (SI 1978/1039 (NI 9)).
[26] CMCHA, s 9(3).
[27] CMCHA, s 9(2).

Regulatory Penalties was published. The review made a number of recommendations including the introduction of new sanctions for criminal courts, these including proposals for 'Corporate Rehabilitation Orders' and publicity orders to be made against corporations following conviction. This appears to have been the genesis for the publicity order created by s 10 of the Act.

7.54 The Sentencing Advisory Panel, in its consultation paper, set out how the Panel's proposed starting point and range for the financial penalty are based on the premise that a publicity order will be imposed in every case of corporate manslaughter and, as such, a court should not need to give any further consideration to the effect of such an order on the overall sentence, that is, it should not consider reducing a fine to reflect the costs of compliance with any order. The Panel have not sought to provide draft detailed guidance on the extent of publicity to be included in any order, but have suggested that minimum standards may be set. For example, the consultation document suggests that if the offender is a local organization, it might normally be appropriate to require publication in the local media; in the case of a large national organization, publication in national media would be more effective. In both cases, a notice in all relevant trade journals should be required. Any shareholders should be notified in order that they may press for enhanced health and safety standards and publication should always be required in an annual report.

7.55 By s 10(1) a court before which an organization is convicted of corporate manslaughter may make a 'publicity order' requiring the organization to publicize in a 'specified manner':

(a) the fact that it has been convicted of the offence;
(b) specified particulars of the offence;
(c) the amount of any fine imposed;
(d) the terms of any remedial order made.

7.56 The Act does not particularize or otherwise limit the 'specified manner' and thus the section appears to give a sentencing judge a very wide power to compel the organization to publicize its conviction in any way.

7.57 In deciding on the terms of a publicity order that it is proposing to make, the court is required to ascertain the views of any such enforcement authorities[28] as it considers appropriate, and to have regard to any representations made by the prosecution or on behalf of the organization.[29]

7.58 A publicity order is required to specify a period within which the requirements in the order are to be complied with and may require the organization to supply, within a specified period, evidence that those requirements have been complied with to any enforcement authority whose views have been ascertained by the court.

7.59 By s 9(4) an organization that fails to comply with a publicity order is guilty of an indictable-only offence punishable by way of fine.

---

[28] For 'enforcement authority' see footnote 23.
[29] CMCHA, s 10(2).

8
INVESTIGATION AND REPRESENTATION

A. Overview	8.01
B. The Investigation of Corporate Manslaughter	8.05
1. The Home Office regulatory impact assessment	8.07
2. The Work-Related Death Protocol	8.14
3. Coroners Act 1988 s 16 and adjourned inquests	8.22
4. Police powers and corporate manslaughter	8.24
C. Representation	8.32

A. OVERVIEW

The investigation and prosecution of corporate manslaughter will remain the responsibility of the police and Crown Prosecution Service. As a result of the passage of the Act into law, the Home Office does not anticipate any significant increase in the number of investigations into work-related deaths for the police and estimates that there will be between 10–13 prosecutions a year. 8.01

The Work-Related Death Protocol will continue to govern investigations of suspected corporate manslaughter offences, with inquests being adjourned pending the completion of such criminal proceedings. 8.02

Police powers of search and seizure may be exercised through warrant under the Police and Criminal Evidence Act 1984 but police powers to arrest and interview under caution may prove to be of very limited application in enquiries involving an allegation of corporate manslaughter. 8.03

The existing terms of employers liability and public liability insurance policies are likely to provide a measure of funding for legal representation in respect of corporate manslaughter. 8.04

B. THE INVESTIGATION OF CORPORATE MANSLAUGHTER

The investigation and prosecution of corporate manslaughter will remain the responsibility of the police and Crown Prosecution Service. No additional police 8.05

8. Investigation and Representation

powers were included in the Act as the Government felt there was, 'not yet sufficient evidence to support the need'[1] for them.

8.06 The subject matter of corporate manslaughter investigations will arise from those killed in work-related incidents. The provisional figure for the number work related deaths[2] in 2006/07 is 241; 90 of whom were classed as being members of the public, in the sense of not having been engaged at work at the time of their death. In 2005/06, the finalized figure was 217 deaths, which was the lowest annual figure on record. While the 2006/07 figure showed an increase, there exists an established long-term downward trend but the rate of decrease has slowed over the last 15 years and there has been very little change in the overall rate over the last five years. The number of member of the public incidents reported has not shown any significant change over time.

1. The Home Office regulatory impact assessment

8.07 A regulatory impact assessment for England and Wales was published by the Home Office with the draft Bill in 2005. This was updated following consultation and amendment to the draft Bill including the incorporation of the application of the offence to Scotland and Northern Ireland in March 2006.

8.08 According to the Home Office,

> An estimate has been made of the likely number of prosecutions under the new offence, in order to make some assessments of the likely costs. It is estimated that there will be between 10–13 additional prosecutions a year, this would be around 3–4 per cent of recorded work related-deaths.[3]

8.09 This revised figure included an estimate that Scotland and Northern Ireland would account for two to three additional cases a year.

8.10 In respect of investigations, the Home Office described how it 'did not anticipate any significant increase in the number of investigations into work-related deaths for the police. In many cases, the offence is likely to facilitate new prosecutions on the basis of evidence that would currently be gathered. Some investigations will need to be fuller in the future than is currently the case and will be the responsibility of the police rather than the HSE or local authorities. However, cases that are most resource intensive, involving major public incidents, are already subject to full investigation. The proposals do not in themselves affect the operation of the current protocol for liaison between enforcement bodies involved in investigating and prosecuting work-related deaths.'[4]

---

[1] The Government Reply to the First Joint Report from the Home Affairs and Work and Pensions Committees Session 2005–06 (Cm 6755), p 31.
[2] Source of statistics: HSE fatal statistics: <http://www.hse.gov.uk/statistics/fatals.htm>.
[3] Corporate Manslaughter and Corporate Homicide: A Regulatory Impact Assessment of the Government's Bill, p 12.
[4] ibid p 13.

B. The Investigation of Corporate Manslaughter

That protocol is the Work-Related Death Protocol, which represents an agreement between the HSE, the Association of Chief Police Officers, the British Transport Police, the Local Government Association and the CPS upon the principles for effective liaison between the parties in relation to the investigation and prosecution of offences relating to work-related deaths. In addition, the Work-Related Death Investigators Guide[5] is intended as practical guidance and offers investigatory systems to be employed in furtherance of the protocol. 8.11

The Home Office Regulatory Impact Assessment recognized that, 'some deaths related to Crown bodies will give rise to an investigation that is wider than current police consideration of the fatality, but as the estimate of prosecutions is fewer than one a year any additional work for the police from Crown cases will arise very infrequently. 8.12

In respect of cases being referred to the Crown Prosecution Service to consider prosecution, the Home Office did not anticipate 'a large increase of entirely new cases being referred to the prosecution services to consider, although there are likely to be some, particularly in the early years, whilst the new offence beds in. . .we expect, in particular in the early years after introduction, that there would be an increase of 20–25 referrals each year. . . We would expect the number of referrals and costs to decrease as familiarity with the new offence increases.'[6] 8.13

2. The Work-Related Death Protocol

The Work-Related Death Protocol's underlying principles are that: 8.14

(a) an appropriate decision concerning prosecution will be made based on a sound investigation of the circumstances surrounding work-related deaths;
(b) the police will conduct an investigation where there is an indication of the commission of a serious criminal offence (other than a health and safety offence), and HSE, the local authority or other enforcing authority will investigate health and safety offences. There will usually be a joint investigation, but on the rare occasions where this would not be appropriate, there will still be liaison and cooperation between the investigating parties;
(c) the decision to prosecute will be co-coordinated, and made without undue delay;
(d) the bereaved and witnesses will be kept suitably informed; and
(e) the parties to the protocol will maintain effective mechanisms for liaison.

The Protocol contains a statement of intent that recognizes that in the early stages of an investigation, whether any serious criminal offence has been committed is not always apparent. The protocol describes that should there be any issue as to who is to be involved in investigating any work-related death, then the parties will work together to reach a conclusion. 8.15

---

[5] <http://www.hse.gov.uk/enforce/investigators.pdf>.
[6] Corporate Manslaughter and Corporate Homicide: A Regulatory Impact Assessment of the Government's Bill, p 13.

8. Investigation and Representation

8.16 The Protocol defines a work-related death as a fatality resulting from an incident arising out of, or in connection with, work. The principles of the protocol are said to apply also to cases where the victim suffers injuries in such an incident that are so serious that there is a clear indication, according to medical opinion, of a strong likelihood of death.

8.17 The Protocol recognizes that there are cases in which it is difficult to determine whether a death is work-related within the terms set out above. It states the principle that each fatality must be considered individually, on its own particular facts, according to organizational internal guidance, and a decision made as to whether it should be classed as a work-related death. The Protocol states that in determining the question, the enforcing authorities will hold discussions and agree upon a conclusion without delay.

8.18 There are principles dealing with initial action, the management of the investigation, decision-making, disclosure of material, special inquiries, advice prior to charge, the decision to prosecute, prosecution, dealings with HM Coroner, and liaison.

8.19 Where the investigation gives rise to a suspicion that a serious criminal offence (other than a health and safety offence) may have caused the death, the Protocol provides that the police will assume primacy for the investigation and will work in partnership with the HSE, the local authority or other enforcing authority. Where it becomes apparent during the investigation that there is insufficient evidence that a serious criminal offence (other than a health and safety offence) caused the death, the investigation should, by agreement, be taken over by HSE, the local authority, or other enforcing authority.

8.20 It is clear in the Protocol that there will also be rare occasions where as a result of the coroner's inquest, judicial review or other legal proceedings, further consideration of the evidence and surrounding facts may be necessary. Where this takes place the protocol states that the police, the enforcing authority with primacy for the investigation, and the CPS will work in partnership to ensure an early decision, but that there may also be a need for further investigation. In practice, such cases, whilst undoubtedly being rare, have occurred with regularity following an 'unlawful killing' verdict by an inquest jury.

8.21 The protocol provides that the police must consult the CPS Casework Directorate for advice when there is any consideration of charging a company or corporation with any serious criminal offence (other than a health and safety offence). In practice, the only serious criminal offences likely to arise in connection with a work-related death within the terms of the protocol are corporate manslaughter and individual gross negligence manslaughter.

3. Coroners Act 1988 s 16 and adjourned inquests

8.22 Schedule 2 to the Act amends the Coroners Act 1988, 16 to add corporate manslaughter to the list of suspected offences in respect of which an inquest will be adjourned pending conclusion of criminal proceedings. The effect of this provision is that whenever the police conduct an investigation into suspected offence

B. The Investigation of Corporate Manslaughter

corporate manslaughter and submit a file to the Crown Prosecution Service, the coroner will be notified and the inquest will be formally opened and adjourned pending the outcome of the police investigation and any CPS prosecution.

No adjourned inquest before a jury with witnesses will be resumed until either a decision is made not to prosecute for corporate manslaughter or such proceedings are completed. The Coroners Act 1988 s 16(7) provides that where a coroner resumed such an adjourned inquest, then the finding of the inquest as to the cause of death must not be inconsistent with the outcome of the relevant criminal proceedings.

8.23

4. Police powers and corporate manslaughter

There are various police powers of search and seizure under the Police and Criminal Evidence Act 1984 (PACE 1984). No individual can be arrested for corporate manslaughter, as no such potential individual liability exists, thus no search of premises following an arrest upon suspicion of having committed corporate manslaughter can occur.

8.24

However PACE 1984, s 8 provides that on an application made by a constable, a magistrate will grant a warrant to enter and search premises if various conditions are met but these include that he is satisfied that there are reasonable grounds for believing that an indictable offence has been committed and that there is material on the premises specified in the application which is likely to be of substantial value (whether by itself or taken together with other material) to the investigation of the offence; that the material is likely to be relevant evidence; and, that it does not consist of, or include, precluded material. Thus, the police would appear to have sufficient powers to obtain a search warrant and thereafter seize relevant documentation in respect of a suspected offence of corporate manslaughter.

8.25

Health and Safety at Work etc. Act 1974 (HSWA) s 20, affords a health and safety inspector extensive powers to obtain evidence, although it does not include any general power of search and seizure, nor does it give inspectors the power to apply for, and obtain, a warrant. In some important respects, the investigatory powers vested in inspectors are far more potent than those enjoyed by police: for example, the power under HSWA s 20(2)(j), 'to require any person whom he has reasonable cause to believe to be able to give any information relevant to any examination or investigation...to answer...questions and to sign a declaration of the truth of his answers'; the power under HSWA, s 20(2)(k) to require the production of, inspect, and take copies of documents. Health and safety inspectors do not have power to investigate corporate manslaughter, their powers being limited to investigations under the HSWA and related provisions.

8.26

(a) Senior management

The real issue in relation to police powers and corporate manslaughter may prove to be in respect of the need to investigate the 'senior management' requirement and the desire to do so through questioning.

8.27

8.28 There are no police powers of compulsory questioning other than the power to interview a suspect under caution, in respect of which, PACE 1984, s 24 provides that an police officer who has reasonable grounds for suspecting that an offence has been committed, may arrest without a warrant anyone whom he has reasonable grounds to suspect of being guilty of guilty of the offence, to allow the prompt and effective investigation of the offence or of the conduct of the person in question, that is including, through interview under caution.

8.29 No individual can be suspected of corporate manslaughter and, whilst police have the power to arrest an individual suspected of common law gross negligence manslaughter or even in respect of an indictable health and safety offence, any interview under caution of such a person would be unlikely to be admissible against the organization in proceedings for corporate manslughter.

8.30 In short, direct evidence against an organization in respect of 'senior management' failings is unlikely to be contained through questioning under caution; instead, the police will have to rely upon documentation and statements obtained from witnesses.

(b) *Organizations and interviews under caution*

8.31 In respect of interviewing a representative of the organization under caution, with no power to arrest such a person, only an invitation can be extended and no compulsion to attend can be applied. Any refusal to attend could not found the drawing of an adverse inference at trial, as the Criminal Justice and Public Order Act 1994, ss 34(1) and 34(2), require a defendant to have failed to mention a fact 'on being questioned under caution', a circumstance that could only occur during interview.

C. REPRESENTATION

8.32 Legal Aid funded representation is not available for organizations. Most organizations the subject of corporate manslaughter investigations will be employers and have the benefit of an insurance policy covering compulsory public and employer's liability. This cover will very often include provision for legal advice and representation during investigation and through the course of any criminal proceedings arising; it may well cover simply the latter.

8.33 A number of insurance policies describe the cover for legal expenses as 'related and limited to proceedings for health and safety offences'. Arguably, this will not cover proceedings for corporate manslaughter. However, insurers have previously extended cover under such policies where proceedings have been instituted in respect of gross negligence manslaughter.

8.34 It is not uncommon for insurance cover in respect of legal representation to be withdrawn. This may happen where the ultimate criminal allegation includes, or the evidence discloses, material suggesting that the insurer had been misled as to the state of risk assessment/control measures that had been required under the policy. In the event of a conviction at trial it is common for the insurer to withdraw cover and not to fund any appeal.

APPENDIX 1

Corporate Manslaughter and Corporate Homicide Act 2007

CONTENTS

Corporate manslaughter and corporate homicide

1. The offence

Relevant duty of care

2. Meaning of 'relevant duty of care'
3. Public policy decisions, exclusively public functions and statutory inspections
4. Military activities
5. Policing and law enforcement
6. Emergencies
7. Child-protection and probation functions

Gross breach

8. Factors for jury

Remedial orders and publicity orders

9. Power to order breach etc to be remedied
10. Power to order conviction etc to be publicised

Application to particular categories of organisation

11. Application to Crown bodies
12. Application to armed forces
13. Application to police forces
14. Application to partnerships

Miscellaneous

15. Procedure, evidence and sentencing
16. Transfer of functions

17 DPP's consent required for proceedings
18 No individual liability
19 Convictions under this Act and under health and safety legislation
20 Abolition of liability of corporations for manslaughter at common law

General and supplemental

21 Power to extend section 1 to other organisations
22 Power to amend Schedule 1
23 Power to extend section 2(2)
24 Orders
25 Interpretation
26 Minor and consequential amendments
27 Commencement and savings
28 Extent and territorial application
29 Short title
Schedule 1 — List of government departments etc
Schedule 2 — Minor and consequential amendments

CORPORATE MANSLAUGHTER AND CORPORATE HOMICIDE ACT 2007

2007 CHAPTER 19

An Act to create a new offence that, in England and Wales or Northern Ireland, is to be called corporate manslaughter and, in Scotland, is to be called corporate homicide; and to make provision in connection with that offence.
[26th July 2007]
BE IT ENACTED by the Queen's most Excellent Majesty, by and with the advice and consent of the Lords Spiritual and Temporal, and Commons, in this present Parliament assembled, and by the authority of the same, as follows:—

Corporate manslaughter and corporate homicide

1 The offence

(1) An organisation to which this section applies is guilty of an offence if the way in which its activities are managed or organised—
   (a) causes a person's death, and
   (b) amounts to a gross breach of a relevant duty of care owed by the organisation to the deceased.
(2) The organisations to which this section applies are—
   (a) a corporation;
   (b) a department or other body listed in Schedule 1;
   (c) a police force;
   (d) a partnership, or a trade union or employers' association, that is an employer.

(3) An organisation is guilty of an offence under this section only if the way in which its activities are managed or organised by its senior management is a substantial element in the breach referred to in subsection (1).
(4) For the purposes of this Act—
 (a) 'relevant duty of care' has the meaning given by section 2, read with sections 3 to 7;
 (b) a breach of a duty of care by an organisation is a 'gross' breach if the conduct alleged to amount to a breach of that duty falls far below what can reasonably be expected of the organisation in the circumstances;
 (c) 'senior management', in relation to an organisation, means the persons who play significant roles in—
  (i) the making of decisions about how the whole or a substantial part of its activities are to be managed or organised, or
  (ii) the actual managing or organising of the whole or a substantial part of those activities.
(5) The offence under this section is called—
 (a) corporate manslaughter, in so far as it is an offence under the law of England and Wales or Northern Ireland;
 (b) corporate homicide, in so far as it is an offence under the law of Scotland.
(6) An organisation that is guilty of corporate manslaughter or corporate homicide is liable on conviction on indictment to a fine.
(7) The offence of corporate homicide is indictable only in the High Court of Justiciary.

Relevant duty of care

2 Meaning of 'relevant duty of care'

(1) A 'relevant duty of care', in relation to an organisation, means any of the following duties owed by it under the law of negligence—
 (a) a duty owed to its employees or to other persons working for the organisation or performing services for it;
 (b) a duty owed as occupier of premises;
 (c) a duty owed in connection with—
  (i) the supply by the organisation of goods or services (whether for consideration or not),
  (ii) the carrying on by the organisation of any construction or maintenance operations,
  (iii) the carrying on by the organisation of any other activity on a commercial basis, or
  (iv) the use or keeping by the organisation of any plant, vehicle or other thing;
 (d) a duty owed to a person who, by reason of being a person within subsection (2), is someone for whose safety the organisation is responsible.
(2) A person is within this subsection if—
 (a) he is detained at a custodial institution or in a custody area at a court or police station;
 (b) he is detained at a removal centre or short-term holding facility;
 (c) he is being transported in a vehicle, or being held in any premises, in pursuance of prison escort arrangements or immigration escort arrangements;
 (d) he is living in secure accommodation in which he has been placed;
 (e) he is a detained patient.
(3) Subsection (1) is subject to sections 3 to 7.
(4) A reference in subsection (1) to a duty owed under the law of negligence includes a reference to a duty that would be owed under the law of negligence but for any statutory provision under which liability is imposed in place of liability under that law.

s 2, Corporate Manslaughter and Corporate Homicide Act 2007

(5) For the purposes of this Act, whether a particular organisation owes a duty of care to a particular individual is a question of law. The judge must make any findings of fact necessary to decide that question.

(6) For the purposes of this Act there is to be disregarded—
   (a) any rule of the common law that has the effect of preventing a duty of care from being owed by one person to another by reason of the fact that they are jointly engaged in unlawful conduct;
   (b) any such rule that has the effect of preventing a duty of care from being owed to a person by reason of his acceptance of a risk of harm.

(7) In this section—
'construction or maintenance operations' means operations of any of the following descriptions—
   (a) construction, installation, alteration, extension, improvement, repair, maintenance, decoration, cleaning, demolition or dismantling of—
      (i) any building or structure,
      (ii) anything else that forms, or is to form, part of the land, or
      (iii) any plant, vehicle or other thing;
   (b) operations that form an integral part of, or are preparatory to, or are for rendering complete, any operations within paragraph(a);

'custodial institution' means a prison, a young offender institution, a secure training centre, a young offenders institution, a young offenders centre, a juvenile justice centre or a remand centre;

'detained patient' means—
   (a) a person who is detained in any premises under—
      (i) Part 2 or 3 of the Mental Health Act 1983 (c. 20) ('the 1983 Act'), or
      (ii) Part 2 or 3 of the Mental Health (Northern Ireland) Order 1986 (S.I. 1986/595 (N.I. 4)) ('the 1986 Order');
   (b) a person who (otherwise than by reason of being detained as mentioned in paragraph (a)) is deemed to be in legal custody by—
      (i) section 137 of the 1983 Act,
      (ii) Article 131 of the 1986 Order, or
      (iii) article 11 of the Mental Health (Care and Treatment) (Scotland) Act 2003 (Consequential Provisions) Order 2005 (S.I. 2005/2078);
   (c) a person who is detained in any premises, or is otherwise in custody, under the Mental Health (Care and Treatment) (Scotland) Act 2003 (asp 13) or Part 6 of the Criminal Procedure (Scotland) Act 1995 (c. 46) or who is detained in a hospital under section 200 of that Act of 1995;

'immigration escort arrangements' means arrangements made under section 156 of the Immigration and Asylum Act 1999 (c. 33); 'the law of negligence' includes—
   (a) in relation to England and Wales, the Occupiers' Liability Act 1957 (c. 31), the Defective Premises Act 1972 (c. 35) and the Occupiers' Liability Act 1984 (c. 3);
   (b) in relation to Scotland, the Occupiers' Liability (Scotland) Act 1960 (c. 30);
   (c) in relation to Northern Ireland, the Occupiers' Liability Act (Northern Ireland) 1957 (c. 25), the Defective Premises (Northern Ireland) Order 1975 (S.I. 1975/1039 (N.I. 9)), the Occupiers' Liability (Northern Ireland) Order 1987 (S.I. 19871280 (N.I. 15)) and the Defective Premises (Landlord's Liability) Act (Northern Ireland) 2001 (c. 10);

'prison escort arrangements' means arrangements made under section 80 of the Criminal Justice Act 1991 (c. 53) or under section 102 or 118 of the Criminal Justice and Public Order Act 1994 (c. 33);
'removal centre' and 'short-term holding facility' have the meaning given by section 147 of the Immigration and Asylum Act 1999;
'secure accommodation' means accommodation, not consisting of or forming part of a custodial institution, provided for the purpose of restricting the liberty of persons under the age of 18.

3 Public policy decisions, exclusively public functions and statutory inspections

(1) Any duty of care owed by a public authority in respect of a decision as to matters of public policy (including in particular the allocation of public resources or the weighing of competing public interests) is not a 'relevant duty of care'.
(2) Any duty of care owed in respect of things done in the exercise of an exclusively public function is not a 'relevant duty of care' unless it falls within section 2(1)(a), (b) or (d).
(3) Any duty of care owed by a public authority in respect of inspections carried out in the exercise of a statutory function is not a 'relevant duty of care' unless it falls within section 2(1)(a) or (b).
(4) In this section—
'exclusively public function' means a function that falls within the prerogative of the Crown or is, by its nature, exercisable only with authority conferred—
   (a) by the exercise of that prerogative, or
   (b) by or under a statutory provision;
'statutory function' means a function conferred by or under a statutory provision.

4 Military activities

(1) Any duty of care owed by the Ministry of Defence in respect of—
   (a) operations within subsection (2),
   (b) activities carried on in preparation for, or directly in support of, such operations, or
   (c) training of a hazardous nature, or training carried out in a hazardous way, which it is considered needs to be carried out, or carried out in that way, in order to improve or maintain the effectiveness of the armed forces with respect to such operations is not a 'relevant duty of care'.
(2) The operations within this subsection are operations, including peacekeeping operations and operations for dealing with terrorism, civil unrest or serious public disorder, in the course of which members of the armed forces come under attack or face the threat of attack or violent resistance.
(3) Any duty of care owed by the Ministry of Defence in respect of activities carried on by members of the special forces is not a 'relevant duty of care'.
(4) In this section 'the special forces' means those units of the armed forces the maintenance of whose capabilities is the responsibility of the Director of Special Forces or which are for the time being subject to the operational command of that Director.

5 Policing and law enforcement

(1) Any duty of care owed by a public authority in respect of—
   (a) operations within subsection (2),
   (b) activities carried on in preparation for, or directly in support of, such operations, or
   (c) training of a hazardous nature, or training carried out in a hazardous way, which it is considered needs to be carried out, or carried out in that way, in order to improve or

maintain the effectiveness of officers or employees of the public authority with respect to such operations, is not a 'relevant duty of care'.
(2) Operations are within this subsection if—
  (a) they are operations for dealing with terrorism, civil unrest or serious disorder,
  (b) they involve the carrying on of policing or law-enforcement activities, and
  (c) officers or employees of the public authority in question come under attack, or face the threat of attack or violent resistance, in the course of the operations.
(3) Any duty of care owed by a public authority in respect of other policing or lawenforcement activities is not a 'relevant duty of care' unless it falls within section 2(1)(a), (b) or (d).
(4) In this section 'policing or law-enforcement activities' includes—
  (a) activities carried on in the exercise of functions that are—
    (i) functions of police forces, or
    (ii) functions of the same or a similar nature exercisable by public authorities other than police forces;
  (b) activities carried on in the exercise of functions of constables employed by a public authority;
  (c) activities carried on in the exercise of functions exercisable under Chapter 4 of Part 2 of the Serious Organised Crime and Police Act 2005 (c. 15) (protection of witnesses and other persons);
  (d) activities carried on to enforce any provision contained in or made under the Immigration Acts.

6 Emergencies

(1) Any duty of care owed by an organisation within subsection (2) in respect of the way in which it responds to emergency circumstances is not a 'relevant duty of care' unless it falls within section 2(1)(a) or (b).
(2) The organisations within this subsection are—
  (a) a fire and rescue authority in England and Wales;
  (b) a fire and rescue authority or joint fire and rescue board in Scotland;
  (c) the Northern Ireland Fire and Rescue Service Board;
  (d) any other organisation providing a service of responding to emergency circumstances either—
    (i) in pursuance of arrangements made with an organisation within paragraph (a), (b) or (c), or
    (ii) (if not in pursuance of such arrangements) otherwise than on a commercial basis;
  (e) a relevant NHS body;
  (f) an organisation providing ambulance services in pursuance of arrangements—
    (i) made by, or at the request of, a relevant NHS body, or
    (ii) made with the Secretary of State or with the Welsh Ministers;
  (g) an organisation providing services for the transport of organs, blood, equipment or personnel in pursuance of arrangements of the kind mentioned in paragraph (f);
  (h) an organisation providing a rescue service;
  (i) the armed forces.
(3) For the purposes of subsection (1), the way in which an organisation responds to emergency circumstances does not include the way in which—
  (a) medical treatment is carried out, or
  (b) decisions within subsection (4) are made.
(4) The decisions within this subsection are decisions as to the carrying out of medical treatment, other than decisions as to the order in which persons are to be given such treatment.

(5) Any duty of care owed in respect of the carrying out, or attempted carrying out, of a rescue operation at sea in emergency circumstances is not a 'relevant duty of care' unless it falls within section 2(1)(a) or (b).
(6) Any duty of care owed in respect of action taken—
  (a) in order to comply with a direction under Schedule 3A to the Merchant Shipping Act 1995 (c. 21) (safety directions), or
  (b) by virtue of paragraph 4 of that Schedule (action in lieu of direction), is not a 'relevant duty of care' unless it falls within section 2(1)(a) or (b).
(7) In this section—
  'emergency circumstances' means circumstances that are present or imminent and—
  (a) are causing, or are likely to cause, serious harm or a worsening of such harm, or
  (b) are likely to cause the death of a person;
  'medical treatment' includes any treatment or procedure of a medical or similar nature;
  'relevant NHS body' means—
  (a) a Strategic Health Authority, Primary Care Trust, NHS trust, Special Health Authority or NHS foundation trust in England;
  (b) a Local Health Board, NHS trust or Special Health Authority in Wales;
  (c) a Health Board or Special Health Board in Scotland, or the Common Services Agency for the Scottish Health Service;
  (d) a Health and Social Services trust or Health and Social Services Board in Northern Ireland;
  'serious harm' means—
  (a) serious injury to or the serious illness (including mental illness) of a person;
  (b) serious harm to the environment (including the life and health of plants and animals);
  (c) serious harm to any building or other property.
(8) A reference in this section to emergency circumstances includes a reference to circumstances that are believed to be emergency circumstances.

7 Child-protection and probation functions

(1) A duty of care to which this section applies is not a 'relevant duty of care' unless it falls within section 2(1)(a), (b) or (d).
(2) This section applies to any duty of care that a local authority or other public authority owes in respect of the exercise by it of functions conferred by or under—
  (a) Parts 4 and 5 of the Children Act 1989 (c. 41),
  (b) Part 2 of the Children (Scotland) Act 1995 (c. 36), or
  (c) Parts 5 and 6 of the Children (Northern Ireland) Order 1995 (S.I. 1995/755 (N.I. 2)).
(3) This section also applies to any duty of care that a local probation board or other public authority owes in respect of the exercise by it of functions conferred by or under—
  (a) Chapter 1 of Part 1 of the Criminal Justice and Court Services Act 2000 (c. 43),
  (b) section 27 of the Social Work (Scotland) Act 1968 (c. 49), or
  (c) Article 4 of the Probation Board (Northern Ireland) Order 1982 (S.I. 1982/713 (N.I. 10)).

Gross breach

8 Factors for jury

(1) This section applies where—
  (a) it is established that an organisation owed a relevant duty of care to a person, and
  (b) it falls to the jury to decide whether there was a gross breach of that duty.

(2) The jury must consider whether the evidence shows that the organisation failed to comply with any health and safety legislation that relates to the alleged breach, and if so—
  (a) how serious that failure was;
  (b) how much of a risk of death it posed.
(3) The jury may also—
  (a) consider the extent to which the evidence shows that there were attitudes, policies, systems or accepted practices within the organisation that were likely to have encouraged any such failure as is mentioned in subsection (2), or to have produced tolerance of it;
  (b) have regard to any health and safety guidance that relates to the alleged breach.
(4) This section does not prevent the jury from having regard to any other matters they consider relevant.
(5) In this section 'health and safety guidance' means any code, guidance, manual or similar publication that is concerned with health and safety matters and is made or issued (under a statutory provision or otherwise) by an authority responsible for the enforcement of any health and safety legislation.

Remedial orders and publicity orders

9 Power to order breach etc to be remedied

(1) A court before which an organisation is convicted of corporate manslaughter or corporate homicide may make an order (a 'remedial order') requiring the organisation to take specified steps to remedy—
  (a) the breach mentioned in section 1(1) ('the relevant breach');
  (b) any matter that appears to the court to have resulted from the relevant breach and to have been a cause of the death;
  (c) any deficiency, as regards health and safety matters, in the organisation's policies, systems or practices of which the relevant breach appears to the court to be an indication.
(2) A remedial order may be made only on an application by the prosecution specifying the terms of the proposed order. Any such order must be on such terms (whether those proposed or others) as the court considers appropriate having regard to any representations made, and any evidence adduced, in relation to that matter by the prosecution or on behalf of the organisation.
(3) Before making an application for a remedial order the prosecution must consult such enforcement authority or authorities as it considers appropriate having regard to the nature of the relevant breach.
(4) A remedial order—
  (a) must specify a period within which the steps referred to in subsection (1) are to be taken;
  (b) may require the organisation to supply to an enforcement authority consulted under subsection (3), within a specified period, evidence that those steps have been taken.
A period specified under this subsection may be extended or further extended by order of the court on an application made before the end of that period or extended period.
(5) An organisation that fails to comply with a remedial order is guilty of an offence, and liable on conviction on indictment to a fine.

10 Power to order conviction etc to be publicised

(1) A court before which an organisation is convicted of corporate manslaughter or corporate homicide may make an order (a 'publicity order') requiring the organisation to publicise in a specified manner—
   (a) the fact that it has been convicted of the offence;
   (b) specified particulars of the offence;
   (c) the amount of any fine imposed;
   (d) the terms of any remedial order made.
(2) In deciding on the terms of a publicity order that it is proposing to make, the court must—
   (a) ascertain the views of such enforcement authority or authorities (if any) as it considers appropriate, and
   (b) have regard to any representations made by the prosecution or on behalf of the organisation.
(3) A publicity order—
   (a) must specify a period within which the requirements referred to in subsection (1) are to be complied with;
   (b) may require the organisation to supply to any enforcement authority whose views have been ascertained under subsection (2), within a specified period, evidence that those requirements have been complied with.
(4) An organisation that fails to comply with a publicity order is guilty of an offence, and liable on conviction on indictment to a fine.

Application to particular categories of organisation

11 Application to Crown bodies

(1) An organisation that is a servant or agent of the Crown is not immune from prosecution under this Act for that reason.
(2) For the purposes of this Act—
   (a) a department or other body listed in Schedule 1, or
   (b) a corporation that is a servant or agent of the Crown, is to be treated as owing whatever duties of care it would owe if it were a corporation that was not a servant or agent of the Crown.
(3) For the purposes of section 2—
   (a) a person who is—
      (i) employed by or under the Crown for the purposes of a department or other body listed in Schedule 1, or
      (ii) employed by a person whose staff constitute a body listed in that Schedule,
      is to be treated as employed by that department or body;
   (b) any premises occupied for the purposes of—
      (i) a department or other body listed in Schedule 1, or
      (ii) a person whose staff constitute a body listed in that Schedule, are to be treated as occupied by that department or body.
(4) For the purposes of sections 2 to 7 anything done purportedly by a department or other body listed in Schedule 1, although in law by the Crown or by the holder of a particular office, is to be treated as done by the department or other body itself.
(5) Subsections (3)(a)(i), (3)(b)(i) and (4) apply in relation to a Northern Ireland department as they apply in relation to a department or other body listed in Schedule 1.

12 Application to armed forces

(1) In this Act 'the armed forces' means any of the naval, military or air forces of the Crown raised under the law of the United Kingdom.
(2) For the purposes of section 2 a person who is a member of the armed forces is to be treated as employed by the Ministry of Defence.
(3) A reference in this Act to members of the armed forces includes a reference to—
   (a) members of the reserve forces (within the meaning given by section 1(2) of the Reserve Forces Act 1996 (c. 14)) when in service or undertaking training or duties;
   (b) persons serving on Her Majesty's vessels (within the meaning given by section 132(1) of the Naval Discipline Act 1957 (c. 53)).

13 Application to police forces

(1) In this Act 'police force' means—
   (a) a police force within the meaning of—
      (i) the Police Act 1996 (c. 16), or
      (ii) the Police (Scotland) Act 1967 (c. 77);
   (b) the Police Service of Northern Ireland;
   (c) the Police Service of Northern Ireland Reserve;
   (d) the British Transport Police Force;
   (e) the Civil Nuclear Constabulary;
   (f) the Ministry of Defence Police.
(2) For the purposes of this Act a police force is to be treated as owing whatever duties of care it would owe if it were a body corporate.
(3) For the purposes of section 2—
   (a) a member of a police force is to be treated as employed by that force;
   (b) a special constable appointed for a police area in England and Wales is to be treated as employed by the police force maintained by the police authority for that area;
   (c) a special constable appointed for a police force mentioned in paragraph (d) or (f) of subsection (1) is to be treated as employed by that force;
   (d) a police cadet undergoing training with a view to becoming a member of a police force mentioned in paragraph (a) or (d) of subsection (1) is to be treated as employed by that force;
   (e) a police trainee appointed under section 39 of the Police (Northern Ireland) Act 2000 (c. 32) or a police cadet appointed under section 42 of that Act is to be treated as employed by the Police Service of Northern Ireland;
   (f) a police reserve trainee appointed under section 40 of that Act is to be treated as employed by the Police Service of Northern Ireland Reserve;
   (g) a member of a police force seconded to the Serious Organised Crime Agency or the National Policing Improvement Agency to serve as a member of its staff is to be treated as employed by that Agency.
(4) A reference in subsection (3) to a member of a police force is to be read, in the case of a force mentioned in paragraph (a)(ii) of subsection (1), as a reference to a constable of that force.
(5) For the purposes of section 2 any premises occupied for the purposes of a police force are to be treated as occupied by that force.
(6) For the purposes of sections 2 to 7 anything that would be regarded as done by a police force if the force were a body corporate is to be so regarded.

(7) Where—
   (a) by virtue of subsection (3) a person is treated for the purposes of section 2 as employed by a police force, and
   (b) by virtue of any other statutory provision (whenever made) he is, or is treated as, employed by another organisation, the person is to be treated for those purposes as employed by both the force and the other organisation.

14 Application to partnerships

(1) For the purposes of this Act a partnership is to be treated as owing whatever duties of care it would owe if it were a body corporate.
(2) Proceedings for an offence under this Act alleged to have been committed by a partnership are to be brought in the name of the partnership (and not in that of any of its members).
(3) A fine imposed on a partnership on its conviction of an offence under this Act is to be paid out of the funds of the partnership.
(4) This section does not apply to a partnership that is a legal person under the law by which it is governed.

Miscellaneous

15 Procedure, evidence and sentencing

(1) Any statutory provision (whenever made) about criminal proceedings applies, subject to any prescribed adaptations or modifications, in relation to proceedings under this Act against—
   (a) a department or other body listed in Schedule 1,
   (b) a police force,
   (c) a partnership,
   (d) a trade union, or
   (e) an employers' association that is not a corporation,
as it applies in relation to proceedings against a corporation.
(2) In this section—
'prescribed' means prescribed by an order made by the Secretary of State;
'provision about criminal proceedings' includes—
   (a) provision about procedure in or in connection with criminal proceedings;
   (b) provision about evidence in such proceedings;
   (c) provision about sentencing, or otherwise dealing with, persons convicted of offences;
'statutory' means contained in, or in an instrument made under, any Act or any Northern Ireland legislation.
(3) A reference in this section to proceedings is to proceedings in England and Wales or Northern Ireland.
(4) An order under this section is subject to negative resolution procedure.

16 Transfer of functions

(1) This section applies where—
   (a) a person's death has occurred, or is alleged to have occurred, in connection with the carrying out of functions by a relevant public organisation, and
   (b) subsequently there is a transfer of those functions, with the result that they are still carried out but no longer by that organisation.
(2) In this section 'relevant public organisation' means—
   (a) a department or other body listed in Schedule 1;

(b) a corporation that is a servant or agent of the Crown;
(c) a police force.
(3) Any proceedings instituted against a relevant public organisation after the transfer for an offence under this Act in respect of the person's death are to be instituted against—
    (a) the relevant public organisation, if any, by which the functions mentioned in subsection (1) are currently carried out;
    (b) if no such organisation currently carries out the functions, the relevant public organisation by which the functions were last carried out. This is subject to subsection (4).
(4) If an order made by the Secretary of State so provides in relation to a particular transfer of functions, the proceedings referred to in subsection (3) may be instituted, or (if they have already been instituted) may be continued, against—
    (a) the organisation mentioned in subsection (1), or
    (b) such relevant public organisation (other than the one mentioned in subsection (1) or the one mentioned in subsection (3)(a) or (b)) as may be specified in the order.
(5) If the transfer occurs while proceedings for an offence under this Act in respect of the person's death are in progress against a relevant public organisation, the proceedings are to be continued against—
    (a) the relevant public organisation, if any, by which the functions mentioned in subsection (1) are carried out as a result of the transfer;
    (b) if as a result of the transfer no such organisation carries out the functions, the same organisation as before.
This is subject to subsection (6).
(6) If an order made by the Secretary of State so provides in relation to a particular transfer of functions, the proceedings referred to in subsection (5) may be continued against—
    (a) the organisation mentioned in subsection (1), or
    (b) such relevant public organisation (other than the one mentioned in subsection (1) or the one mentioned in subsection (5)(a) or (b)) as may be specified in the order.
(7) An order under subsection (4) or (6) is subject to negative resolution procedure.

17 DPP's consent required for proceedings

Proceedings for an offence of corporate manslaughter—
    (a) may not be instituted in England and Wales without the consent of the Director of Public Prosecutions;
    (b) may not be instituted in Northern Ireland without the consent of the Director of Public Prosecutions for Northern Ireland.

18 No individual liability

(1) An individual cannot be guilty of aiding, abetting, counselling or procuring the commission of an offence of corporate manslaughter.
(2) An individual cannot be guilty of aiding, abetting, counselling or procuring, or being art and part in, the commission of an offence of corporate homicide.

19 Convictions under this Act and under health and safety legislation

(1) Where in the same proceedings there is—
    (a) a charge of corporate manslaughter or corporate homicide arising out of a particular set of circumstances, and
    (b) a charge against the same defendant of a health and safety offence arising out of some or

all of those circumstances, the jury may, if the interests of justice so require, be invited to return a verdict on each charge.
(2) An organisation that has been convicted of corporate manslaughter or corporate homicide arising out of a particular set of circumstances may, if the interests of justice so require, be charged with a health and safety offence arising out of some or all of those circumstances.
(3) In this section 'health and safety offence' means an offence under any health and safety legislation.

20 Abolition of liability of corporations for manslaughter at common law

The common law offence of manslaughter by gross negligence is abolished in its application to corporations, and in any application it has to other organisations to which section 1 applies.

General and supplemental

21 Power to extend section 1 to other organisations

(1) The Secretary of State may by order amend section 1 so as to extend the categories of organisation to which that section applies.
(2) An order under this section may make any amendment to this Act that is incidental or supplemental to, or consequential on, an amendment made by virtue of subsection (1).
(3) An order under this section is subject to affirmative resolution procedure.

22 Power to amend Schedule 1

(1) The Secretary of State may amend Schedule 1 by order.
(2) A statutory instrument containing an order under this section is subject to affirmative resolution procedure, unless the only amendments to Schedule 1 that it makes are amendments within subsection (3). In that case the instrument is subject to negative resolution procedure.
(3) An amendment is within this subsection if—
   (a) it is consequential on a department or other body listed in Schedule 1 changing its name,
   (b) in the case of an amendment adding a department or other body to Schedule 1, it is consequential on the transfer to the department or other body of functions all of which were previously exercisable by one or more organisations to which section 1 applies, or
   (c) in the case of an amendment removing a department or other body from Schedule 1, it is consequential on—
      (i) the abolition of the department or other body, or
      (ii) the transfer of all the functions of the department or other body to one or more organisations to which section 1 applies.

23 Power to extend section 2(2)

(1) The Secretary of State may by order amend section 2(2) to make it include any category of person (not already included) who—
   (a) is required by virtue of a statutory provision to remain or reside on particular premises, or
   (b) is otherwise subject to a restriction of his liberty.
(2) An order under this section may make any amendment to this Act that is incidental or supplemental to, or consequential on, an amendment made by virtue of subsection (1).
(3) An order under this section is subject to affirmative resolution procedure.

24 Orders

(1) A power of the Secretary of State to make an order under this Act is exercisable by statutory instrument.
(2) Where an order under this Act is subject to 'negative resolution procedure' the statutory instrument containing the order is subject to annulment in pursuance of a resolution of either House of Parliament.
(3) Where an order under this Act is subject to 'affirmative resolution procedure' the order may not be made unless a draft has been laid before, and approved by a resolution of, each House of Parliament.
(4) An order under this Act—
    (a) may make different provision for different purposes;
    (b) may make transitional or saving provision.

25 Interpretation

In this Act—
'armed forces' has the meaning given by section 12(1);
'corporation' does not include a corporation sole but includes any body corporate wherever incorporated;
'employee' means an individual who works under a contract of employment or apprenticeship (whether express or implied and, if express, whether oral or in writing), and related expressions are to be construed accordingly; see also sections 11(3)(a), 12(2) and 13(3) (which apply for the purposes of section 2);
'employers' association' has the meaning given by section 122 of the Trade Union and Labour Relations (Consolidation) Act 1992 (c. 52) or Article 4 of the Industrial Relations (Northern Ireland) Order 1992 (S.I. 1992/807 (N.I. 5));
'enforcement authority' means an authority responsible for the enforcement of any health and safety legislation;
'health and safety legislation' means any statutory provision dealing with health and safety matters, including in particular provision contained in the Health and Safety at Work etc. Act 1974 (c. 37) or the Health and Safety at Work (Northern Ireland) Order 1978 (S.I. 1978/ 1039 (N.I. 9));
'member', in relation to the armed forces, is to be read in accordance with section 12(3);
'partnership' means—
    a partnership within the Partnership Act 1890 (c. 39), or
    a limited partnership registered under the Limited Partnerships Act 1907 (c. 24),
or a firm or entity of a similar character formed under the law of a country or territory outside the United Kingdom;
'police force' has the meaning given by section 13(1);
'premises' includes land, buildings and moveable structures;
'public authority' has the same meaning as in section 6 of the Human Rights Act 1998 (c. 42) (disregarding subsections (3)(a) and (4) of that section);
'publicity order' means an order under section 10(1);
'remedial order' means an order under section 9(1);

'statutory provision', except in section 15, means provision contained in, or in an instrument made under, any Act, an Act of the Scottish Parliament or any Northern Ireland legislation;
'trade union' has the meaning given by section 1 of the Trade Union and Labour Relations (Consolidation) Act 1992 (c. 52) or Article 3 of the Industrial Relations (Northern Ireland) Order 1992 (S.I. 1992/807 (N.I. 5)).

26 Minor and consequential amendments

Schedule 2 (minor and consequential amendments) has effect.

27 Commencement and savings

(1) The preceding provisions of this Act come into force in accordance with provision made by order by the Secretary of State.
(2) An order bringing into force paragraph (d) of section 2(1) is subject to affirmative resolution procedure.
(3) Section 1 does not apply in relation to anything done or omitted before the commencement of that section.
(4) Section 20 does not affect any liability, investigation, legal proceeding or penalty for or in respect of an offence committed wholly or partly before the commencement of that section.
(5) For the purposes of subsection (4) an offence is committed wholly or partly before the commencement of section 20 if any of the conduct or events alleged to constitute the offence occurred before that commencement.

28 Extent and territorial application

(1) Subject to subsection (2), this Act extends to England and Wales, Scotland and Northern Ireland.
(2) An amendment made by this Act extends to the same part or parts of the United Kingdom as the provision to which it relates.
(3) Section 1 applies if the harm resulting in death is sustained in the United Kingdom or—
  (a) within the seaward limits of the territorial sea adjacent to the United Kingdom;
  (b) on a ship registered under Part 2 of the Merchant Shipping Act 1995 (c. 21);
  (c) on a British-controlled aircraft as defined in section 92 of the Civil Aviation Act 1982 (c. 16);
  (d) on a British-controlled hovercraft within the meaning of that section as applied in relation to hovercraft by virtue of provision made under the Hovercraft Act 1968 (c. 59);
  (e) in any place to which an Order in Council under section 10(1) of the Petroleum Act 1998 (c. 17) applies (criminal jurisdiction in relation to offshore activities).
(4) For the purposes of subsection (3)(b) to (d) harm sustained on a ship, aircraft or hovercraft includes harm sustained by a person who—
  (a) is then no longer on board the ship, aircraft or hovercraft in consequence of the wrecking of it or of some other mishap affecting it or occurring on it, and
  (b) sustains the harm in consequence of that event.

29 Short title

This Act may be cited as the Corporate Manslaughter and Corporate Homicide Act 2007.

SCHEDULES

SCHEDULE 1
SECTION 1

List of Government Departments Etc

Assets Recovery Agency
Attorney General's Office
Cabinet Office
Central Office of Information
Crown Office and Procurator Fiscal Service
Crown Prosecution Service
Department for Communities and Local Government
Department for Constitutional Affairs (including the Scotland Office and the Wales Office)
Department for Culture, Media and Sport
Department for Education and Skills
Department for Environment, Food and Rural Affairs
Department for International Development
Department for Transport
Department for Work and Pensions
Department of Health
Department of Trade and Industry
Export Credits Guarantee Department
Foreign and Commonwealth Office
Forestry Commission
General Register Office for Scotland
Government Actuary's Department
Her Majesty's Land Registry
Her Majesty's Revenue and Customs
Her Majesty's Treasury
Home Office
Ministry of Defence
National Archives
National Archives of Scotland
National Audit Office
National Savings and Investments
National School of Government
Northern Ireland Audit Office
Northern Ireland Court Service
Northern Ireland Office
Office for National Statistics
Office of the Deputy Prime Minister
Office of Her Majesty's Chief Inspector of Education and Training in Wales
Ordnance Survey

Privy Council Office
Public Prosecution Service for Northern Ireland
Registers of Scotland Executive Agency
Revenue and Customs Prosecutions Office
Royal Mint
Scottish Executive
Serious Fraud Office
Treasury Solicitor's Department
UK Trade and Investment
Welsh Assembly Government

SCHEDULE 2
SECTION 26

Minor And Consequential Amendments

Coroners ACT 1988 (c. 13)

1 (1) The Coroners Act 1988 is amended as follows.
(2) In the following provisions, after 'manslaughter' there is inserted
', corporate manslaughter'—
   (a) section 11(6) (no finding of guilt at coroner's inquest) (twice);
   (b) subsection (1)(a)(i) of section 16 (adjournment of inquest in event of criminal proceedings);
   (c) subsections (1)(a) and (2)(a) of section 17 (coroner to be informed of result of criminal proceedings).
(3) In section 35(1) (interpretation), after the definition of 'Greater London' there is inserted—
'"person", in relation to an offence of corporate manslaughter, includes organisation;'.

Criminal Justice Act 2003 (c. 44)

2 In Schedule 4 to the Criminal Justice Act 2003 (qualifying offences for purposes of section 62), after paragraph 4 there is inserted—
'*Corporate manslaughter* 4A An offence under section 1 of the Corporate Manslaughter and Corporate Homicide Act 2007.'
3 (1) Schedule 5 to that Act (qualifying offences for purposes of Part 10) is amended as follows.
(2) After paragraph 4 there is inserted—
'Corporate manslaughter
4A An offence under section 1 of the Corporate Manslaughter and
Corporate Homicide Act 2007.'
(3) After paragraph 33 there is inserted—
'Corporate manslaughter
33A An offence under section 1 of the Corporate Manslaughter and
Corporate Homicide Act 2007.'

Criminal Justice (Northern Ireland) Order 2004 (S.I. 2004/1500 (N.I. 9))

4   In Schedule 2 to the Criminal Justice (Northern Ireland) Order 2004 (qualifying offences for purposes of Article 21), after paragraph 4 there is inserted—
'*Corporate manslaughter*
4A An offence under section 1 of the Corporate Manslaughter and Corporate Homicide Act 2007.'

APPENDIX 2

A Guide to the Corporate Manslaughter and Corporate Homicide Act 2007

CONTENTS

Introduction
Background
Who is covered by the offence?
What is the scope of the new offence?
When will an organisation be convicted?
Penalties
Jurisdiction
Investigation and prosecution

INTRODUCTION

The 2007 Act puts the law on corporate manslaughter (in Scotland, corporate culpable homicide) onto a new footing, setting out a new statutory offence. In summary, an organisation is guilty of the offence if the way in which its activities are **managed or organised** causes a death and amounts to a **gross breach** of a relevant duty of care to the deceased. A substantial part of the breach must have been in the way activities were managed by **senior management**.

The offence addresses a key defect in the law that meant that, prior to the new offence, organisations could only be convicted of manslaughter (or culpable homicide in Scotland) if a 'directing mind' at the top of the company (such as a director) was also personally liable. The reality of decision making in large organisations does not reflect this and the law therefore failed to provide proper accountability, and justice for victims.

The new offence allows an organisation's liability to be assessed on a wider basis, providing a more effective means of accountability for very serious management failings across the organisation. The new offence is intended to complement, not replace, other forms of accountability such as prosecutions under health and safety legislation and is specifically linked to existing health and safety requirements. The offence will support well managed organisations by targeting those which cut costs by taking unjustifiable risks with people's safety.

> This guidance applies throughout the UK. However, it is non-statutory and is for guidance. It should not be regarded as providing legal advice, which should be sought if there is any doubt as to the application or interpretation of the legislation.

Appendix 2: A Guide to the CMCHA 2007

Implementation

The Act was given Royal Assent on 26 July and the majority of it will come into force on 6 April 2008. The Act applies across the UK.

Provisions relating to **publicity orders** will be commenced when supporting sentencing guidelines in England and Wales are available. The Sentencing Advisory Panel expects to publish a consultation paper on publicity orders (and the assessment of financial penalties) in November. A final guideline is expected to be ready by the autumn of 2008, paving the way for publicity orders to be brought into force at that point. The application of the offence to the management of **custody** will also commence at a later stage. The Government is working to implement that aspect of the legislation within 3 years of the offence itself, but has indicated that a period of up to 5 years might be necessary.

Copies of the Act

The Act, and Explanatory Notes, are published by The Stationery Office and available from the website of the Office of Public Sector Information.

BACKGROUND

Prior to this legislation it was possible for a corporate body, such as a company, to be prosecuted for a wide range of criminal offences, including manslaughter. To be guilty of the common law offence of gross negligence manslaughter, a company had to be in gross breach of a duty of care owed to the victim. The prosecution of a company for manslaughter by gross negligence was often referred to as 'corporate manslaughter'. As the law stood, before a company could be convicted of manslaughter, a 'directing mind' of the organisation (that is, a senior individual who could be said to embody the company in his actions and decisions) also had to be guilty of the offence. This is known as the identification principle.

In 1996 the Law Commission's report 'Legislating the Criminal Code: Involuntary Manslaughter' (Law Com 237) included proposals for a new offence of corporate killing that would act as a stand-alone provision for prosecuting companies to complement offences primarily aimed at individuals. The Law Commission's report, including its proposals on corporate killing, provided the basis for the Government's subsequent consultation paper in 2000 'Reforming the Law on Involuntary Manslaughter: the Government's Proposals'. These papers, and a summary of responses to the consultation paper, are available on the Home Office website

A draft Corporate Manslaughter Bill (Cm 6497) was published in March 2005. This set out the Government's proposals for legislating for reform and proposed an offence based on the Law Commission's proposals, with some modifications, including the application of the new offence to Crown bodies. The draft Bill was subject to pre-legislative scrutiny by the Home Affairs and Work and Pensions Committees in the House of Commons that autumn. Their report was published in December 2005 (HC 540 I-III) and the Government responded in March 2006 (Cm 6755).

Difficulties with prosecuting corporate bodies for gross negligence manslaughter were also relevant to Northern Ireland, where the common law was substantially the same. Policy responsibility for the criminal law lies with the Secretary of State for Northern Ireland and consultation there, following the publication of the Government's draft Bill, supported extension of the Westminster legislation.

In Scotland, although the criminal law on culpable homicide differs from the law of manslaughter elsewhere in the UK, the same issues of identifying a directing mind had arisen.

A Guide to the CMCHA 2007

Criminal law is generally a matter for the Scottish Parliament and in 2005 Scottish Ministers convened an Expert Group to review the law in Scotland on corporate liability for culpable homicide. The Group reported on 17 November 2005 and the report and other papers are available on the Scottish Executive website. After detailed consideration of the Group's proposals and the draft Bill, it was concluded that both were too closely linked to the reserved matters of health and safety and business associations to be within the Scottish Parliament's competence. The Westminster Act therefore extends to Scotland.

WHO IS COVERED BY THE OFFENCE?

Key information

The Act applies to:

- companies incorporated under companies legislation or overseas
- other corporations including:
- public bodies incorporated by statute such as local authorities, NHS bodies and a wide range of non-departmental public bodies;
- organisations incorporated by Royal Charter;
- limited liability partnerships
- all other partnerships, and trade unions and employer's associations, if the organisation concerned is an employer
- Crown bodies such as Government departments
- police forces.

THE POSITION OF INDIVIDUALS

The offence is concerned with the corporate liability of the organisation itself and does not apply to individual directors, senior managers or other individuals. Nor is it possible to convict an individual of assisting or encouraging the offence (see section 18).

However, individuals can already be prosecuted for gross negligence manslaughter/culpable homicide and for health and safety offences. The Act does not change this and prosecutions against individuals will continue to be taken where there is sufficient evidence and it is in the public interest to do so.

Questions and answers

Who will be prosecuted and who will stand in the dock?

- Prosecutions will be brought against the organisation itself and not specific individuals. As with prosecutions against companies at present, organisations will be represented by their lawyers in court, although individual directors, managers and other employees may be called as witnesses.

How will it be possible in practice to prosecute an unincorporated association, such as a partnership, which has no legal personality?

- The Act makes provision (section 14) for a prosecution to be brought in the name of a partnership and not against individual members, and for any fine to be paid out of

Appendix 2: A Guide to the CMCHA 2007

partnership funds. This reflects the approach taken under other legislation, such as the Companies Act 2006 and means that partnerships will be dealt with in a similar manner to companies and other incorporated defendants.
- This will already be the case where a partnership is a legal person under the law by which it is governed (for example, under Scots law). Section 14 does not therefore apply to partnerships of this type, because the offence applies to these partnerships without the need for special provision.

Why are only certain partnerships, trade unions and employers associations covered?
- We think it is right to take a cautious approach in extending the offence to unincorporated associations: this will represent a new extension of the criminal law to these organisations. Extending the offence to partnerships will ensure that an important range of employing organisations, already subject to health and safety law, is within the offence and that large firms are not excluded because they have chosen not to incorporate.
- The Act makes provision for the range of organisations covered by the offence to be extended by secondary legislation (section 21).

Can a parent company be convicted because of failures within a subsidiary?
- No. Companies within a group structure are all separate legal entities and therefore subject to the offence separately. In practice, the relevant duties of care that underpin the offence are more likely to be owed by a subsidiary than a parent.

Does the new offence apply to foreign companies?
- Yes – the new offence applies to all companies and other corporate bodies operating in the UK, whether incorporated in the UK or abroad.
- Because of the way the new offence applies in relation to a group structure (see above), where a company incorporated abroad is operating through a locally registered subsidiary, the subsidiary is likely to be the relevant organisation to be investigated and prosecuted if appropriate.
- The Act sets out specific rules for the jurisdiction of the new offence – that is to determine whether a death in a particular place will fall under the new offence. These are explained in the section on 'Jurisdiction'.

Does the new offence apply to sub-contractors?
- The new offence applies to all companies and employing partnerships, including those in a contracting chain. However, whether a particular contractor might be liable for the new offence will depend in the first instance on whether they owed a relevant duty of care to the victim. The Act does not impose new duties of care but the new offence will apply in respect of existing obligations on the main contractor and sub-contractors for the safety of worksites, employees and other workers which they supervise.

Does the new offence apply to charities and voluntary organisations?
- As with the law of manslaughter/culpable homicide at present, the new offence will apply where a charity or voluntary organisation has been incorporated (for example, as a company or as a charitable incorporated organisation under the Charities Act 2006). A charity or voluntary organisation that operates as any other form of organisation to which the offence applies, such as a partnership with employees, will also be liable to the new offence.

A Guide to the CMCHA 2007

What is Crown immunity?

- This is a long established legal doctrine that means that Crown bodies (such as Government departments) cannot be prosecuted. Section 11(1) makes it clear that this principle does not apply to prosecutions under the Act.
- Because, in law, Government departments operate in the name of the Crown, there is a need for a number of technical provisions to ensure the new offence operates in respect of Crown bodies in the same way that it operates for corporations. This is dealt with in sections 11 and 12. Whilst not Crown bodies, similar issues arise for police forces, and this is addressed by section 13.

Which Crown bodies will be covered by the offence?

- Schedule 1 sets out a list of Government departments etc to which the offence applies. In addition, the offence will apply to Crown bodies that are incorporated, such as the Northern Ireland departments, Charity Commission, Office of Fair Trading and Postal Services Commission.
- The Act will also apply to a wide range of statutory public bodies which are not part of the Crown, including local authorities, NHS bodies and many non-departmental public bodies with executive responsibilities.

What about Executive Agencies?

- Agencies come under the responsibility of a parent department. All departments are covered by the offence (either through Schedule 1 or by virtue of being a corporate body) and this will extend the offence to fatalities caused by Executive Agencies.

What happens when there are changes to government departments?

- This is dealt with by section 16. The general rule is that any prosecution will be taken against the body that currently has responsibility for the functions connected with the death. This reflects the reality that when functions transfer, large parts of departments frequently transfer too. If appropriate, there is scope for the Secretary of State to vary which department or Crown body is to be prosecuted.
- If a function is transferred out of the public sector entirely, proceedings will be against the public body by which the function was last carried out.

WHAT IS THE SCOPE OF THE NEW OFFENCE?

Key information

The new offence builds on the responsibilities that employers and organisations already owe to their employees, in respect of the premises they occupy and for the activities that they carry out. For the new offence to apply, the organisation concerned must have owed a '**relevant duty of care**' to the victim. This term is explained further below. The offence itself occurs where an organisation is in gross breach of a relevant duty because of the way its activities were managed and organised and this causes a death.

The Act sets out a number of **exemptions** covering deaths connected with certain public and government functions. The management of these functions involves wider questions of public

---

Appendix 2: A Guide to the CMCHA 2007

> policy and is already subject to other forms of accountability. Areas in which exemptions apply include military operations, policing, emergency response, child protection work and probation. A fuller description of the exemptions is also below.
>
> The new offence will apply to the management of custody, but this part of the Act will not come into force on 6 April 2008. The Government is working to commence this within 3 to 5 years.

Owing a relevant duty of care

A **duty of care** is an obligation that an organisation has to take reasonable steps to protect a person's safety. These duties exist, for example, in respect of the systems of work and equipment used by employees, the condition of worksites and other premises occupied by an organisation and in relation to products or services supplied to customers. The Act does not create new duties – they are already owed in the civil law of negligence and the new offence is based on these.

The duty must be a **relevant** one for the offence. Relevant duties are set out in section 2 of the Act and include:

- Employer and occupier duties.
- Duties connected to:
  - Supplying goods and services
  - Commercial activities
  - Construction and maintenance work
  - Using or keeping plant, vehicles or other things.
- Duties relating to holding a person in custody.

Are statutory duties owed under health and safety law 'relevant' duties for the new offence?

- No – only a duty of care owed in the law of negligence will be a relevant duty of care (see section 2(1)). In practice, there is a significant overlap between these types of duty. For example, employers have a responsibility for the safety of their employees under the law of negligence and under health and safety law (see for example section 2 of the Health and Safety at Work etc Act 1974 and article 4 of the Health and Safety at Work (Northern Ireland) Order 1978). Similarly, both statutory duties and common law duties will be owed to members of the public affected by the conduct of an organisation's activities.
- The common law offence of gross negligence manslaughter in England and Wales and Northern Ireland is based on the duty of care in the law of negligence, and this has been carried forward to the new offence. In Scotland, the concepts of negligence and duty of care are familiar from the civil law.

Who will decide if a duty of care is owed?

- The Act requires the judge to decide if a duty of care is owed – section 2(5).

What about circumstances where a person cannot be sued in negligence?

- In certain circumstances, a person cannot be sued under the civil law of negligence. Nevertheless, the new offence may still apply. This will be the case, for example, where a statute has replaced liability under the law of negligence with a 'no fault' scheme for damages. The new offence will also apply where an organisation is engaged jointly in unlawful conduct with another person (for example, in cases of illegal employment) and where a person has voluntarily accepted the risks involved. This is set out in sections 2(4) and 2(6).

A Guide to the CMCHA 2007

Exemptions

Sections 3-7 of the Act set out specific exemptions. These mean that the offence will not apply to deaths that are connected with the management of particular activities. They fall into two broad types:

Comprehensive exemptions:

Where a comprehensive exemption exists, the new offence does not apply in respect of any relevant duty of care that an organisation owes. These apply to:

- *Public policy decisions* (section 3(1)). This covers, for example, strategic funding decisions and other matters involving competing public interests. But it does not exempt decisions about how resources were managed.
- *Military combat operations*, including potentially violent peacekeeping operations and dealing with terrorism and violent disorder. Related support and preparatory activities and hazardous training are also exempt. This is set out in section 4.
- *Police operations dealing with terrorism and violent disorder*. This also extends to support and preparatory activities and hazardous training. This is set out in sections 5(1) and 5(2).

Partial exemptions:

In these circumstances, the new offence does not apply unless the death relates to the organisation's responsibility as employer (or to others working for the organisation) or as an occupier of premises. These include:

- Policing and law enforcement activities[1] (section 5(2)).
- The emergency response of:
  - fire authorities and other emergency response organisations;
  - NHS trusts (including ambulance trusts) – this does not exempt duties of care relating to medical treatment in an emergency, other than triage decisions (determining the order in which injured people are treated);
  - the Coastguard, Royal National Lifeboat Institution and other rescue bodies; the armed forces.
- Carrying out statutory inspection work (section 3(3)), child-protection functions or probation activities (section 7).
- The exercise of 'exclusively public functions' (section 3(2)). This covers:
  - functions carried out by the Government using prerogative powers, such as acting in a civil emergency; and
  - functions that, **by their nature**, require statutory (or prerogative) authority. This does not exempt an activity simply because statute provides an organisation with the power to carry it out (as is the case, for example, with legislation relating to NHS bodies and local authorities). Nor does it exempt an activity because it requires a licence (such as selling alcohol). Rather, the activity must be of a sort that cannot be independently performed by a private body. The type of activity involved must intrinsically require statutory or prerogative authority, such as licensing drugs or conducting international diplomacy.

Further information can be found in the Explanatory Notes to the Act. These are published by The Stationery Office and available from the website of the Office of Public Sector Information.

---

[1] Where the comprehensive exemption described above does not apply.

Appendix 2: A Guide to the CMCHA 2007

What is the position of private companies carrying out exempt functions?

- Private companies that carry out public functions are broadly in the same position as public bodies. A number of exemptions are written in a general way, to exclude a particular activity regardless of what sort of organisation is carrying it out. In other cases, an exemption applies to all public authorities. This will include private organisations that exercise public functions. In some instances, the Act makes specific provision for organisations in both the public and private sectors. Overall, the Act is intended to ensure a broadly level playing field under the new offence for public and private sector bodies when they are in a comparable situation.

Working out if the new offence applies to a particular case

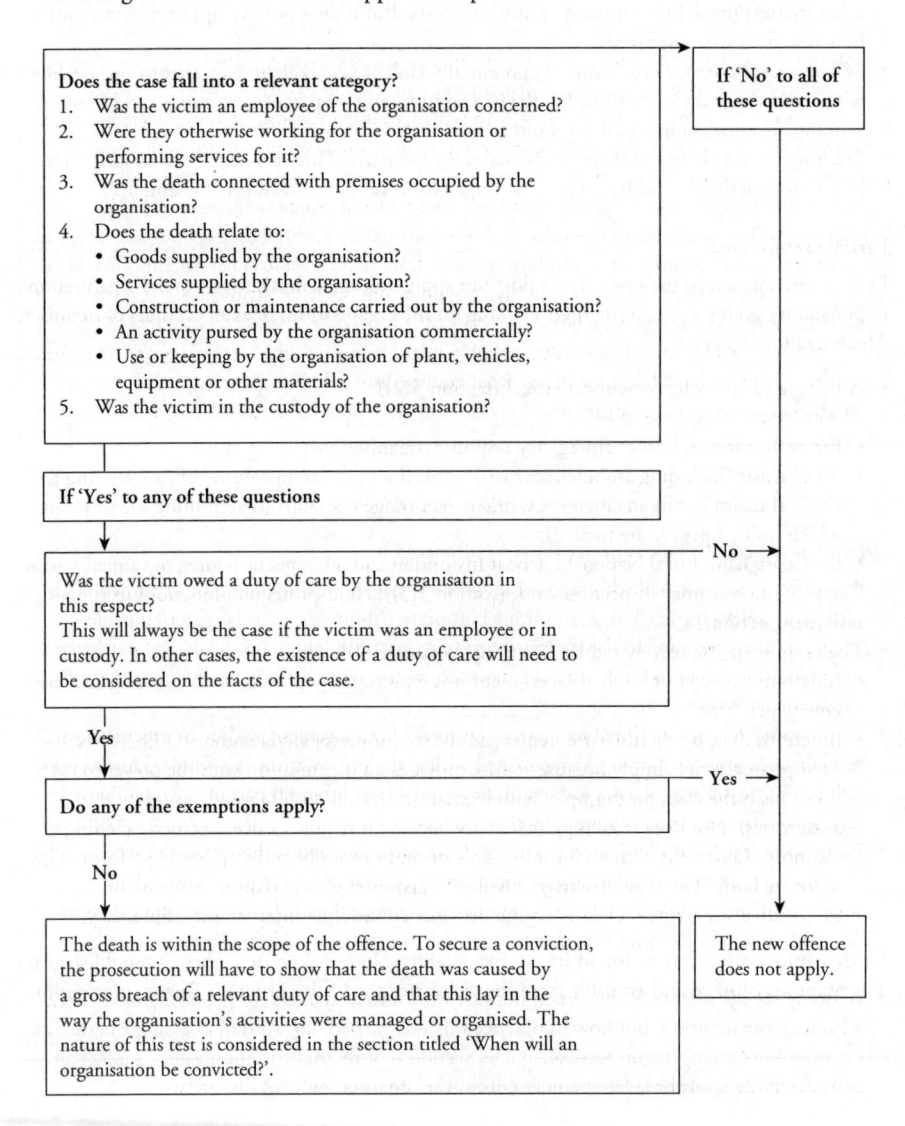

Does the case fall into a relevant category?
1. Was the victim an employee of the organisation concerned?
2. Were they otherwise working for the organisation or performing services for it?
3. Was the death connected with premises occupied by the organisation?
4. Does the death relate to:
   - Goods supplied by the organisation?
   - Services supplied by the organisation?
   - Construction or maintenance carried out by the organisation?
   - An activity pursed by the organisation commercially?
   - Use or keeping by the organisation of plant, vehicles, equipment or other materials?
5. Was the victim in the custody of the organisation?

→ **If 'No' to all of these questions**

If 'Yes' to any of these questions

↓

Was the victim owed a duty of care by the organisation in this respect?
This will always be the case if the victim was an employee or in custody. In other cases, the existence of a duty of care will need to be considered on the facts of the case.

→ No

↓ Yes

Do any of the exemptions apply?

→ Yes

↓ No

The death is within the scope of the offence. To secure a conviction, the prosecution will have to show that the death was caused by a gross breach of a relevant duty of care and that this lay in the way the organisation's activities were managed or organised. The nature of this test is considered in the section titled 'When will an organisation be convicted?'.

The new offence does not apply.

In some circumstances, it may be easier to consider first whether the activity which the death relates is exempt, for example, deaths involving the armed forces, policing and law enforcement, the response of the emergency services or rescue operations, child protection and probation work. This might also be a useful early consideration in cases involving significant public policy questions and types of activity requiring statutory powers.

WHEN WILL AN ORGANISATION BE CONVICTED?

Key information

> Corporate manslaughter/homicide will continue to be an extremely serious offence, reserved for the very worst cases of corporate mismanagement leading to death.
>
> The offence is concerned with the **way in which an organisation's activities were managed or organised.** Under this test, courts will look at management systems and practices across the organisation, and whether an adequate standard of care was applied to the fatal activity.
>
> A substantial part of the failing must have occurred at **a senior management level.**
>
> Juries will be required to consider the extent to which an organisation was in breach of health and safety requirements, and how serious those failings were. They will also be able to consider wider cultural issues within the organisation, such as attitudes or practices that tolerated health and safety breaches.
>
> The threshold for the offence is **gross negligence**. The way in which activities were managed or organised must have fallen far below what could reasonably have been expected.
>
> The failure to manage or organise activities properly must have **caused** the victim's death.

Questions and answers

What will the courts look at under the new offence?

- The offence is concerned with the way in which activities were managed or organised. This represents a new approach to establishing corporate liability for manslaughter/culpable homicide and does not require the prosecution to establish failure on the part of particular individuals or managers. It is instead concerned with how an activity was being managed and the adequacy of those arrangements.
- This approach is not confined to a particular level of management within an organisation: the test considers how an activity was managed within the organisation as a whole. However, it will not be possible to convict an organisation unless a substantial part of the organisation's failure lay at a senior management level.
- Factors that might be considered will range from questions about the systems of work used by employees, their level of training and adequacy of equipment, to issues of immediate supervision and middle management, to questions about the organisation's strategic approach to health and safety and its arrangements for risk assessing, monitoring and auditing its processes.
- In doing so, the offence is concerned not just with formal systems for managing an activity within an organisation, but how in practice this was carried out. And in assessing whether an organisation's arrangements were adequate, section 8 of the Act specifically allows a jury to consider evidence of broader attitudes within the organisation towards safety.

Appendix 2: A Guide to the CMCHA 2007

What standards are expected of organisations?

- The offence does not require organisations to comply with new regulatory standards and creates an explicit link with existing requirements under health and safety law. Section 8 requires juries to consider, when assessing whether there has a gross breach of a relevant duty of care, the extent and seriousness of failures to comply with health and safety obligations, and the degree of danger this posed.
- Juries may also have regard to any relevant health and safety guidance. This includes statutory Approved Codes of Practice and other guidance published by regulatory authorities that enforce health and safety legislation. Employers do not have to follow guidance and are free to take other action. But guidance from regulatory authorities may be helpful to a jury when considering the extent of any failures to comply with health and safety legislation and whether the organisation's conduct has fallen far below what could reasonably have been expected.
- Guidance on health and safety at work in England and Wales and Scotland is available from the Health and Safety Executive and in Northern Ireland from the Health and Safety Executive Northern Ireland, as well as from local authorities as appropriate.
- However, HSE, HSENI and local authorities are not the only health and safety regulatory authorities. There are specific regulatory bodies, and in some cases separate legislation too, for certain sectors of industry (for example, in the various transport sectors: rail, marine, air and roads) and for dealing with particular safety issues (such as food and environmental safety). Further information about the standards that apply in these circumstances should be obtained from the relevant regulatory authority.

Who are an organisation's senior management?

- These are the people who make significant decisions about the organisation, or substantial parts of it. This includes both those carrying out headquarters functions (for example, central financial or strategic roles or with central responsibility for, for example, health and safety) as well as those in senior operational management roles.
- Exactly who is a member of an organisation's senior management will depend on the nature and scale of an organisation's activities. Apart from directors and similar senior management positions, roles likely to be under consideration include regional managers in national organisations and the managers of different operational divisions.
- The Act does not require the prosecution to prove specific failings on the part of individual senior managers. It will be sufficient for a jury to consider that the senior management of the organisation collectively were not taking adequate care, and this was a substantial part of the organisation's failure.

Can the offence be avoided by senior management delegating responsibility for health and safety?

- No. The Act is concerned with the way an activity was being managed or organised and will consider how responsibility was being discharged at different levels of the organisation. Failures by senior managers to manage health and safety adequately, including through inappropriate delegation of health and safety matters, will therefore leave organisations vulnerable to corporate manslaughter or corporate homicide charges.
- This does not mean that responsibility for managing health and safety cannot be made a matter across the management chain. However, senior management will need to ensure that they have adequate processes for health and safety and risk management in place and are implementing these.

A Guide to the CMCHA 2007

- New guidance 'Leading health and safety: leadership actions for directors and board members' is being drawn up jointly by the Health and Safety Commission and Institute of Directors and will be published UK-wide later this year.

How is the threshold for the offence changing?

- The offence will continue to apply only in cases of gross negligence. The new offence makes it clear that the standard is whether the organisation's conduct fell far below what could reasonably have been expected. This is intended to be broadly equivalent to the sort of threshold applied under the common law.

Won't the cause of death always be a more immediate, front line matter than failure to manage properly?

- It will not be necessary for the management failure to have been the sole cause of death. The prosecution will, however need to show that 'but for' the management failure (including the substantial element attributable to senior management), the death would not have occurred. The law does not, however, recognise very remote causes, and in some circumstances the existence of an intervening event may mean that the management failure is not considered to have caused the death.

PENALTIES

Key information

An organisation convicted of the new offence can receive:
- A **fine**. There is no upper limit to what this can be.
- A **publicity order**. This requires an organisation to publicise the fact of its conviction and certain details of the offence, in a way specified by the court. Publicity orders are not being brought into force on 6 April 2008, but will be commenced when supporting guidelines are available.

In addition, the court can set a **remedial order**, requiring the organisation to address the cause of the fatal injury. These are not currently available for organisations convicted of manslaughter/culpable homicide, although they can be imposed under health and safety legislation.

Questions and answers

How will courts determine the size of a fine?

- This will be a matter for the courts and any sentencing guidelines. In England and Wales, the Sentencing Guidelines Council is working on a guideline to support the new offence. The Sentencing Advisory Panel is expected to publish a consultation paper in November. A final guideline is expected to be in place by the autumn of 2008.
- Generally, we would expect the courts to consider the sort of issues taken into account when setting fines under health and safety legislation, but with the additional recognition that an organisation has been found guilty of an offence of homicide.
- Factors considered in health and safety proceedings include whether the breach was with a view to profit, the degree of risk and the extent of the danger involved, and the objective of

Appendix 2: A Guide to the CMCHA 2007

achieving a safe environment for the public and need to bring that message home. In England and Wales, the leading case on setting fines for health and safety offences is R v F Howe & Co (Engineers) Limited[2].
- Generally, fines need to reflect the relative size of the offender and the scale of the offending. The courts have shown an increasing willingness to hand down very severe penalties in very serious cases. As an illustration:
    - In 1999 Great Western Trains was fined £1.5million in proceedings resulting from the 1997 Southall train crash.
    - In 2003 Thames Trains was fined over £2 million and Network Rail £4million in relation to health and safety breaches that led to the fatal train crash at Ladbroke Grove in 1999.
    - In 2005, Transco was fined £15million for health and safety breaches behind a fatal explosion in Larkhall in 1999.
    - In 2006, the highest ever fines were seen against railway organisations in relation to the fatal derailment of a train near Hatfield in 2000. Network Rail was fined £3.5million and, after appeal, Balfour Beatty's fine was £7.5million.
- In appropriate cases, fines on this scale, and even higher, are of the sort that we would expect to see for corporate manslaughter.

How will remedial orders be set?

- A remedial order may only be made where the prosecution apply. An application from the prosecution must be accompanied with the proposed terms of the order. Before making the application, the prosecution must consult the appropriate regulatory authority (or authorities), such as the Health and Safety Executive, Office of Rail Regulation, Food Standards Agency or local authority.
- In practice, we expect prosecutors will wish to discuss the possibility of a remedial order with the relevant regulatory body in general liaison over the handling of the case. As the relevant enforcement experts, the regulatory body will be closely involved in drafting the proposed terms of the order, and suggesting a period in which the necessary steps must be taken.

When will remedial orders be used? How will they be enforced?

- We expect the courts to impose a remedial order in relatively rare circumstances since the relevant regulator will have been involved in the case from the outset and will have been able to use their existing enforcement powers to address any dangerous practices long before a case comes to court. Nevertheless, this power enables the judge to impose an order if it still appears necessary.
- From a practical perspective, the relevant regulator will already be closely involved in the case and will have been consulted on the terms of any remedial order. We would expect this authority to take a key interest in the progress the organisation is making to address the cause of the fatality, including taking the steps identified in the remedial order. An order may require an organisation to supply details of compliance to the regulatory body.
- An organisation that fails to take the action set out in the order can be prosecuted for failure to do so. This would be the responsibility of the general prosecuting authorities (the Crown Prosecution Service in England and Wales, the Public Prosecution Service in Northern Ireland and the Procurator Fiscal in Scotland). An unlimited fine can be imposed on conviction.

---

[2] [1999] 2 Cr App R(S) 37.

A Guide to the CMCHA 2007

When will publicity orders be made available to the courts?

- This new sort of order will be brought into force when sentencing guidelines are available in England and Wales. The Sentencing Advisory Panel expects to publish a consultation paper on publicity orders (and the assessment of financial penalties) in November. A final guideline is expected to be ready by the autumn of 2008, paving the way for publicity orders to be brought into force at that point.

JURISDICTION

Key information

- The Act applies across the UK.
- The new offence can be prosecuted if the harm resulting in death occurs:
  - in the UK
  - in the UK's territorial waters (for example, in an incident involving commercial shipping or leisure craft)
  - on a British ship, aircraft or hovercraft
  - on an oil rig or other offshore installation already covered by UK criminal law.

Questions and answers

What is the 'harm resulting in death'?

- Typically, this will be a physical injury that is fatal. In the majority of cases, the injury causing the death and the death will occur at the same time, in the same location. But death may occur some time after an injury or harm takes place. The courts will still have jurisdiction for the new offence if the death has occurred abroad, provided the relevant harm was sustained in the UK.
- In the case of fatalities connected with ships, aircraft and hovercraft, the new offence will still apply if the death does not actually occur on board (for example, the victim drowns), provided it relates to an on-board incident – see section 28(4).

Does the new Act apply to British companies responsible for deaths abroad?

- No. The new offence only applies where the harm that leads to death occurs within the UK or in one of the other places described in the box above.
- Where a death occurs abroad, the practical issues for investigators are acute – there will be no control of the crime scene or of the gathering of evidence relating to the cause of death. This evidence will be located overseas and collected and held to different standards, but would be a crucial part of the investigation and prosecution.

Appendix 2: A Guide to the CMCHA 2007

INVESTIGATION AND PROSECUTION

Key information

- It is for the police to investigate general criminal offences and investigations relating to corporate manslaughter/homicide will be led by them. However, it is important that the knowledge and expertise of the regulatory enforcing authorities (such as the Health and Safety Executive, the Office of Rail Regulation, Food Standards Agency and local authorities) are properly harnessed in any corporate manslaughter investigation, and protocols currently exist to facilitate this.
- The Rail, Air and Marine Accident Investigation Branches will continue to be responsible for separate investigations to determine the cause of an incident and to issue reports.
- Proceedings for the new offence will be the responsibility of the general prosecuting authorities: the Crown Prosecution Service in England and Wales, the Public Prosecution Service in Northern Ireland and the Procurator Fiscal in Scotland. Proceedings will not therefore be brought by regulatory bodies

Questions and answers

What arrangements exist to ensure that the relevant agencies work together?

- In England and Wales, the Work-Related Deaths Protocol, first published in 1998, has worked well to bring the police, the Crown Prosecution Service and regulatory authorities closer together when investigating and prosecuting work-related deaths.
- Work has continued since then to improve this. A revised Protocol was published in 2003, and in 2004 in response to requests from investigators, the National Liaison Committee on the Work-Related Deaths Protocol published an 'Investigators' guide' to improve consistency in its application. The National Liaison Committee will continue to keep the Protocol under review. A copy of the Protocol can be obtained from the Health and Safety Executive website.
- Liaison in Northern Ireland is covered by a separate and broadly equivalent document 'Investigation of Work-related Deaths: Northern Ireland agreement for liaison'.
- In Scotland, a Protocol on Work-Related Deaths was published in October 2006 and has encouraged partner agencies to adopt a collaborative approach to the investigation of work-related deaths in Scotland.

What support will bereaved families receive?

England and Wales

- The Code of Practice for Victims of Crime sets out what services victims can expect to receive in England and Wales from each of the criminal justice agencies. This will apply to corporate manslaughter investigations and prosecutions under the new Act, as it does to manslaughter cases at present.
- The Code requires a dedicated family liaison police officer to be assigned to bereaved relatives in homicide cases and provides a right to information, including notification of court cases.
- Family members are entitled to make a personal statement about how a crime has affected them, which will become part of the case papers. A pilot scheme (the Victim Advocate Scheme) operating in a number of Crown Courts allows families an opportunity to present

their family impact statement orally to the court, or to have this done on their behalf. Additionally, from October this year, the Crown Prosecution Service's Victim Focus Scheme will ensure that prosecutors meet with families in cases of this nature to explain the charging decision and possibility of the prosecution reading out in court the impact statement. Family Liaison Officers will be able to provide further details about where the Victim Advocate Scheme operates and advise on the Victim Focus Scheme.
- The Health and Safety Executive does not provide a family liaison function. However, they and other regulatory bodies seek to follow the Code of Practice as far as possible when dealing with cases of work-related death that are not pursued by the police as manslaughter investigations. Further information about HSE's policy towards victims can be found on the HSE website.

Scotland

- In Scotland, the National Standards for Victims of Crime set out what standards victims can expect in their dealings with agencies and voluntary organisations in the criminal justice system.
- It is the duty of the relevant Procurator Fiscal to enquire into all sudden, suspicious, accidental, unexpected and unexplained deaths. The Victim Information and Advice Service, which is part of the Crown Office and Procurator Fiscal Service, provides a dedicated service that helps bereaved next of kin through the criminal justice process by keeping them informed of key developments and identifying other organisations that can offer them practical and emotional support.
- A victim statement scheme has been piloted in some parts of Scotland, giving victims of certain crimes the right to make a written statement about the emotional, physical and financial impact the crime had on them. In cases where the victim had died, this right passed to their next of kin. Information about the current availability of this scheme can be obtained from the Victim Information and Advice Service.

Northern Ireland

- The Police Service of Northern Ireland will assign specialist Family Liaison Officers to bereaved relatives in homicide cases. These officers will provide appropriate support and information about the investigation, and will ensure that families are treated appropriately, professionally and with respect for their needs.
- It is the current policy and practice of the Public Prosecution Service to take account of the need to ensure that all relevant information on the effects of the crime on the victim is brought to the attention of the court and this has been included as a specific requirement in their new Code for Prosecutors.
- In addition, it is normal practice, in cases involving death, for the court to seek a victim impact report, from the appropriate relative, to help inform sentencing. The Judge may also consider any correspondence provided by the next of kin or relatives of the deceased.

Where is further information available?

England and Wales

- The Code of Practice and information about family impact statements, as well as further information for victims of crime, can be found on the cjsonline website. Guidance on the Victim Focus Scheme can be found on the Crown Prosecution Service website.
- Victim Support provides free and confidential support. Local Victim Support Schemes are listed in the local phone book, or the Victim Supportline can be contacted on 0845 30 30 900.

Appendix 2: A Guide to the CMCHA 2007

Scotland
- The National Standards for Victims of Crime as well as other useful information can be found on the Victims of Crime in Scotland website.
- The Victim Support Scotland Helpline can be contacted on 0845 60 39 123.

Northern Ireland
- Further information to assist victims of crime, particularly in explaining the roles, responsibilities and processes of those organisations working within the criminal justice system, can be found on the CJSNI website.
- Victim Support NI provides free and confidential support. Local Victim Support Offices are listed in the local telephone directory, or the Victim Supportline can be contacted on 0845 30 30 900.

Will compensation be available for bereaved families?
- The families of victims will be able to seek compensation in the same way as at present. This will generally be via the civil courts, which are best placed to assess the detail of a claim for damages.

Can a private prosecution be brought for the new offence?
- Individuals in England and Wales and Northern Ireland will be able to bring a private prosecution for the new offence, as is the case at present with gross negligence manslaughter. However, proceedings for the new offence must have the consent of the Director of Public Prosecutions or, in Northern Ireland, the Director of Public Prosecutions for Northern Ireland. In England and Wales, the Director's consent can be given by any Crown Prosecutor. Further information about consent should be obtained from the Crown Prosecution Service or the Public Prosecution Service for Northern Ireland.
- In Scotland, all prosecutions are initiated by the Procurator Fiscal.

Is the reform retrospective?
- No. It is a general principle that criminal law does not apply retrospectively. The offence will only apply to fatalities caused by gross management failings that occur after the new law comes into force on 6 April 2008. Section 27(3) makes this explicit.

Will the existing law remain in force?
- In England and Wales and Northern Ireland, it will no longer be possible to bring proceedings for gross negligence manslaughter against a company or other organisation to which the offence applies. That part of the common law is abolished – see section 20.
- In Scotland, where the law on culpable homicide differs in certain respects from the law on gross negligence manslaughter, the common law will continue in force. It will be for the Procurator Fiscal to determine the appropriate charge in light of the circumstances of each individual case.

What about cases that occur before 6 April?
- The Act includes a saving (section 27(4)) for cases that occur wholly or partly before the new offence comes into force. Prosecutions in those cases will therefore continue to be possible, even after 6 April, on the basis of the existing common law.

Index

References are to paragraph and Appendix numbers

adjourned inquests 8.22, 8.23
affirmative duties 3.54
agency workers 4.40, 4.41
aggravating factors 7.07, 7.21
armed forces 5.41–5.48

breach of duty 6.01–6.06
  causation
    contributory negligence 6.37–6.40
    Environmental Agency v Empress Cars 6.28–6.32
    Law Commission's report 6.21–6.26
    management failure 2.89–2.95, 6.36, 6.41–6.45
    novus actus interveniens 6.33–6.35
    usual principles 6.27
  gross breach 6.46–6.58
    health and safety legislation 6.64–6.104, 6.112–6.116
    jury factors 6.59–6.78, 6.104, 6.105, 6.112
    organizational culture 6.109–6.111
    senior management requirement 6.117–6.158
  management failure 2.89–2.95, 6.07–6.45
    gross breach 6.46–6.58
    senior management 6.117–6.158

causation *see* **breach of duty**
child protection 5.84, 5.85, 5.87, 5.88
Clapham rail crash 1.32
Codes of Practice 6.112–6.116
common law
  corporate attribution 1.04–1.06
    directing mind 1.08–1.15
    identification doctrine 1.07
  duty of care 1.13–1.15, 1.20, 3.33–3.37
    affirmative duties 3.54
    Caparo Industries plc v Dickman 3.38–3.45
    ex turpi causa 1.22, 1.24, 4.15
    'fair, just and reasonable' 3.52, 3.53
    foreseeability of harm 3.34, 3.38, 3.46, 3.47
    omissions 3.54, 3.55
    proximity 3.36, 3.38, 3.48–3.51
    standard of care 6.53, 6.54
    versus statutory offence 1.25–1.27, 1.30, 1.31
    volenti non fit injuria 4.16–4.19, 4.47, 4.48
    see also **relevant duty of care**
  gross negligence manslaughter 1.01, 1.11, 1.12, 1.16–1.18, 2.01
    need for reform 1.32–1.37
    recent authorities 1.19–1.29

company directors 2.15
construction operations 4.75–4.86
contributory negligence 6.37–6.40
convictions *see* sentencing
corporate attribution 1.04–1.06
  directing mind 1.08–1.15
  identification doctrine 1.07
corporate culture 6.109–6.111
corporate manslaughter 2.01–2.05
  breach of duty *see* **breach of duty**
  causation *see* **breach of duty**
  company directors 2.15
  definition and elements of the offence 2.06–2.08
  individual and secondary liability 2.13, 2.14
  institution of proceedings 2.12
  investigation *see* **investigation**
  relevant duty of care *see* **relevant duty of care**
  secondary liability in respect of non-natural persons 2.16–2.20
  sentencing *see* **sentencing**
  territorial extent 2.09–2.11
  work-related deaths 2005/07 8.06
Corporate Manslaughter and Corporate Homicide Act 2007
  commencement and orders 2.26–2.32
  disclaimer 1.37
  exemptions *see* **exemptions**
  full text of the Act App 1
  Guide to the Act App 2
  health and safety legislation and 2.21–2.25
  history of the Act 1.38–1.49
  organizations subject to *see* **organizations subject to the Act**
  previous common law 1.01–1.03, 2.01
  procedural provisions and consequential amendments 2.33–2.46
  procedure against corporations 2.35–2.44
  relevant duty of care *see* **relevant duty of care**
  sentencing *see* **sentencing**
corporations
  procedure against 2.35–2.44
  subject to the Act 2.50–2.53
Crown bodies 2.54–2.65
Crown Prosecution Service (CPS) 8.01, 8.05, 8.11, 8.133, 8.20, 8.21, 8.22 *see also* **investigation**
custody duty of care 4.99
  common law duty 4.111–4.113
  detention outside of s 2(2) 4.107, 4.108
  potential commencement 4.100–4.102

Index

custody duty of care (*cont.*)
  power to amend categories of detained
    person in s 2(2) 4.109, 4.110
  relevant duty 4.103–4.106
  suicide/self harm 4.114–4.121

dangerous activities 6.87
detained persons *see* **custody duty of care**
duty of care 1.13–1.15, 1.20, 3.33–3.37
  affirmative duties 3.54
  Caparo Industries plc v Dickman 3.38–3.45
  ex turpi causa 1.22, 1.24, 4.15
  'fair, just and reasonable' 3.52, 3.53
  foreseeability of harm 3.34, 3.38, 3.46, 3.47
  omissions 3.54, 3.55
  organizations subject to the Act 2.83–2.88
  proximity 3.36, 3.38, 3.48–3.51
  standard of care 6.53, 6.54
  statutory offence versus common law offence
    1.25–1.27, 1.30, 1.31
  volenti non fit injuria 4.16–4.19, 4.47, 4.48
  see also **relevant duty of care**

emergencies 5.65–5.83
employers' associations 2.72–2.76
employer's duty of care 4.20–4.29
  agency workers 4.40, 4.41
  control test 4.37–4.39
  definition of employee 4.30–4.36
  non-employee workers 4,42
  statutory health and safety duties 4.44–4.46
  vicarious liability 4.43
  volenti non fit injuria 4.47, 4.48
ex turpi causa 1.22, 1.24, 4.15
exemptions 5.01–5.06
  child protection 5.84, 5.85, 5.87, 5.88
  emergencies 5.65–5.83
  military activities 5.41–5.48
  policing 5.49–5.64
  probation functions 5.86–5.88
  public authorities 5.08
    as defendants 5.21, 5.22
    Prerogative, statutory powers, statutory duties
      and discretion 5.23–5.31
  public functions 5.12–5.19, 5.35, 5.36
  public policy 5.09–5.11, 5.32–5.36
  statutory inspections 5.37–5.40

fines *see* **sentencing**
foreseeability of harm 3.34, 3.38, 3.46, 3.47

goods 4.67–4.71
Government bodies 2.54, 2.59–2.65
gross breach *see* **breach of duty**
gross negligence manslaughter 1.01, 1.11, 1.12,
  1.16–1.18, 2.01
  company directors 2.15
  gross breach and 6.52

need for reform 1.32–1.37
recent authorities 1.19–1.29
relevant duty of care 3.06–3.09

Hampton Review 7.53
Hatfield train crash 1.28, 1.32
Health and Safety Executive (HSE)
  8.11, 8.14, 8.19
health and safety guidance 6.112–6.116
health and safety inspectors 8.26
health and safety legislation 2.21–2.25, 4.44–4.46
  gross breach 6.64–6.104, 6.112–6.116
  organizational culture 6.109–6.111
  reasonable practicability 6.87–6.92
Herald of Free Enterprise 1.32
Home Office Regulatory Impact
  Assessment 8.07–8.13

identification doctrine 1.07
individual liability 2.13, 2.14
  company directors 2.15 *see also* **gross**
    negligence manslaughter
institution of proceedings 2.12
insurance cover 8.33, 8.34
interviews under caution 8.31
investigation 8.01–8.06
  adjourned inquests 8.22, 8.23
  Coroners Act 1988 s16 8.22, 8.23
  Home Office Regulatory Impact
    Assessment 8.07–8.13
  interviews under caution 8.31
  police powers 8.24–8.27
  senior management 8.27–8.30
  Work-Related Death Protocol 8.02, 8.11,
    8.14–8.21

juries 3.30–3.32
  consideration of gross breach issues 6.59–6.78,
    6.104, 6.105, 6.112

King's Cross fire 1.32

Law Commission 6.21–6.26
law enforcement 5.49–5.64
legal representation 8.32–8.34

Macrory Review of Regulatory Penalties 7.53
maintenance operations 4.75–4.79, 4.87–4.91
management failure 2.89–2.95, 6.07–6.45
  gross breach 6.46–6.58
  senior management 6.117–6.158
manslaughter by gross negligence *see* **gross**
  negligence manslaughter
Marchioness pleasure boat 1.32
medical treatment 5.70–5.72
military activities 5.41–5.48
misfeasance 3.55
mitigating factors 7.07, 7.08, 7.22

172

Index

negligence *see* duty of care; gross negligence manslaughter; relevant duty of care
non-natural persons 2.16–2.20
nonfeasance 3.55
novus actus interveniens 6.33–6.35

occupiers' liability 4.49–4.65
organizational culture 6.109–6.111
organizations subject to the Act 2.47–2.49
    causation and breach 2.89–2.95 *see also* breach of duty
    corporations 2.50–2.53
    Crown bodies 2.54–2.65
    duty of care owed to the deceased 2.83–2.88
    employers' associations 2.72–2.76
    Government bodies 2.54, 2.59–2.65
    legal representation 8.32–8.34
    partnerships 2.72–2.82
    police forces 2.66–2.71
    trade unions 2.72–2.76

partnerships 2.72–2.82
Piper Alpha oil platform 1.32
plant 4.97, 4.98
police custody *see* custody duty of care
police forces 2.66–2.71, 5.49–5.64
police investigations *see* investigation
Prerogative 5.23–5.31
prisons *see* custody duty of care
probation functions 5.86–5.88
proceedings 2.12
proximity 3.36, 3.38, 3.48–3.51
public authorities 5.08
    as defendants 5.21, 5.22
    Prerogative, statutory powers, statutory duties and discretion 5.23–5.31
    sentencing 7.29–7.32
public disasters
    Clapham rail crash 1.32
    Hatfield train crash 1.28, 1.32
    Herald of Free Enterprise 1.32
    King's Cross fire 1.32
    Marchioness 1.32
    Piper Alpha 1.32
    Southall rail disaster 1.11, 1.32
public functions 5.12–5.19, 5.35, 5.36
public policy 5.09–5.11, 5.32–5.36
publicity orders 7.44, 7.53–7.59

rail disasters 1.11, 1.28, 1.32
reasonable practicability 6.87–6.92
relevant duty of care 3.01–3.05, 4.01–4.03
    carrying on activities on a commercial basis 4.922–4.96
    common law limitations disregarded 4.14
        ex turpi causa 4.15
        volenti non fit injuria 4.16–4.19

construction operations 4.75–4.86
custody *see* custody duty of care
    definition 4.04–4.09
    directing the jury 3.30–3.32
    employer's duty of care to employees 4.20–4.29
        agency workers 4.40, 4.41
        control test 4.37–4.39
        definition of employee 4.30–4.36
        non-employee workers 4.42
        statutory health and safety duties 4.44–4.46
        vicarious liability 4.43
        volenti non fit injuria 4.47, 4.48
    exemptions *see* exemptions
    individual gross negligence manslaughter 3.06–3.09
    maintenance operations 4.75–4.79, 4.87–4.91
    occupier of premises 4.49–4.65
    procedure for determining the existence of 3.20–3.30
    section 2(5) 3.10–3.19
    superseding statutory duties 4.10–4.13
    supply of goods 4.67–4.71
    supply of services 4.67–4.69, 4.72–4.74
    use or keeping of any plant, vehicle or other thing 4.97, 4.98
remedial orders 7.44–7.52
representation 8.32–8.34
rescue at sea 5.82, 5.83

sea rescue 5.82, 5.83
secondary liability 2.13, 2.14, 2.16–2.20
self harm 4.114–4.121
senior management 6.117–6.158, 8.27–8.30
sentencing
    aggravating factors 7.07, 7.21
    by way of fine 7.01–7.05
    financial means of the organization 7.33–7.40
    health and safety cases 7.18–7.28
    mitigating factors 7.07, 7.08, 7.22
    organization part of a wider group 7.24–7.27
    public bodies 7.29–7.32
    publicity orders 7.44, 7.53–7.59
    R v Balfour Beatty Rail Infrastructure Services Ltd 7.24–7.27
    R v Howe & Sons 7.21–7.23, 7.33, 7.40
    R v Transco plc 7.28, 7.34, 7.38
    remedial orders 7.44–7.52
Sentencing Advisory Panel consultation paper 7.06–7.17, 7.54
services 4.67–4.69, 4.72–4.74
Southall rail disaster 1.11, 1.32
standard of care 6.53, 6.54
statutory duty 1.25–1.27, 1.30, 1.31
statutory inspections 5.37–5.40
statutory powers and duties 5.23–5.31
suicide 4.114–4.121

173

Index

supply of goods 4.67–4.71
supply of services 4.67–4.69, 4.72–4.74

territorial limits 2.09–2.11
trade unions 2.72–2.76
train crashes 1.11, 1.28, 1.32

vehicles 4.97, 4.98
vicarious liability 4.43

violent events 5.56–5.59
volenti non fit injuria 4.16–4.19, 4.47, 4.48

Work-Related Death Protocol 8.02, 8.11, 8.14–8.21
work-related deaths
    2005/07 8.06